Toward an Imperfec Education

Interventions: Education, Philosophy & Culture
Michael A. Peters & Colin Lankshear, Series Editors

Toward an Imperfect Education

Facing Humanity, Rethinking Cosmopolitanism

Sharon Todd

Routledge
Taylor & Francis Group
LONDON AND NEW YORK

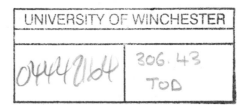
First published 2009 by Paradigm Publishers

Published 2016 by Routledge
2 Park Square, Milton Park, Abingdon, Oxon OX14 4RN
711 Third Avenue, New York, NY 10017, USA

Routledge is an imprint of the Taylor & Francis Group, an informa business

Library of Congress Cataloging-in-Publication Data

Todd, Sharon, 1962–
    Toward an imperfect education : facing humanity, rethinking cosmopolitanism / Sharon Todd.
        p. cm. — (Interventions : education, philosophy, and culture)
    Includes bibliographical references and index.
    ISBN 978-1-59451-621-4 (hardcover : alk. paper)
    ISBN 978-1-59451-622-1 (paperback : alk. paper)
    1. Education—Social aspects.   2. Cosmopolitanism.   I. Title.
    LC191.T54 2008
    306.43—dc22

                                                                            2008028754

ISBN13: 978-1-59451-621-4 (hbk)
ISBN13: 978-1-59451-622-1 (pbk)

Designed and typeset by Straight Creek Bookmakers.

Contents

Acknowledgments

This book has been conceived at a juncture of my own grappling with upheavals of identity, place, and language. In some respects, my recent move to a new country, and all that such relocation entails, has brought home to me the urgency of thinking through the borders of belonging and what kind of demands we make on ourselves and others to make a new place in the world. I have benefited enormously from conversations with colleagues and students, friends and family, which have challenged my own thinking across borders. In particular, I would like to thank the Social Science and Humanities Research Council of Canada under whose auspices I conducted research into human rights education and social justice, some of which is reflected in chapters 3, 4, and 5. In this connection, I extend my gratitude specifically to Sharon Sliwinski and Trent Davis, whose work as researchers on the project has proved invaluable to my discussion here. I also am indebted to the Swedish National Research Council whose funding for the project "Gendering the Cosmopolitan Ethic: A Feminist Inquiry into Intercultural and Human Rights Issues in Education" enabled me to undertake a large portion of the writing. In particular, I wish to thank Lovisa Bergdahl for her thoughtfulness and astute conversations about the ongoing complexities of cosmopolitanism, feminism, and cultural and religious diversity.

Without the time spent at University of Glasgow in the fall of 2007, this book would not have seen the light of day. I particularly wish to acknowledge the hospitality afforded me by Jim Conroy, Penny Enslin, and Bob Davis. It was the kind of sojourn that has left me with a desire to return. I also extend my thanks to Michael Peters for inviting me to contribute to his and Colin Lankshear's series, to my first editor, Beth Davis, whose attentiveness and understanding went beyond the call of duty and to Carol Smith whose smooth editorial support in the final stages of production I counted on to get me through some difficult weeks.

Many parts of this book have been the subject of seminars, conference presentations, and lectures in various venues. But it is the fine collegiality of our Post-structural Studies group (DICE) at Stockholm University, which has been of tremendous intellectual support and source of creativity. For their comments on various chapters I thank Lovisa Bergdahl, Klara Dolk, Silvia Edling, Bodil Halvars-Franzén, Karin Hultman, Elisabet Langmann, Hillevi Lenz-Taguchi, Margaret Obondo, Anna Palmer, and Cathrine Ryther. Finally, to Carl Anders, my colleague and partner—with love and gratitude.

Parts of various chapters have been published previously and are reworked here with kind permission from the publishers:

Chapter 4 appeared as "Promoting a Just Education: Dilemmas of Rights, Freedom and Justice" in *Educational Philosophy and Theory* 39, no. 3 (2007): 592–603.

Chapter 8 appeared as "Teachers Judging without Scripts, or Thinking Cosmopolitan" in *Ethics and Education* 2, no. 3 (2007): 25–38.

Parts of chapters 2 and 5 have drawn on "Ambiguities of Cosmopolitanism: Difference, Gender and the Right to Education." In *Education in the Era of Globalization*, ed. Klas Roth and Ilan Gur Ze'ev. 67–84. Dordrecht: Springer, 2007.

Parts of chapter 6 were drawn from an article coauthored with Carl Anders Säfström, "Democracy, Education and Conflict: Rethinking Respect and the Place of the Ethical" *Journal of Educational Controversy* 3 (1: 2008): http://www.wce.wwu.edu/Resources/CEP/eJournal/.

Prologue

Education and an Imperfect Garden

The humanist enterprise could never bring itself to a halt. It rejects the dream of a paradise on earth, which would establish a definitive order. It envisages men in their current imperfection and does not imagine that this state of things can change; it accepts, with Montaigne, the idea that their garden remains forever imperfect.

Tzvetan Todorov, Imperfect Garden

Todorov (2002), in his conversation with the legacy of French humanism, reminds us of a crucial insight: that human beings are imperfect. A rather simple thought that would seem to be so self-evident that one could legitimately question whether a sustained discussion on the topic is indeed even warranted. After all, we live with our imperfections daily, in petty envies, sharp words and indifference to others. On a larger scale, of course, we are reminded of the great heights to which such imperfection can accede: civil breakdown, enforced poverty, racist hatred, and the sheer murderous violence which threatens to erupt on streets, in schools, and at work. Such imperfection, it seems to me, has been the reason why education has taken upon itself various projects that focus on social justice and more peaceful forms of coexistence. For it is because of our imperfection that we seem to need the civilizing force that education appears to offer. To be taught virtuous habits of mind, to develop our capacities for concern for others, to learn how to become subjects that can make the world a better place to live in, are all commonsensical renderings of what education can do for us. Education tenders the hope that we can be rescued from the bed of destruction.

Yet, we lie in the bed we made for ourselves. No one knew this better than Nietzsche, perhaps, who insisted on our "all too human" propensity for creating the very conditions of life which we continually seek to overcome. I realize that in saying this I seem to be dismissing the ways individuals do not usually choose to live in violence or strife, that such conditions are inflicted upon them, with little regard for their integrity as persons. However, my point is to suggest here that there is something unsettlingly human about that violence which we live with—albeit against our will.

Although human imperfection has been a primary reason for why education needs to salve the wounds that have been inflicted on individuals and communities, it has done so largely on the basis that such imperfection does not exist as part of humanity as such. Thus it is often taken for granted that humanity is itself the remedy for violence, as if violence could be divorced from the actual human subjects who commit it. Indeed, humanity has been conflated with human life and goodness in such a commonplace way, that imperfection has been expunged from its meaning. It is this idea of humanity insofar as it relegates imperfection under the sign of "inhumanity" upon which I set my critical focus. In particular, I take as my point of departure the way in which this idea of humanity has become a hallmark of the recent turn to cosmopolitanism in education (and other disciplines).

Cosmopolitanism is not easy to define, as I explore in detail in chapter 2, and has a long conceptual history dating back to the Roman Stoics, and developed in subsequent eras by Augustine and Kant. Generally speaking, it takes on the task of broadening those borders we have conventionally used to define our place in the world, and has, at a most fundamental level, advocated for world citizenship. As human beings who belong to a world we share with others, so it is argued, we cannot be so narrow in our sights that we only see ourselves in relation to our nearest and dearest: our family, our tribe, our compatriots. Its current reappearance has come hand-in-hand with the focus on economic globalization, ever-increasing mixtures of populations, and technological advances that make neighbors out of the most distant of inhabitants. But equal to this infusion of diversity into our daily midst has been the attention paid to those apparently universal aspects of coexistence, most notably, human rights. Along with democracy and global citizenship, human rights have become the supposed guarantors of a harmonious world order. Cosmopolitanism, then, simultaneously recognizes both the importance of cultural diversity and the centrality of universal human rights to its project for global harmony and peace. In education, there is now a proliferation of programs and courses on world or cosmopolitan citizenship in universities and schools; human rights education organizations have appeared all around the globe; and democratic, citizenship, and civic education have begun to embrace more global features. Although cosmopolitanism is not the exclusive proprietor of these areas of educational interest, it nonetheless brings them together into a more or less unified constellation and aspects of cosmopolitanism have been evident in world agencies such as UNESCO for many years. As we will see, however, throughout various chapters, cosmopolitanism bases its understanding of these new terms of belonging upon an idea of humanity that is reflective of precisely the kind of disavowal of imperfection that I touched on above.

For this reason, then, my task here is to examine critically the edifice of cosmopolitanism—and its building blocks in the shape of its commitments to diversity, human rights, democracy, and citizenship—locating its keystone in an idea of humanity purged of imperfection. My intent here is to show how shaky this keystone is for supporting the claims being made in cosmopolitanism's name. That is, as long as the idea of humanity disavows what is "inhuman" and imperfect about us, cosmopolitanism cannot give an adequate response to the question of violence and antagonism which plague our lives, despite its own attestations to the contrary. Indeed, I question here its suitability to sustain a notion of social justice without some serious rebuilding and, in fact, question whether this new edifice can any longer be recognized as cosmopolitanism as we have come to know it. For if we begin with the task of facing humanity in all its imperfection, we end up with a very different construction than the one we set out with. Although there are many things I admire and support in the quest to build a human future beyond those nefarious borders of ethnic nationalism, religious fanaticism, economic servitude, and patriarchal oppression, and although education clearly has a central place in the building of such future, I do think that appealing to an idea of humanity divorced from the particular ways humanity is lived and experienced presents us with a false sense of who we think we are and therefore of what we can hope to accomplish. In challenging this idea of humanity, my intent is not to provide some grand truth about human nature, nor is it to demolish the working toward more just forms of coexistence, but to do two things: to expose the limits of educational thought in order to pose currently unasked questions about the nature of the educational enterprise; and to propose ways of responding to those questions that take the cosmopolitan commitments to diversity, human rights, democracy, and citizenship seriously. In so doing, the book as a whole affirms these latter commitments through its reframing of imperfection as central to humanity.

Yet, admittedly, it does seem slightly risky to be challenging humanity in this way, and still retain a promising sense of education. The difficulties of walking this line, of proclaiming that education needs to face imperfection and what has been designated "inhuman," became clear to me after a tragic event that gripped the headlines in November, 2007.

A school shooting occurred in Finland, a land that is a close neighbor to my current country of residence, Sweden. The incident brought home for many in Scandinavia the fragility of a social fabric long seen to be relatively free from the mass violence often associated with American society. But this particular event was also for me personally a source of deep ambivalence. The boy who killed his classmates had filmed himself prior to the event, and posted a short clip to YouTube. Not only did he display a chilling ease in his handling of the gun, but he sported a T-shirt with a message that I found most jarring and which haunted my thoughts over the subsequent few weeks:

HUMANITY IS OVERRATED

Deeply immersed in the writing and editing of the essays contained in this book, I experienced an uncanny moment of both recognition and profound discomfort. Recognition in that my very topic deals with challenging a certain idea of humanity as a ground for cosmopolitan education. Could not my own inquiry also be interpreted as a claim that humanity was overrated? This indeed seemed to be where the recognition lay. At the same time, I was distressed by my own seeming complicity in this statement of repudiation of humanity, which, it is to be remembered, was borne by a boy intent on taking others' lives. Yet it wasn't simply the repudiation of "humanity" that disturbed me (repudiating ideas is, after all, a part of what we academics do); it was the apparent repudiation of human life itself which was the source of my anxiety. In that moment of disturbance, I perceived humanity as corresponding to a certain truth about human existence. Thus, despite my own critical intellectual stance toward an idea of humanity, I nonetheless also responded in the moment *as if* "humanity" corresponded to the lives of actual persons. In this way, the statement operated on two levels, one that took humanity as an idea that was considered to be overrated (hence my recognition), the other taking humanity as persons who in-the-flesh were considered to be overrated and therefore presumably dispensable (hence my disturbance). As a signifier, then, "humanity" simultaneously signified for me two different signifieds.

What my divided response to this statement so ominously laid bare was the easy equation that can be made between the term "humanity" and "human life," and the difficulties we have at separating the two. The power of the word, then, made it plain to me that I need to be most clear about what I am up to in this book. Because I am in no way challenging human life, but critiquing an idea of humanity currently operative in cosmopolitan approaches to education. So the burden lies on me in these pages to articulate the shift I seek to make with respect to how humanity can signify differently.

The primary focus for making this shift lies in the attention I pay to human pluralism. I advocate in these pages for an attention to pluralism that goes much deeper than simply claiming that cultural diversity ought to be recognized. Often this kind of approach operates only to further the claim that "underneath we are all the same." Thus it is not so uncommon to see the appeal to respect cultural diversity alongside the appeal to recognize our "shared humanity." It is precisely this tension that reveals, I think, a need to take pluralism seriously; for pluralism necessarily involves the idea that each of us is different in particular ways. Human pluralism is not simply about the aggregation of identities, or communities to which one belongs, but is specific to the relationships, communicative contexts, languages, and internal dynamics through which one makes attachments to the world. Pluralism on this view, then, has led me to ask questions from a perspective of specificity, and I largely draw on the work of Hannah Arendt, Emmanuel Levinas, Chantal Mouffe, and Luce Irigaray in framing and discussing questions such as: How do universal rights matter to lived persons? How do such universals get translated and negotiated in specific contexts? How does democracy come to name a particular moment of political association? How might citizenship reflect the very lives of women and men across cultures? Part of this focus on pluralism and specificity involves a commensurate view of the antagonistic aspects of social life. This is to suggest, following Chantal Mouffe, that subjectivities, since they are formed in relation to specific contexts which no two subjects entirely share, inevitably lead to disagreement and sometimes incommensurability. The task at hand, then, is not to hide behind appeals to cosmopolitan harmony or a shared humanity, but to take pluralism and its attendant conflicts seriously as part of a political and ethical commitment in education.

The chapters that follow set out precisely to do just that. The first two chapters can be read as introductions to the framework and approach I take throughout the rest of the book. "Facing Humanity: Crisis and Inevitability" lays out in more detail my critique of the idea of humanity underwriting cosmopolitan commitments in education. It positions this book beyond the polarities of humanism and antihumanism in asserting that humanity as a term does not need to be dispensed with, but that it must nonetheless be read in and against the "inhuman" aspects of the human condition. I offer a reading of Kant's views on the cosmopolitan direction of education through a critique of his idea of humanity which underwrites it. I bring into the discussion the work of Hannah Arendt, Luce Irigaray and Emmanuel Levinas to move us beyond the apparent innocence of humanity and education. The second chapter, "Rethinking Cosmopolitanism along the Fault Lines of a Divided Modernity," outlines the breadth of cosmopolitan theory and focuses on the split within it as one based on an inevitable yet paradoxical double commitment: respect for cultural diversity and a commitment to the universal right of humanity. This split forms the bedrock for future chapters, and I explore the way three contemporary thinkers have commented on this divide in their efforts to focus on human pluralism as a condition for cosmopolitanism: Seyla Benhabib, Julia Kristeva, and Jacques Derrida.

Chapters 3, 4, and 5 focus explicitly on human rights. Collectively, they question the nature of the subject, freedom, and justice in human rights theory and educational practice. Chapter 3 discusses the difficulties and incomplete nature of human rights, and gives an overview, through a reading of Arendt's notion of the "right to have rights," of three major themes that have shaped the foundation and educational significance of human rights declarations: the state's relation to the individual; the issue of universality; and the relation between rights and suffering. Chapter 4 focuses on the pedagogical aspects of teaching human rights, particularly when rights are seen to be based on the "necessary fiction of freedom" and the communicative nature of justice. Here, I propose that it is only by facing the dilemmas posed by freedom, rights, and justice that we can better construct pedagogical approaches to the teaching of rights, particularly as they are reflective of responsibility to others and are not merely entitlements. Chapter 5 brings the discussion of rights to bear on questions of cultural diversity and sexual difference. Here I discuss the background struggles that have accompanied the reformulation of rights and discuss the ways in which rights have been caught within a culture-sex divide. In proposing that rights need to be negotiated in specific contexts and to undergo acts of cultural translation (following Judith Butler), I draw extensively upon the French law prohibiting the wearing of religious symbols to schools in order to highlight the ways in which such an approach to rights can be beneficial to creating meaningful democratic spaces for Muslim girls.

The next two chapters have as their focus democracy and citizenship. Chapter 6 challenges the idea of consensus that permeates dialogic and deliberative approaches to democracy, which cosmopolitan theory often supports. I draw on proponents of radical democratic theory in order to explore how conflict, not consensus, is necessary to the creation of robust democratic action. The chapter argues that the idea of humanity that supports consensus actually works against democratic possibility and suggests ways in which education can move beyond consensus in promoting the promise of democracy. The next chapter, "Educating the Sexed Citizen: Irigaray and the Promise of a Humanity that is Yet to Come," centers on the work of feminist philosopher Luce Irigaray, who proposes that humanity is itself divided along the lines of sexual difference. I deal in particular with Irigaray's writing on sexuate rights, civil codes, and education in order to propose that educating for sexed citizenship involves an education in human becoming.

Chapter 8, "Teachers Judging without Scripts, or Thinking Cosmopolitan," serves to advance the shift I have made throughout the preceding pages. Here, I discuss judgment and thinking as central to a renewed sense of a cosmopolitan project, one which moves away from an "ism" which risks merely becoming a frame for the "how-to's" of teaching toward the idea that it is really how one adjudicates between universals and particulars against the horizon of our "cosmopolitan existence" that lies at the heart of cosmopolitan education. Here, I focus on the work of Arendt and Levinas in order to claim how thought and judgment are founded on one's relationship to others. I conclude this book with an epilogue on what I see to be the fundamental features of working toward an imperfect education.

Throughout these pages, then, I put into question the conventional hope that given the right kind of education we can live up more fully to those positive qualities that are seen to inhere in humanity: dignity, rationality, compassion, and freedom, to name but a few. Instead, I ask what education might be like if we begin with an entirely different premise, with the imperfection of humanity itself, and seek not to cultivate a garden of shared humanity but live in and with an imperfect garden thoughtfully. I leave the reader to judge whether the premise and the conclusions this book leads to can frame a new sense of the cosmopolitan direction in education.

1

Facing Humanity: Crisis and Inevitability

They spoke to me of people, and of humanity.
But I've never seen people, or humanity.
I've seen various people, astonishingly dissimilar,
Each separated from the next by unpeopled space.

Fernando Pessoa[1]

Why speak of humanity when we speak of education—particularly if, as Pessoa so eloquently expresses, we cannot meet "humanity" but only people in all their diversity? Do we not risk endangering our concern for actual persons in our appeals to a humanity we can never face, greet, confront, or listen to? It appears nonetheless to be a common enough assumption that there is some intrinsic connection between the project of education and the idea of humanity itself. This connection has been a central feature of a wide range of educational viewpoints, most notably in the grand humanistic traditions of *bildung* and liberal arts education.[2] On these views, education is fundamentally about the development of those qualities that are seen to contribute to a sense of human flourishing: dignity, respect, creativity, freedom, and rationality, to name but a few. Though debates exist about which qualities deserve the most attention, the appeal to humanity as a condition of becoming not merely an educated person but a human subject who is deeply connected to others, both morally and politically, has resonated quite loudly. Indeed, as early as Kant's 1803 treatise on education, the modern idea of humanity has been used as a way of framing education's contribution to the creation of a more humane future.[3]

On the face of it, this appears to be a welcomed line of thinking, especially given the present scope of social breakdown and violence around the globe. And it is precisely this line of thinking which is reflected in the current turn to a cosmopolitan direction in education, with its blending of concerns for world citizenship, human rights, democracy, and cross-cultural understanding (e.g., Kemp 2005; Noddings 2005; Nussbaum 1997a). In particular, as we will see in more detail in the next chapter, the cosmopolitan project also seeks to educate for global awareness and unquestionably positions a "shared humanity" as a condition of world citizenship beyond the narrow borders of national identities

(Heater 2002). As one of the most cogent apologists for cosmopolitanism, Martha Nussbaum writes:

> The accident of where one is born is just that, an accident; any human being might have been born in any nation. Recognizing this, we should not allow differences of nationality or class or ethnic membership or even gender to erect barriers between us and our fellow human beings. We should recognize humanity—and its fundamental ingredients, reason and moral capacity—wherever it occurs, and give that community of humanity our first allegiance. (1997a, 58–59)

Calling for such an allegiance can be seen, I think, as a complex moral, political, and educational response to a seeming "failure" of humanity, in which the bettering of the human condition is thought to be at least partially accomplished by educating youth in the arts of human coexistence founded on what we share we others. Not only confined, then, to a philosopher's dream of a better world, the term humanity is also regularly placed in the company of such words as "cultivating," "nurturing," "promoting," or "caring for" by organizations such as UNESCO—words which suggest that humanity is something indeed desirable to educate for even if it is not immediately in evidence.

Although such appeals to humanity are constructed on supposedly positive, universal ideals, such as dignity, reason, respect, and freedom, there is an unsightly side to the apparent idea of "goodness" that is contained in the term humanity itself. What such affirmative statements on humanity reveal about the possibilities of education is nothing other, it seems to me, than an admission that the present human condition is in crisis.[4] After all, when organizations such as UNESCO, or when cosmopolitan educationalists appeal to humanity, they are hoping to counteract the very devastating realities of social dissolution that plague societies throughout the world and to unite us under a banner of respect for what we share as human beings. Schools, then, often are called upon to educate—and yes, to socialize—the young into becoming more humane citizens. Derek Heater (2002) has noted that "there is such an abundance of hatred, injustice and violence in this world that one would properly court ridicule by naïvely suggesting that schools could readily replace this condition with cosmopolitan harmony" (164). Yet equally, he suggests, we cannot think that education can make no contribution at all in addressing injustice. Instead, Heater claims, it is more fruitful to embrace an *equivocal* position when it comes to making lofty educational claims about the amelioration of the human condition (2002, 165).

Taking a modest, equivocal position with regard to what education can accomplish in responding to violence and inequity across human differences requires, in my view, a critical re-evaluation of the idea of humanity itself. My main reason for advancing such a position emerges in light of what I see as the way humanity is conceived along the lines of an oppositional stance to all that is undesirable in human interaction. To use it, therefore, as an appeal to politics, ethics, or education means blinding ourselves to the very *human* aspects of our *inhuman* actions.[5] Thus the idea that education can ameliorate certain global conditions under the sign of humanity is a worrying proposition, not least because it fails to recognize that the very injustices and antagonisms which are the targets of such education are created and sustained precisely through our human talent for producing them.

Simon Critchley (2007) has recently voiced a warning along similar lines. He remarks that since humanity has been used to justify the exclusion of those with whom we are in conflict, "the slightly further left amongst us should also be careful about invoking the signifier of humanity in any oppositional politics" (143). Humanity, in his view, has been used as a justification for the so-called legitimate annihilation of those whom have been deemed enemies. Similarly, Chantal Mouffe (2005) notes that throughout history the "wars raged in the name of humanity were particularly inhuman since all means were justified once the enemy had been presented as an outlaw of humanity" (78).[6] Thus the tendency to use the idea of the humanity as a moralistic ground for exclusion should raise suspicion about our use of the term in educational circles. If one of the purposes of education is indeed to transform the small injustices which plague our lives in the social (and not the grander scope of global violence, as Heater intimates), it must, in my view, take a more critical attitude to the idea of humanity which serves to underpin this very purpose. My task here, then, in offering such a reconsideration of humanity in relation to education in general, and cosmopolitanism more particularly, is not to plea for a new humanism, which states—*unequivocally*—what counts as human "flourishing" and "fulfillment"; nor is it a call for a more definitive picture of human nature. Instead, I focus here on the idea that the possibility of acting in the name of humanity lies in our capacity for betraying it. That is, the idea of humanity itself must include human limits as well as human possibilities and needs to be read in relation to the very violence and antagonism that inheres in specifically *human* interaction. Therefore what follows shifts from a position in which education is seen to "cultivate" an ideal of humanity, to a position in which education concerns itself with the more concrete—and difficult—work of "facing" humanity. For if education is going to work toward a more peaceful future that fully recognizes the plurality of human lives, I argue that it must do so without appealing to an idealized humanity that is solely based on universal and intrinsic goodness. The primary question to be addressed, therefore, is how do we imagine an education that seeks not to *cultivate* humanity, to borrow from Nussbaum (1997a), but instead seeks to *face* it—head-on, so to speak, without sentimentalism, idealism, or false hope?

In response to this question, the first section of this chapter discusses the inhuman in relation to the idea of humanity and suggests that humanity needs to be thought beyond the polarities of humanism and antihumanism. The second section delves more directly into the question humanity poses for education, drawing primarily on Kant, Hannah Arendt, and Luce Irigaray. Here I identify the problem of equating humanity with goodness and universalism, and discuss the limitations of education itself in promoting humanity as a justification for its aims. The next section discusses violence and suffering as inevitably intertwined with ethical (nonviolent) possibility and how this challenges an equation of humanity with any simple notion of the Good (Levinas 1969; 1998a). It, moreover, puts forth the view that it is only in *facing* humanity that we can more adequately conceive of advocating an educational responsibility for dealing with injustice. I conclude with a few ideas about how facing humanity can act as a motivation for what education can hope to accomplish, and how this promotes a rethinking of cosmopolitanism as an aim of education (a task which is taken up more fully in the next chapter).

HUMANITY AND THE INHUMAN

The idea of humanity historically often appears on the scene as a sort of compensation for the devastation and suffering humans themselves have been responsible for creating. The various appeals to humanity in foundational documents such as the American Bill of Rights, the French Droits de l'Homme et du Citoyen, and the UN Universal Declaration followed precisely on the heels of the devastation wrought by colonialism, the ancien régime, and the Holocaust, respectively. Similarly, the European fascination with various aspects of the cosmopolitan project in the fairly recent past has come about in the shadow of the wars and ethnic cleansing in the former Yugoslavia. Even more recent, the urgency with which democratic, global, intercultural, and interreligious themes have been placed on the educational agenda is directly related to the highly polarized situation created after the US terrorist attacks and the subsequent wars in Afghanistan and Iraq. The idea of humanity seems to have become a sign under which to mobilize forces against our "human, all too human" gift for mutual hatred and destruction. With this said, it would appear that our very hope in promoting the kind of humanity these rights-based documents call for is also paradoxically bound up with the idea that our humanity has abandoned us, or, more to the point perhaps, has been abandoned *by* us. Thus the rhetorical force of "humanity" is actually made more meaningful against the very backdrop of its seeming negation.

Yet, appealing to humanity as a ground for nonviolence, conflict resolution, or civil peace—that is, as the *opposite* of that which we find difficult to bear—risks, to my mind, the erasure of the very human element to be found in "inhuman" violence, suffering, and civil hardship. Indeed, as Drucilla Cornell (2003) warns us, while violence is inexcusable on ethical grounds, there is nonetheless a human face that belongs to those who commit it (174). She argues that even terrorists are covered under the Kantian "ideal of humanity" umbrella; for without this protection, she warns, one falls easily into a justification of "inhumanity" itself. Although I am sympathetic to Cornell's attempts to complicate what has become in the US a black-and-white portrayal of the human-inhuman divide, unlike Cornell, my purpose here is not so much to argue that everyone is part of some *ideal* of humanity as to propose that the *idea* of humanity itself can be rethought as containing the human capacity for violence without seeing that violence merely as its negation. On this view, an idea of humanity includes within it both the capacity for dignity and freedom as well as the capacity to do harm to others. What needs to be explored further, of course, is how conceiving humanity on these terms can effectively motivate us to an ethical position of nonviolence. By this I mean an ethical position that does not sidestep the very question of violence as a human possibility and that does not return to certain humanistic accounts of the "goodness" of humankind that merely serve to mask our undesirable elements.

Alain Badiou, in his recent book, *The Century* (2007), explores two positions which he claims have attempted to rewrite the discourse of humanism in the postwar European context: a radical humanism envisaged by Jean-Paul Sartre and a radical antihumanism advocated by Michel Foucault. In the first account, the human is conceived as filling the emptiness left by the "death of God." On Badiou's reading, this radical humanism builds on a view of philosophy as anthropology—that is, philosophy begins in the idea that human beings create their own systems of meaning for which they must assume responsibility. In the second account, the human is to be thought in terms of the void created by the "death of Man" as a universal or transcendent subject. Badiou argues that such radical antihumanism sees philosophy as thought, as "a thinking which lets an inhuman beginning arrive" (2007, 172). What is of importance to note for my purposes here is that both positions largely have been abandoned. In Badiou's eyes, these now have been replaced by a classical humanism "without a God," which merely reduces humans to a species, to a biological body, to DNA and cellular composition; it has, he claims, become a "projectless humanism," an "animal humanism" (2007, 175). What have been eclipsed as well are the inhuman aspects of the human condition, which have the possibility of opening new beginnings for philosophical reflection. Badiou suggests that what is needed is a rethinking of the human that moves beyond both radical humanism and radical antihumanism without falling back on depictions of "man" in crass materialistic terms of genes, cells, and neurons. He is adamant that where we need to start our thinking is with the inhuman truths of human existence itself (2007, 175).

It is in light of this call for inhuman beginnings that the present work situates itself—not in order to revive (or continue) the radical antihumanist project of Foucault, but in order to rethink the human element within our appeals to humanity as containing something of the inhuman as well. Jean-François Lyotard (1991) articulates a most fundamental question: "What shall we call human in humans ...?" (3). In raising this query, Lyotard's point is not to suggest that we can give a definitive answer, but that we interrogate our assumptions about the exclusion of the inhuman in our appeals to humanity. Indeed, Lyotard claims that it is precisely the inhuman element inherent in the human condition that premises our educational endeavors (4). He writes:

> If humans are born human, as cats are born cats (within a few hours), it would not be ... I don't even say desirable, which is another question, but simply possible, to educate them. That children have to be educated is a circumstance which only proceeds from the fact that they are not completely led by nature,

not programmed. The institutions which constitute culture supplement this native lack. (1991, 3)

Raising the possibility that education actually deals face-to-face with the "inhuman" as a condition of possibility for creating the "human" suggests to me that educational thought needs to begin not with the projection of an already secured and perfected ideal of what counts as human, but upon other terms altogether. Lyotard points out that humanism erases the "unharmonizable" aspects of our existence in seeking a common project and destiny for humankind, and he sees one such unharmonizable aspect lying in the humanity/inhumanity of the child:

> Shorn of speech, incapable of standing upright, hesitating over the objects of its interest, not able to calculate its advantages, not sensitive to common reason, the child is eminently the human because its distress heralds and promises things possible. Its initial delay in humanity, which makes it the hostage of the adult community, is also what manifests to this community the lack of humanity it is suffering from, and which calls on it to become more human. (1991, 3–4)

What Lyotard indicates here is how the idea of humanity actually rests upon the concealment of an inhuman element essential to its survival. In turn, education, he claims, enacts upon the child its own inhumanity in seeking to render the child "human" through "constraint," "terror," and even "castration" (4–5). That is, education must impose a humanity that is traumatic to the nascent human subject that is the child.[7] In this way, then, education can never be an innocent purveyor of humanistic goods but is an institutionalized practice that is fraught with ambiguity, living in the aporetic space that opens up in the encounter between the human and inhuman. What Lyotard points to is that the child (and the student more generally) must learn to become a member of the "community of humanity," as both Nussbaum (1997a) and Arendt (1992) put it. It is not that the child is "inhuman" in and of itself; but acts as a reminder to adults of both the fragility of humanity and the learning required to become human. In thus moving beyond the terms of humanism and antihumanism what Lyotard asks us to consider is to think of humanity as a *problem*, as a *question* for education, and not simply as a solution or justification for it.

RETHINKING HUMANITY AS AN EDUCATIONAL PROBLEM

One response to the relation between humanity and education, if I may be permitted an oversimplification here, has often led to the development of ideas about what constitutes a shared human existence, how each individual might fulfill its potential in partaking in that existence, and the ways in which education can then structure a path toward the fulfillment of that existence in relation to others. With respect to the pursuit of projects concerning, in particular, social justice, cosmopolitanism, and human rights, education's roots in the idea of humanity find familiar expression in Kant's educational thought:

> One *principle of education* which those men especially who form educational schemes should keep before their eyes is this—children ought to be educated, not for the present, but for a possibly improved condition of man in the future; that is, in a manner which is adapted to the *idea of humanity* and the whole destiny of man ...

> But the basis of a scheme of education must be cosmopolitan. And is, then, the idea of the universal good harmful to us as individuals? Never! for [sic] though it may appear that something must be sacrificed by this idea, an advance is also made towards what is the best even for the individual under his present conditions. And then what glorious consequences follow! It is through good education that all the good in the world arises. For this the germs which lie hidden in man need only to be more and more developed; for the rudiments of evil are not to be found in the natural disposition of man. Evil is only the result of nature not being brought under control. In man there are only germs of good. (1906, 14–15)

In these short passages, Kant offers here a complex, multilayered account of education in relation to the idea of humanity. First, it is at once outward looking in its cosmopolitan purpose, as well as inward looking in appealing to the "germs" of basic human goodness—even if those germs, as Kant claims, lie well hidden. Secondly, it relies on a universalistic account of humanity, delineated by the appeal to the whole destiny of "man," and thereby unites differences in its cosmopolitan frame. Thirdly, education is to be put in the service of an idea of humanity, which entails working toward the future-oriented improvement of the condition of "man".[8]

On the surface, at least, these paragraphs crystallize that dream of education, which many of us, as teachers, hold close to our hearts: through our acts as educators we can indeed contribute to creating a better place to live. Even more compelling, I suggest, is Kant's rendering of this dream in the name of universal humanity, for it lends purpose and significance to teachers' daily work with students. In times that seem ripe with violence and disruption, the call to humanity lends hope to the enduring powers of education to transform the conditions under which people can coexist more peacefully. Without wishing to disregard these comforts entirely, for they do feed and sustain the work of teachers and breathe life into what can otherwise seem meaningless activities geared toward state examinations and classroom tests, I do wish to question three points: first, how the goodness of humanity is premised on a paradoxical rendering of our capacity for evil; secondly, how the universal subject of "man" rubs against the grain of the particularity embedded within the cosmopolitan emphasis on plurality; and thirdly, the conception of education underlying Kant's views as one that is geared toward the future destiny of man.

With respect to my first point, what Kant gives us here is an image of humanity as building on a seemingly natural germ of goodness that lies in opposition to our human capacity for evil. The conventional reading of Kant's thesis is that evil is an ever-present threat to our well-being—an aspect of our nature gone awry—and through bringing it under the control of our rational faculty the seeds of human goodness thereby have the opportunity to grow. However, there is something about his characterization of evil here which suggests that a slightly different reading is in order. Evil is itself rendered paradoxically as being at once an "uncontrolled," uneducated aspect of "nature" *and* as that which cannot be found entirely within man's "natural" disposition. Indeed, there is an apparent struggle at play here: at one moment Kant introduces evil *as* nature insofar as it must be brought under control, and the next he claims that it is a deformation of man's "natural" goodness. It appears, then, that evil is something *not quite* naturally human; it is depicted as belonging to the spheres of *both* human potentiality and of human impossibility. Kant ultimately positions evil outside the boundaries of a more "fundamental" aspect of human nature—namely, the good—and thereby turns evil into a betrayal of humanity itself. Yet, what he also curiously reveals (without discussing its consequences) is that it is a betrayal that exists precariously on the border of what is evidently or factually human (evil acts *are* committed by particular persons) and what is a seeming distortion of "man's" universal nature. Hence rather than dealing directly with this problematic of evil through education, Kant's retreat to the goodness "within man" neatly accomplishes its banishment from educational concern. That is, it is only by repressing this capacity for evil that education can begin its task of cultivating humanity—a humanity that is now effectively cut off from the very terrors of evil that "naturally" seem to threaten it. I am not claiming that Kant sees evil *definitively* in this way (and many discussions of his concept of radical evil attest to this), but in his proffering of humanity as a condition of cosmopolitan education rooted in an intrinsic goodness, he sacrifices human complexity in the move to deny evil a definitive place in the field of human nature. Education thus serves the future not by facing the undesirable aspects of our being human but through nurturing those seeds of goodness that lie "within." My concern is that current educational projects that one-sidedly take up the goodness of humanity risk repeating this same banishment of evil, leaving us without a language for dealing with the antagonistic elements of human interaction, which are indeed rife in educational and social encounters.

The second point to be raised concerns the universalism of "man" as a signifier for humanity. Without rehearsing what has by now become fairly standard fare in feminist critiques of such universalism, I do wish to reflect on how the importation of the idea of the humanity into current forms of cosmopolitanism in education actually might be reproducing those same limitations—despite various appeals to "gender" (see the quote from Nussbaum above). As Luce Irigaray (1996; 2002) has noted, such claims to humanity fail to account adequately for the specificity not only of women's lives, but of men's lives as well. That is, as long as "humanity" seeks to suture over differences in the name of "man" or even "humankind" without acknowledging itself as a reflection of a particular conceptual history, we do a violence to the very ways that humanity can be differentially experienced, symbolized, and imagined (Irigaray 1996). So, even if we rewrite Kant's appeal in gender-neutral terms so it reads the "whole destiny of *humankind*," the point remains is that it is the universalizing impulse that lies behind the appeal which cannot account for the fundamental differences within human existence*s*—in the plural. Thus for Irigaray, it is not simply a matter of replacing "man" with "woman" or even "human", but of reimagining the idea of humanity altogether. Indeed, the inhuman element of Kant's universalism is connected to the very nature of a thought that seeks to unify the experiences of multiple existences. Irigaray proposes, then, that if education is to have anything at all to do with humanity, it needs to challenge this inhuman element of universality. Its task, in her mind, is to develop new relations through which what is human reveals itself through its difference (Irigaray 2001, 9). On Irigaray's view, then, education would have a very different function than of providing for the universal destiny of mankind, which brings me to my third point.

While not wishing to claim that all cosmopolitanists agree with Kant on the specific direction he takes with respect to education, there nonetheless lies at the kernel of his thought an idea about educating *for* humanity that raises the question of what education can itself actually bear and, moreover, the weight that children themselves should shoulder. Creating a hopeful future for humanity as a whole is not an unusual aim, particularly amongst educators and policy makers who wish to see education as one ingredient, if not *the* ingredient, to creating a more humane future. Yet, as Hannah Arendt (1965) has warned us, education risks posing as a danger to itself if it takes on the task of "constructing" a new world for children, instead of embracing the very ambiguity that lies at the core of education: the task of teaching for a "world that is or is becoming out of joint" (192). This view is important for my argument that education cannot ever simply embrace "humanity" without risking its very purpose. Let me explain.

Arendt's ideas on education largely rest, first, on her notion of natality: that each child brings a unique specificity into the world and thus by virtue of this will create it anew; and secondly, on her notion of education as that which has the responsibility to teach that which is already known as part of a project of conserving tradition and introducing children to the already existing world into which they born. In this sense, education resides in a dilemma. It is caught between preparing children for the world as it is—with all its difficulties and pleasures—and recognizing the hope that youth's newness brings. She cautions, however, that as soon as teachers try to direct or control this hope, despite our best intentions, we endanger it. "It is in the nature of the human condition that each new generation grows into an old world, so that to prepare a new generation for a new world can only mean that one wishes to strike from the newcomers' hands their own chance at the new" (Arendt 1965, 177). Connected to this is her view that any political use of education results in a mere "dictatorial intervention, based on the absolute superiority of the adult" (1965, 176). Thus, as she sees it, the task for education is not to consign children to a "destiny" but to pre-serve newness in an old world. To quote a rather famous passage:

> Education is the point at which we decide whether we love the world enough to assume responsibility for it and by the same token save it from that ruin which, except for renewal, except for the coming of the new and young, would be in-evitable. And education, too, is where we decide whether we love our children enough not to expel them from our world and leave them to their own devices, nor to strike from their hands their chance of undertaking something new, something unforeseen by us, but to prepare them in advance for the task of re-newing a common world. (Arendt 1965, 196)

Whether or not one agrees with Arendt's idea that education is necessarily about conservation and not about advancing any political agendas, she nonetheless raises a crucial point for my discussion here, and that is how in educating *for* humanity, we run the risk of creating for children a world that does not respond to it *as it is*, and create instead a harmonious image of what we adults *want the world to be*. On Arendt's account, the greatest risk to the future is to claim, as Kant does, that children can be raised for the explicit benefit of man's destiny without having a say in what that destiny could look like or how it might be re-newed. Thus I read Arendt's concern with the renewal of the common world as specifically not rooted in idealized conceptions of intrinsic goodness or even the universality of humanity, but with the complexities of the human condition, in all its plurality. For Arendt, belonging to a community of humanity means be-longing to a world where pluralism is prized above all else.

What I have attempted here is to reconsider some of the ideas that lie be-hind a commitment to humanity and read humanity as an educational problem—one caught up in the expulsion of evil, of difference, and of newness from edu-cational concern. In both Irigaray's and Arendt's eyes, it is pluralism and differ-ence that needs to be made meaningful in creating possibilities for a better fu-ture. I am thus worried that in appealing to a "shared humanity" as a way of achieving respect for pluralism, we actually diminish pluralism in its name and thereby risk our ability to teach responsively in troubled times. With respect to the cosmopolitan direction education has taken, how can a rethinking of human-ity actually provide us with a new sense of educational promise and a new sense of responsibility?

BEYOND INTRINSIC GOODNESS AND UNIVERSALITY: HUMANITY *AS* RESPONSIBILITY

In rethinking the terms upon which the idea of humanity rest—intrinsic good-ness and universality—I turn here to the thought of Emmanuel Levinas. What I think Levinas's work so well expresses is precisely its resistance to the kind of Kantian universalism that would see us all as caught within the net of a pre-scribed *idea* of what humanity consists of, and its questioning of the belief that this idea can make exacting ethical claims upon us. For where Levinas locates the ethical demand is neither in ideas nor principles, but in the goodness that is only to be found in relation to the other. Thus, what I am proposing here in discussing Levinas in this context is that an attention to alterity and the way the individual "I" is commanded by it, opens up the terms of humanity to pluralism and to a reconceptualization of the good based on radical difference.

In the conception of the face-to-face relation, Levinas recognizes the potentiality for violence that invites itself as a response to the complete exposure, or nakedness, of the other's face. "The skin of the face is that which stays most naked, most destitute.... The face is exposed, menaced, as if inviting us to an act of violence" (1985, 86). Paradoxically, however, Levinas also states "the ethical presence is both other and imposes itself without violence" (1969, 218). What are we to make of such a perplexing assertion—that the face invites violence *and* imposes itself without violence? In the relation to the face, where ethics is located (particularly in his earlier work), Levinas claims that there arises a possibility for violence *at the same moment* as it encounters its injunction. That is, the naked vulnerability of the face simultaneously tempts violence as it forbids it through its ethical challenge: "thou shalt not kill." It is not that violence acts as a *condition* for nonviolence, it is that the possibility for nonviolence appears in the space where violence is capable of being committed. Levinas's task is to depict that trajectory, that time and space of ethical responsibility, which signifies a relationship of nonviolence without banishing or denying the risk of the eruption of violence itself—for without a reminder of such a possibility, nonviolence becomes a meaningless signifier; it literally makes no sense. When he writes, for instance, that "only beings capable of war can rise to peace" (1969, 222), he is not suggesting that war is a necessary prelude to peace, but that peace cannot itself be *thought* without considering our capacity for war. So, too, then is the ethical possibility for nonviolence unthinkable without admitting of the violent story of human interaction.

But where Levinas's theory really takes on its most compelling depictions of violence is in his portrayal of the subject's responsibility for the other in terms that suggest the pain, suffering, and trauma involved. Thus not only does the encounter with the face tempt a violence that is prohibited, giving rise to the possibility for nonviolent interaction—but the violence also works in the other direction as well. The other actually disturbs the apparent serenity and complacency of the ego's identity. It is this "traumatic wounding," as he calls it, that ushers in a renewed sense of responsibility beyond conventional notions of the good.

Responsibility, in Levinas's later work, emerges in the proximity between self and other and it is here that he locates both the trauma of subjectivity and the meaning of humanity itself: "Proximity is quite distinct from every other relationship, and has to be conceived as a responsibility for the other; it might be called humanity, or subjectivity, or self" (1998a, 46). It is here, in such proximity, that the other commands the self to respond by calling that very self into question. Not through a literal posing of the question "Who are you?" but through the experience of address from which the self cannot flee.

> Vulnerability, exposure to outrage, to wounding, passivity more passive than all patience, passivity of the accusative form, trauma of accusation suffered by a hostage to the point of persecution, implicating the identity of the hostage who substitutes himself for the others: all this is the self, a defecting or defeat of the ego's identity. (1998a, 15)

It is in this relation of heteronomy—as a power that exists over the ego—that the subject is propelled into submission to the other. And in a typically Levinasian counterintuitive move, it is precisely this relation of subjection that Levinas names the Good.

The Good, he claims, does not arise from a "germ" within the subject, or by virtue of the subject's belonging to an idea of "humanity"; it comes from the other. It is a goodness only conceived in relation—not in rationality or autonomous freedom. This goodness, moreover, "persecutes" the ego: the I is haunted by it, ensnared within its demand without having a choice in the matter. Levinas writes: "The Good cannot become present or enter into a representation. The present is a beginning in my freedom, whereas the Good is not presented to freedom; it has chosen me before I have chosen it. No one is good voluntarily" (1998a, 11). The Good, in other words, comes before me, comes prior to any decision I make to be good. What Levinas is getting at here has to do with the way in which the proximity to the other brings about an ineluctable responsibility with no hope for escape. It is not that the I cannot "refuse" to respond to others—we do so all the time in failing to meet the eyes of people who address us in the street, and in committing harms, both large and small. Yet, in Levinas's terms, the "Evil" that is committed in refusing responsibility reveals that responsibility in spite of itself (2003, 50). Evil is only a momentary refusal of what is a basic (ethical) condition of human subjectivity.

Contra Kant, the Good can neither be taught as a positive moral quality, nor can it exist as that which is intrinsic to the human being. The Good, on Levinas's terms, as we have seen, cannot enter into the present, where the subject is a free and willing individual that autonomously decides to choose goodness, nor can the Good be represented as a principle or as a guide for action. And this is because the Good emanates from *within* the relation to the other, from within the proximity to difference; it cannot be found "within man himself" or in any ideal that lies outside the human encounter. Since this proximity is marked by trauma, ironically, for Levinas, the Good is not "good," in our conventional meaning of the term. It is inextricably linked to the very violent structure of facing alterity. Again, he reasserts his meaning of the Good: "For the Good cannot enter into a present nor be put into a representation. But being Good it redeems the violence of its alterity, even if the subject has to suffer through the augmentation of this ever more demanding violence" (1998a, 15). To my mind, Levinas casts goodness in terms of "violence" because there is an inevitable affliction of pain and a consequent experience of suffering, which admits of the difficulties—and indeed traumas—that incur in facing difference. It is, therefore, not part of some idea of a predefined Being, or humanity; instead, "Goodness gives to subjectivity its irreducible signification" (1998a, 18).

Thus beyond humanism and antihumanism, Levinas attempts to recuperate a subject of humanity, but not one sanitized from the sheer difficulties of *facing* that humanity, both literally and figuratively. While obviously proposing that such a facing is the place where the ethical structure of subjectivity itself emerges, where the possibility for goodness emerges, Levinas recognizes nonetheless that there is something frightful and awesome to this facing. Even if we do not accept the intricacies involved in the Levinasian position and the exaggerated language through which he depicts the Good and the prospect of ethics, I nonetheless think that his work has the potential to suggest a more complicated picture of what humanity can entail, for it focuses on the specificity of human relations as a condition for respecting human pluralism. For Levinas, humans are not humans by virtue of a prior, shared existence in humanity; the ego only comes into being through the traumatic encounter with an other whose existence is radically different from the ego's own. Thus humanity is not a preconceived ideal, but is located in the proximity where self and other meet. Humanity's name *is* the responsibility that is forged out of trauma and the ever-present threat of violence.

HUMANITY, RESPONSIBILITY, AND COSMOPOLITAN EDUCATION

What I have attempted in preceding pages to show is how the idea of "cultivating" humanity, which is so often taken for granted in educational thought focusing on global citizenship, human rights, and democracy, can actually preclude responding to the pluralism into which cosmopolitan projects also put so much of their energy. Moreover, I have attempted to clarify how both the conception of intrinsic goodness that leads to calls for "cultivation," "flourishing," and "caring for" humanity, and the universalism implicit in those calls, hinders the way we reflect on the very antagonisms that cosmopolitanists work so hard to counter. My suggestion is that if education—cosmopolitan or otherwise—can take a more equivocal position on what it can hope to achieve, then it needs to confront such antagonism, violence, and hatred as part and parcel of humanity itself. To repeat, this is not an antihumanist stance, whereby the language of humanity no longer is seen to be valid; it is rather to read humanity as distinctly connected to the concrete situations in which we find ourselves. There is, I suggest, an inevitability to this task, in that a refusal to face humanity on terms which we might find disagreeable thwarts our attempts to engage rigorously with the very ethical and political dilemmas that frame our educational commitments. In a major sense, this is a plea for developing a *perspective of specificity* in which humanity reveals itself as a sometimes very difficult aspect of our work as teachers in our encounters with students. In calling for the *facing* of humanity, I am therefore highly critical of the work we do in humanity's name, particularly when it is only about our putting our best face forward; at the same time, though, I think we need to inform the work we do with reimagining humanity *as* we confront the particular difficulties, conflicts, and tensions in our encounters with others.

Thus, I do not see that facing humanity is about abandoning hope for working against injustices. Quite the contrary. My view is that in facing humanity, in assuming the responsibility that comes from the relation to the other, we have a much better chance at alleviating at least some of those conditions. Facing humanity allows us, I think, to resist the condemning moralization that turns others into nonhumans, or into emblems of inhumanity. Instead, if we think that humanity actually comes into being at the point where we acknowledge the risk of its impossibility, then education can be reimagined as a site of response to human difference.

In drawing on Levinas, I have suggested that the respect, dignity, and freedom which have become signifiers of humanity are not bred from within, but from the relation to the disturbing and provocative event of being confronted by another person. It is here, in this provocation, where I see the promise of education itself. For it allows into education the difficult prospect of responding to others as an actual *practice* of justice—however incomplete such practices might be—without deferring it to some future that will one day arrive. I say difficult here, for Levinas's responsibility is not a salve for soothing the wounds of the world couched in some nice language of "care," "love," or "empathy"; his is not a comforting philosophy. It is a relentless examination of the ways in which violence plagues our lives and our capacities for responding in the face of them.

Since education exists on that precarious border between the world we live in and the world that will come into being, as Arendt so passionately depicts it, it must deal with the present without disenabling the chance for children to reimagine the future. To construct educational models based on cosmopolitan harmony, then, does a disservice to the existing lives of those children we teach. For on the one hand, adults claim that the world is partially a horrible place which we have to fix and that children have, at least in part, inherited the responsibility for fixing it; and on the other hand, the real, lived experiences of conflict, including racial slurs, bullying, religious taunts, and the like, can seem so far removed from the hopes for the future that adults themselves project onto children. It is not that I disagree with encouraging political engagement or global awareness in education (quite the opposite, in fact, as will become clearer in future chapters), it is that if humanity is to guide our teaching, it must do so in ways that acknowledge the profound difficulties faced by the children themselves—difficulties which originate in particularly fragile relations across difference. Although, as I pointed out above, goodness in the Levinasian sense cannot be taught, it does compel us to consider the ways in which teachers can offer a language of responsibility as a direct, concrete response to the lives of children themselves. I realize that cosmopolitanism is driven by the need for youth to think beyond themselves and their own backyards, but in the attempt to forge "global" identities on the grounds of an idea of humanity seems to me to be displacing the problem of humanity onto abstract notions that fail to respect the very particular ways humanity is itself "revealed" in the tangible relations in which we find ourselves. To assume that humanity exists in the universal risks diminishing concrete forms of existing, in all their rich variety and diversity. Thus coupled with a goodness that comes from relations to others, is the idea that humanity is, in a most fundamental way, plural.

In this, then, the cosmopolitan emphasis on a "shared humanity" is not something that I think we should advocate if we are really concerned with relieving injustice. This is not to say that we do not share anything with one another (we do indeed share values, love, suffering, and joy). Nor is it to claim that people—children included—cannot forge alliances and friendships across these shared spaces. My point is, rather, that to educate on the basis that we already know what humanity is, risks counting some persons "in" while leaving others (those who express violence and hatred, for instance) "out" and it further masks how each one of us is capable of committing harm in the first place. Humanity is, as I have discussed above, not an ideal, but an orientation (a responsibility) that responds to human difference; it is here that dignity resides. So long as cosmopolitanism aims to mould, encourage, or cultivate in youth a humanity that is already seen as "shared," it prevents us from confronting the far more difficult and much closer task at hand of facing the troublesome aspects of human interaction that emerge in specific times and places. As Lyotard insists, we are not born human (unless we take human merely to be a particular biological constellation of cells, genes, and the like), but learn to become human through the specific encounters with those who people our lives. It this emphasis on specificity that Arendt, Irigaray, and Levinas illustrate so well, I think, in their various commitments to human pluralism and in their reconsiderations of humanity. To return to the observations of the poet Fernando Pessoa, we do not see humanity, only particular people—and this, it seems to me, is both the hope and the tragedy of the human condition which we must face.

NOTES

1. Pessoa (1987). I read this quote originally in Simon Critchley's *Infinitely Demanding* (2007, 143).

2. For a contemporary discussion of the role of humanity in education see, for example, Aloni (2002); Nussbaum (1997a); Seymour and Levin (2005). See also the contributions in Løvlie, Mortensen, and Nordenbo (2003) for a critical discussion of bildung in postmodern society.

3. I discuss this Kantian position more fully below.

4. This claim was just as true in Kant's time as it is in our own. It is the impending sense of crisis, in my view, which creates the retreat into idealistic accounts of the human condition. Not that we can totally dispense with the idea of humanity as such, but my plea

here is that it needs to be reframed within the very context of injustice it is often mobilized to challenge.

5. Taking a slightly different view, Pheng Cheah (2006) discusses the inhuman conditions of capitalist globalization as constitutive of forms of humanity. Although these are not the terms under which I am addressing the inhuman here, her work highlights the peculiar structures of subjectivity as they are shaped in relation to inhuman social, economic and political forces. She writes, for instance, "We commonly oppose the human to inhuman forces that oppress and degrade humanity, such as social engineering or capitalist accumulation. The aporias of development, however, indicate a constitutive making of the inhuman within the human that renders indeterminate the borderline between the two terms. They force us to acknowledge that what we know as human has always been given to us by an inhuman temporality and spacing that we cannot fully grasp or control" (230).

6. Both Critchley and Mouffe are here referring to Carl Schmitt's work, which pointedly criticized liberal democracies, from a perspective of the right, for the way humanity is used to legitimate certain acts of violence. Mouffe further emphasizes that the cosmopolitan focus on universal humanity and the denial of the antagonism inherent to democracy is deeply problematic: "To believe in the possibility of cosmopolitan democracy with cosmopolitan citizens with the same rights and obligations, a constituency that would coincide with 'humanity', is a dangerous illusion" (Mouffe, 2005, 106–107). See my discussion of this theme in chapters 2 and 5.

7. For a further discussion of the violence inherent to education, see Chapter 1 in Todd (2003).

8. This is further illustrated in Kant's suggestion that we should encourage youth "in love towards others, as well as to feelings of cosmopolitanism. There exists something in our minds which causes us to take an interest (a) in ourselves, (b) in those with whom we have been brought up, and (c) there should also be an interest in the progress of the world. Children should be made acquainted with this interest, so that it may give warmth to their hearts. They should learn to rejoice at the world's progress, although it may not be to their own advantage or to that of their country" (1906, 121).

2

Rethinking Cosmopolitanism Along the Fault Lines of a Divided Modernity

> The peoples of the earth have thus entered in varying degrees into a universal community, and it has developed to the point where a violation of rights in *one* part of the world is felt *everywhere*. The idea of a cosmopolitan right is therefore not fantastic and overstrained; it is a necessary complement to the unwritten code of political and international right, transforming it into a universal right of humanity. Only under this condition can we flatter ourselves that we are continually advancing towards a perpetual peace.
>
> Immanuel Kant, *Perpetual Peace*

Kant's two hundred year old plea for a universal right of humanity now seems almost prophetic in light of the contemporary culture of human rights around the globe. As an idea that entertains the possibility of universal right as a unifying force across various nations, cultures, and societies, Kant's cosmopolitanism foreshadows, to a degree, current responses to the complexities of living in and with the effects of that hotly contested term "globalization"—a term that variously refers to rampant capitalism, vast international migration, ecological fragility, technological interconnectivity, cultural hybridity, and reconfiguration of political power.[1] Indeed all these themes are present, to greater and lesser degrees, in the recent turn to cosmopolitanism, particularly within political philosophy, social theory, cultural studies, education, and ethics.[2] Reflective of a struggle to articulate norms and standards through which it might be possible to work toward peace, security, and human dignity, discussions of cosmopolitanism have surfaced at a time when debates over citizenship and the borders of belonging as well as over the obligations we have to others from cultures different from our own are occurring at a fevered pitch.

In chapter 1, I outlined some of my concerns with the idea of humanity that underwrites educational projects seeking to put forth a cosmopolitan agenda, one largely based on cross-cultural understanding, human rights, global democracy, and world citizenship. But the question remains, in what specific ways does cosmopolitanism embrace such an idea? This question is not as easy to answer as it may first appear, partly because cosmopolitanism does not itself comprise a singular worldview, but mirrors, rather, a somewhat diverse collection of interests with respect to the "worldliness" of the human condition. In this chapter, I begin with a discussion of this diversity and then turn to a reading of Kant's cosmopolitanism, since it is traces of his legacy that are most prominent in the current attention being paid to this notion. Here, I sketch out what I see as some of the primary tensions operating within cosmopolitanism which come about through its double commitment both to universal rights and to respect for cultural diversity and pluralism. Articulating this as a connected to what Amanda Anderson (1998) calls the features of a "divided modernity" inherent to modern formulations of cosmopolitanism, I analyze this double commitment through the work of three theorists who have taken on directly—and have sought to transform—the central tensions of cosmopolitanism through their focus on the question of the other: namely, Seyla Benhabib, Julia Kristeva, and Jacques Derrida. In particular, I explore their work through two themes that, to my mind, raise important questions for rethinking education's relationship to cosmopolitanism that are discussed in subsequent chapters: (a) citizenship and belonging; and (b) hospitality as universal right. But first I turn to examine how cosmopolitanism has been theorized recently across a range of disciplines, in order to provide the reader with a sense of the vastness of the conceptual landscape.

THE MANY FACES OF CONTEMPORARY COSMOPOLITANISM

Seyla Benhabib has identified cosmopolitanism as "one of the keywords of our times" (Benhabib 2006, 17). Like most keywords (e.g., globalization, human rights, and democracy), cosmopolitanism is difficult to pin down. It has been described, variously, as "a) a socio-cultural condition; b) a kind of philosophy or world-view; c) a political project towards building transnational institutions; d) a political project for recognizing multiple identities; e) an attitudinal or dispositional orientation; and/or f) a mode of practice or competence" (Vertovec and Cohen 2002, 9). Yet, under the banner of cosmopolitanism there are nonetheless some important overarching consistencies: "In general, cosmopolitanism endorses reflective distance from one's cultural affiliations, a broad understanding of other cultures and customs, and a belief in universal humanity" (Anderson 1998, 267).

Amanda Anderson (1998) sees that the weight given to these various constituent elements has largely accounted for the differences amongst cosmopolitan theories. However, Anderson, along with a number of others, further directs our attention to a deeper split in the wide range of theorizing devoted to cosmopolitanism, which can be captured by two general orientations: new cosmopolitanism and classic cosmopolitanism. It is a breach, moreover, that appears to be cavernous in that edited collections devoted to cosmopolitanism either take one or the other perspective. Indeed advocates of new cosmopolitanism rarely appear in volumes alongside their classic counterparts.[3]

Classic Cosmopolitanism

Classic cosmopolitanism has emanated primarily from the Stoics in classical times, and from Kant in modern times. Largely occupying the disciplines of philosophy, political theory, and international relations, most contemporary revivals of cosmopolitanism, however, are indebted to the Kantian tradition as opposed to the Stoic one (Martha Nussbaum [1997a; 1997b] is a noted exception in this regard, drawing on both). Indeed, many have attempted to redefine Kant's early articulations of a world federation, the idea of belonging to a common world, and the fostering of values that cultivate a sense of our shared humanity. Such redefinitions are put in the service of rethinking political institutions and alliances, and the moral ground upon which such political reforms can take place. And this is often accomplished through appeals both to pluralism and to universal principles.

For example, David Held (2005) identifies cosmopolitan principles as "the conditions of taking cultural diversity seriously and of building a democratic culture to mediate clashes of the cultural good" (16). He advocates for a "cosmopolitan democracy" based on the realignment of international institutions that would promote democracy globally. Underlying Held's pluralism are familiar Kantian commitments to autonomy and impartial reasoning, which he identifies as the "meta-principles" of cosmopolitanism. (As I take up in chapter 6, this cosmopolitan idea of democratic culture rooted in the universal idea of rationality bases itself on the hope that some degree of harmony and consensus are indeed possible to strive for.[4]) Daniele Archibugi (2003; 1998) also aligns himself with cosmopolitan democracy, stressing the benefits of creating a new "global world order" in which citizens' voices can be heard on the international stage, even if they might be silenced at home (2003, 8). Although less committed to an overtly Kantian view of humanity, he nonetheless identifies the project of cosmopolitanism with principles for regulating global institutions, among which the universality of human rights plays an eminent role. Similar commitments, along with principles of justice, have informed the work of a range of cosmopolitan thinkers (Anderson-Gold 2001; Moellendorf 2005; and Beck 2006). Moellendorf (2005) suggests, for instance, that "the central claim of cosmopolitanism is that we owe duties of justice to all the persons in the world" (148). He outlines how this commitment to "all persons" needs to be rooted in liberal principles of justice that can be universally applied.

Taken together, then, such revivals of classic cosmopolitanism base their views on appeals to universal humanity, rights, and/or world citizenship, taking these (in varying degrees) as fundamental to the project of working toward a more just, harmonious, and peaceful world order.

New Cosmopolitanism

As for the second strand, the new cosmopolitanism that emerged in the 1990s can be seen in direct response to the mounting pluralism in societies around the globe, to postcolonialism's emphasis on the importance of this pluralism for

founding new moments of social and political thought, and to poststructural accounts of the production of subjectivity as something not founded on abstract
notions of human nature but as something that proliferates in encounters with
language, discourses, and embodied others. Most often appearing in literary theory and cultural studies this new cosmopolitanism distances itself (most vocifer-
ously) from its classical political cousins. Indeed, as Pollock et al. (2002) suggest:

> cosmopolitanism is not some known entity existing in the world, with a clear
> genealogy from the Stoics to Immanuel Kant, that simply awaits more detailed
> description at the hands of scholarship.... Cosmopolitanism may instead be a
> project whose conceptual content and pragmatic character are not only as yet
> unspecified but also must always escape positive and definite specification,
> precisely because specifying cosmopolitanism positively and definitely is an
> uncosmopolitan thing to do. (2002, 1)

Instead, what motivates these theorists' appeals to cosmopolitanism is a focus on
it as a way of life. Thus although they share with classic forms of cosmopolitanism the fostering of "reciprocal and transformative encounters between strangers" (Anderson 1998, 269), new cosmopolitan theories do so less through an
appeal to abstract notions of human nature or to metaprinciples of autonomy,
impartial reasoning, democracy, or justice, and more through radical appeals to
the way individuals and groups inhabit and create spaces of cross-cultural exchange. Sami Zubaida (2002), in his examination of Middle Eastern forms of
cosmopolitanism, identifies cosmopolitanism "in the old-fashioned sense of
communally deracinated and culturally promiscuous groups and milieux" (41).
There is thus a "loosening up" of the universal terms through which cosmopolitanism is often understood. Malcomson (1998) coins the term "actually-existing
cosmopolitanisms" as a way of suggesting that it is the lived realities of transnational border crossing—both in terms of movement of populations and the flow
and exchange of ideas—which are the defining feature of cosmopolitanisms, in
the plural.[5] In addition, the idea that cosmopolitanism itself is differentially experienced and theorized according to one's location in the world acts to frame
our political attention. Hence there is also a shift evident in this literature toward
renaming cosmopolitanisms as "cosmopolitics."

Within this view, cosmopolitanism as a singular body of shared commitments is difficult to situate in any precise sense. These new cosmopolitanisms,
as Bruce Robbins (1998) notes, "take off from a double assumption: first, that
any cosmopolitanism's normative or idealizing power must acknowledge the
actual historical and geographical contexts from which it emerges, and second,
that such an acknowledgement need not prove fatal" (2). What is evident in the
literature, as a result, is a built-in reflexivity about the nature of the term itself:
how it shifts its meaning according to the time and location in which it is articulated. Hence discussing cosmopolitanisms, in the plural, means that the content
of the term alters according to whether one is discussing postcolonial Mumbai,
Byzantium during the Ottoman Empire, or present-day New York.

Thus these new theories refuse to see cosmopolitanism merely as a reflection of western enlightenment principles. Cheah (1998), for one, positions it as a framework for analyzing those social, economic, and political formations that have become increasingly integrated into global systems. With a definite focus on human plurality, these new theories seek to reposition cosmopolitanism as a political and ethical intervention into already existing ways of life, and what is highlighted here is not so much a unified ideal but a set of ideas that are deeply contingent upon specific times and places.

A Divided Modernity

In an astute discussion of both these strands of contemporary cosmopolitanism, Amanda Anderson claims that they do not so much constitute polar opposites but represent different threads in the rent fabric of modernity itself. She identifies universalism as one of keystones of modernity and reads cosmopolitanism (both new and old) as historically providing a direct response to the demand for universalism in a fragmented world: "Cosmopolitanism has repeatedly emerged at times when the world has suddenly seemed to expand in unassimilable ways; it is at these moments that universalism needs the rhetoric of worldliness that cosmopolitanism provides" (Anderson 1998, 272). She therefore draws the distinctions between new and classic cosmopolitanisms along the lines of their differing invocations of universalism. Taking a stand against any robust conception of universalism, on the grounds that it undermines the very cosmopolitan commitments to cultural exchange it seeks to be underpinning, Anderson puts forth an alternative vision: "Ultimately, a too rigorous or bald universalism seems at odds, for the cosmopolitan, with the requisite moral task of developing delicate intersubjective competence within a culturally diverse horizon" (275). She defines this "delicate intersubjective competence" as "join[ing] the language of universalist ethics with an emphasis entirely foreign to that tradition—the emphasis on tact, sensibility, and judgment (*phronesis*), which seem fundamental to the cosmopolitan's reconfigured relation to universality" (275).

What Anderson makes so clear in her essay is that although new cosmopolitanism eschews the universalism of an enlightenment version of human nature and the idea of humanity, it cannot (and ought not) completely abandon all forms of universalism outright. Indeed, invoking the work of Judith Butler, Ernesto Laclau, and other poststructuralist thinkers who have been influential to rethinking universalism as contingent, she identifies the centrality of negotiating—or translating, in her words—the relation between universal appeals to humanity and rights, on the one hand, and the "actually existing" ways people live in the context of ongoing cultural exchange, on the other. Of the possibilities that inhere in poststructural accounts of cosmopolitanism, she writes:

> This does not mean we should not deploy the term *universal*; we should in fact continuously attempt to give it fuller articulation, so as to include groups that have hitherto been excluded from its purview. One key way to forward this goal is to set different conceptions of universality and of rights in dialogue with

one another, in order to aggravate our awareness of cultural divergence and to hone our capacity for transformative intercultural encounters. (1998, 281)

Anderson raises the important point that it is not so much the modern idea of humanity that anchors universalism; rather it is that universalism needs to take into account the diversity of humanity. This means that universalism is not a fixed assumption which underlies cosmopolitan theory; instead cosmopolitan theory continually works toward new articulations of universalism through the provocation occasioned by cross-cultural encounters.

Walter Mignolo (2002), in a fascinating essay promoting the idea of critical cosmopolitanism, takes up a similar thread. For Mignolo, cosmopolitanism, and the way it invokes both human rights and democracy, has in its conceptualization far too often been linked to past and present forms of coloniality. Instead, he argues that cosmopolitanism needs to shed its modernist ties to principles of an unquestioned universality in order to put diversity at the center of any appeal to cosmopolitanism. With this move, Mignolo seeks to reinvest the universality of rights, for instance, with what he calls a "diversality":

> Diversality can be imagined as a new medievalism, a pluricentric world built on the ruins of ancient, non-Western cultures and civilizations with the debris of Western civilization. A cosmopolitanism that only connects from the center of the large circle outward, and leaves the outer places disconnected from each other, would be cosmopolitanism from above, like Vitoria's and Kant's cosmopolitanism in the past and Rawls's and Habermas's cosmopolitanism today, and like the implications of human rights discourse, according to which only one philosophy has it 'right.' (2002, 183–184)

This focus on diversality as a way of reframing (not abandoning) universalism represents an important shift in cosmopolitan thought, one that allows us to ask questions such as: Who is excluded in our continual appeal to universal rights? Whose belonging counts? What responsibility do states have to previously excluded individuals and groups? How do cross-cultural encounters reinform our understanding of rights, democracy, citizenship, and justice?

What becomes clear from my brief depiction of the many faces of contemporary cosmopolitanism is that there is a deep ambivalence that lies at its core, which is mirrored not only in the division between new and classic cosmopolitanisms but also within their respective theories. As we have seen, exponents of the classic strand position themselves as responding to cultural diversity through the appeals to a somewhat strong universalism, which actually seems to undermine (or at the very least raise questions about) the status of diversity as having a serious role to play in the formation of the ideas of global justice, global democracy, or world citizenship. With respect to new cosmopolitanism, it is the emphasis on cultural diversity and its role in creating new social and political formations within global societies that take prime place; these calls are sometimes prefaced by a dismissal of the universal altogether. I read these differing emphases not only as an effect of philosophical (or political or ethical) preference, but also as an effect of the very conceptual tradition of cosmopolitanism itself. Although advocates of classic cosmopolitanism have more in common with Kant's project of universalism than the new cosmopolitans do, I believe the conceptual split within cosmopolitanism that both strands enact also reveals the trace of a divided modernity—to borrow from Anderson—that we continue to live with in cosmopolitan theory. That is, the modern commitment to universal humanity, human rights, global citizenship, and respect for cultural diversity, which Kant himself embraced, as we shall see, is a deeply ambivalent one. It is not as if each element can be held together in some kind of equal balance; rather it is that the tensions between them and the weight given to one or another of these commitments define particular orientations to cosmopolitanism. Moreover, it is a divide that we cannot simply ignore. As both Anderson and Mignolo indicate, it is rather more a question of refashioning the divide. After all, we do not choose our conceptual heritage, but we can work within and against it simultaneously.

Education and a Divided Modernity

The universalism/pluralism divide also makes its appearance in the adoption of cosmopolitanism within the field of education. What is curious about most educational initiatives is that they reflect more clearly the classical strand of cosmopolitan thought, leaving discussions of "actually existing cosmopolitanisms" largely to the side. For instance, the themes of global justice (e.g., Enslin and Tjiattas 2004), human rights (e.g., Reardon 1995), and global or cosmopolitan citizenship (e.g., Osler and Starkey 2003) are prominent in the attempt to articulate new directions for forms of belonging and for heightening awareness of one's responsibility in the world. Interestingly, although taken together they insist on greater respect for other cultures and on developing conversations across cultural borders, they also simultaneously embrace appeals to a shared humanity and largely stay within the frame of the universalism that underpins classic approaches to cosmopolitanism. Thus even with the emphasis on cross-cultural exchange, they cannot be said to reflect the issues and concerns of the "new cosmopolitanism" camp, which has a tendency to be suspicious of such appeals to humanity.[6]

Martha Nussbaum's (1997a) by now classic treatise on cosmopolitan education serves as a good example of how the intertwining of universalism and diversity emerges in educational thinking on cosmopolitanism. As mentioned in the previous chapter, Nussbaum appeals to a sense of shared humanity, one that invokes the universality of reason and moral capacity. Drawing inspiration from the Roman Stoics, she observes that our first allegiance should be given "to the moral community made up by the humanity of all human beings" (1997a, 59). This moral idea, she claims, is about treating with respect "the dignity of reason and moral choice in every human being, no matter where that person was born, no matter what that person's rank or gender or status may be" (1997a, 59).

> Becoming a citizen of the world is often a lonely business…. If one begins life
> as a child who loves and trusts its parents, it is tempting to want to reconstruct
> citizenship along the same lines, finding in an idealized image of a nation a sur-
> rogate parent who will do one's thinking for one. Cosmopolitanism offers no
> such refuge; it offers only reason and the love of humanity, which may seem at
> times less colorful than other sources of belonging. (1994, http://www.soci
> .niu.edu/☐phildept/Kapitan/nussbaum1.html)

In proposing an education for world citizenship, Nussbaum summons forth,
alongside her humanism, a strong need for encountering other cultures and a
respect for the plurality of human life. Cosmopolitan education is a multicultural
education, according to Nussbaum, one in which "the task of world citizenship
requires the would-be world citizen to become a sensitive and empathic inter-
preter. Education at all ages should cultivate the capacity for such interpreting"
(1997a, 63).

Note the apparently easy slide here from the universal idea of shared humanity (based on reason and moral capacity) to promoting an understanding of
other cultures (based on empathy and sensitivity). To my mind, such a slide
should not—and cannot—be taken for granted. Indeed, it appears as though the
whole point of developing cultural awareness (which is also echoed by Noddings [1995]) is merely a means for recognizing what we share with others (as
"interpreters") rather than being a means for facing cultural differences as they
appear in encounters with actual people, texts, and the like. As Papastephanou
(2002) notes, Nussbaum's position is based on a naïve assumption about the
nature of cross-cultural relations. Papastephanou insists that the "historical en-
tanglements" between cultures, which have been marked at times by conflict and
violence, makes Nussbaum's particular appeal to diversity seem idealistic at
best.

> The linchpin that is missing is a mode of studying the past of each culture that
> adequately recognizes the way that that past has been shaped through cross-
> cultural contact. But past (and often contemporary) cross-cultural encounters
> involve at least two chief elements: an exchange of cultural material but also
> violence, aggression and pain. (Papastephanou 2002, 79)

As I interpret it, what is being sutured in Nussbaum's appeals to learning
about other cultures is the very problematic structure of intelligibility (reason
and moral capacity) through which we supposedly accomplish this learning.
Exposure to cultures other than our own is put in the service here of making
"us" better people on "our" own terms. Thus, in educating for world citizenship,
it is the universal which serves to filter diversity, making the latter more palat-
able and less acidic to digest than it can sometimes be. What we see here, in my
view, is evidence of the tendency to *incorporate* diversity, while leaving the
main body of reason and moral capacity intact. There is not, therefore, much
reflection offered on the very possibility for *exchange* that would actually alter
the very content of what counts as reason and moral capacity.

Like other educational writers, Nussbaum's cosmopolitanism is haunted by the specter of a divided modernity, where universal rights and principles actually jockey for primary place alongside the commitment to diversity and the particularism this inevitably involves. Insofar as this tension continues to play a role in the development of cosmopolitanism in political theory, cultural studies, and education, it is worth exploring it in further detail. I begin with Kant here, for in recent articulations of cosmopolitanism that also attempt to redraw the boundaries of the universal (exemplified here by Benhabib, Kristeva, and Derrida), it is his account of cosmopolitanism that has had the most lingering effects on the question of citizenship and its relation to rights, and of both in relation to cultural difference. My reason for going into Kant's formulations is to flag what I perceive to be the fault lines of cosmopolitanism in light of its modernist heritage. My task here is to resituate these fault lines in ways that take human pluralism seriously. Although, as will become evident through my critique, I am much more firmly committed to the expressions of diversity to be found in the new cosmopolitanism, I do not situate my project solely there. Instead, I seek to uncover the fissures within cosmopolitan thinking and argue that they present us with a number of ambivalences, paradoxes, and tensions that no cosmopolitanism—new or classic—can fully address.

THE KANTIAN COSMOPOLITAN PROJECT

Kant's 1795 essay "On Perpetual Peace: A Philosophical Sketch" was penned in the headiness of 18th century political change. Written at a time of the burgeoning development of nation states in Europe, and on the heels of the Treaty of Basel that brokered a suspension of all hostilities between revolutionary France and Prussia, Kant's 1795 essay proffers a view of peace as embodying a cosmopolitan orientation. Strongly influenced by both the American and French revolutions, Kant's essay sought to outline those conditions that would enable peaceful coexistence among all states. Distinguishing these conditions for *peace* from the mere *laying down of arms* (Kant 1991, 93)—which is the primary aim of treaties—Kant instead calls for a new understanding of (a) the role of states, (b) interstate cooperation, and (c) the basic rights of humanity, in three definitive articles of *perpetual* peace.

The Role of States

The first of these articles defines the kind of state needed for peace to be attained. Here, Kant outlines the need for each state to develop a republican civil constitution that is founded on three principles: the freedom of all in society "as men"; the dependence of all upon a unified body of law "as subjects"; and legal equality for all "as citizens" (1991, 99). Kant viewed this securing of what we now recognize as human and civil rights as essential to any possibilities for peaceful coexistence. What is worthy of note here is that he outlines states as embodying a responsibility to individuals (not groups) in three different dimensions: as man, as subject, and as citizen. His republican sensibilities, however, should not be seen as promoting democracy, as we understand it today. Indeed, it is the task of a republic to secure the freedom of individuals, not the freedom of "the people" as such:

> *Republicanism* is that political principle whereby the executive power (the government) is separated from the legislative power. Despotism prevails in a state if the laws are made and arbitrarily executed by one and the same power.... Of the three forms of sovereignty [autocracy, aristocracy, and democracy], *democracy*, in the truest sense of the word, is necessarily a *despotism*, because it establishes an executive power through which all the citizens may make decisions about (and indeed against) the single individual without his consent, so that decisions are made by all the people and yet not by all the people; and this means that the general will is in contradiction with itself, and thus also with freedom. (1991, 101)

Thus whilst Kant, in his formulation of a responsible state that has contractual obligations toward individuals, anticipates in large measure the current constitutions of modern liberal democratic states, there nonetheless lies at the core of his thought an idea of an autonomous, rational individual whose political freedom lies in the hands of the enlightened state.

Interstate Cooperation

The second article involves the establishment of a "pacific federation" between such republican states, in accordance with "international right [law]" (1991, 104).[7] Each nation-state has the right to demand of others to enter into a constitution (not unlike a civil one) that would guarantee the rights of all states to exist in peaceful relations with others. This requires the capacity of international law to "preserve and secure the *freedom* of each state in itself" and sees that states need to make some binding concessions in order to create new forms of political association (1991, 104). Kant claims that such a federation is not the same thing as a single international state; indeed he proposes federalism since the prospects for a world republic seem unlikely given the contemporary situations of nations. Yet, he does allow himself to dream of its possibility:

> There is only one rational way in which states coexisting with other states can emerge from the lawless condition of pure warfare. Just like individual men, they [states] must renounce their savage and lawless freedom, adapt themselves to public coercive laws, and thus form an *international* state (*civitas gentium*), which would necessarily continue to grow until it embraced all the peoples of the earth. But since this is not the will of the nations, according to their present conception of international right ... the positive idea of a *world republic* cannot be realized. If all is not to be lost, this can at best find a negative substitute in the shape of an enduring and gradually *federation* likely to prevent war. (105)

Thus Kant seems to settle for a federation when the real goal—the rational solution—is for a world republic. In this sense, it is no wonder that in light of his discussion, this second article has received much attention by proponents of cosmopolitan or world government and international law—proponents who seek to extend peace through increased global legislation and/or the creation of a global state.

The Rights of Humanity

The third article is devoted to what Kant refers to as a "cosmopolitan right" as limited to the "conditions of universal hospitality" (1991, 105). Here, Kant formulates the basic "right of humanity" as "the right of the stranger not to be treated with hostility when he arrives on someone else's territory" (1991, 105). Lest we think that hospitality is merely a voluntary gesture, Kant stipulates that in his view hospitality is "concerned not with philanthropy, but with *right*" (1991, 105). What is important to note in Kant's formulation is that this cosmopolitan right is not a right to citizenship or membership in a state, it is a right of welcome.

> If it can be done without destroying him, he can be turned away; but, as long as he behaves peaceably he cannot be treated as an enemy. He may request the *right* to be a *permanent visitor* (which would require a special, charitable agreement to make him a fellow inhabitant for a certain period), but the *right to visit*, to associate, belongs to all men by virtue of their common ownership of the earth's surface; for since the earth is a globe, they cannot scatter themselves infinitely, but must, finally, tolerate living in close proximity, because originally no one had a greater right to any region of the earth than anyone else. (Kant 2003, 16)[8]

Indeed, hospitality is not "a virtue of sociability, as the kindness and generosity one may show to strangers" (Benhabib 2004, 26), but a right which requires a moral obligation on the part of the state *and* its individual members to receive all others, independent of cultural, national, or social membership. Hospitality becomes the condition upon which discussions of a world federation or republic may be entertained:

> But this natural right of hospitality, i.e. the right of strangers, does not extend beyond those conditions which make it possible for them to *attempt* to enter into relations with the native inhabitants. In this way, continents distant from each other can enter into peaceful mutual relations which may eventually be regulated by public laws, thus bringing the human race nearer and nearer to a cosmopolitan constitution. (Kant 1991, 106)

It is this article in particular that establishes fully the cosmopolitanism direction of Kant's treatise on perpetual peace. For although the requirements of peace also depend upon civil constitutions and state adherence to international law, it is here, in establishing cosmopolitan right as a right of hospitality, where the kernel of cosmopolitanism is to be found. Yet, much that is written on cosmopolitanism (particularly within the classic strand) seems to consider the first two articles as central to developing new forms of political association, while often leaving the intricacies of hospitality out of the picture altogether. Indeed, emphases on world citizenship, international rights, global government, and cosmopolitan justice do not treat hospitality fully as a political concept, particularly with respect to those whose belonging to a host state is precarious. Thus authors who embrace a classic cosmopolitan position in line with—or more appropriately as an extension of—Kantian formulations of world government, international rights, and transnational law miss the entire cosmopolitan point of hospitality, which is fundamentally about *establishing a relation to human difference as a condition for political association.* For what Kant is so keen on doing here is to establish a cosmopolitan framework driven by a "natural right" to hospitality, since he is all too aware of the trickery states can play with respect to securing the freedom of individuals who are *not* full citizens. Kant develops a cosmopolitan world-view that is conditional upon equal treatment under the law based on the universal freedom accorded to all members of society (at least all male members) while at the same time being also contingent upon the upholding the universal right to hospitality. It is no small thing, then, that the state can place limits on accepting members fully into their fold while also being obligated to grant temporary sojourn to outsiders. Thus what we have here is a cosmopolitanism that recognizes the state's legitimate right to declare itself as self-determining, at the same time as it has a universal moral duty to be hospitable. In addition, we have state commitment to uphold human rights by virtue of the common dignity and freedom of each human being and its right to grant citizenship only to those it deems worthy.

It is precisely around these issues where the fault lines of cosmopolitanism reveal themselves. That is, Kant's cosmopolitan formulation leads to very real tensions about what the cosmopolitan project actually is, how it is to be defined, and whether, or if, it can be pursued as an integrated political and ethical response to human pluralism in an increasingly globalized world.

If hospitality is about welcoming nonmembers into one's community, and into the community based on a "cosmopolitan constitution," then how do states deal with the demands of particularism in terms of the universal hospitality that is accorded to all others by right? Coupled with the state's right to self-determination to secure for itself its own membership and define for itself the conditions of freedom for its citizens, the obligation required to meet the right of hospitality can often lead to a tension between what it means on the part of strangers to feel welcomed, and what the state is prepared to offer. To be hospitable necessarily requires attentiveness to accommodation that suits the other's particular needs. And this would seem to rub against the grain of the very universalism that underpins the idea of humanity upon which this right rests. That is, the Kantian formulation of the universal freedom and rationality that bind us together as human beings becomes somewhat difficult to sustain in light of the attention to the particular that both hospitality and respect for human pluralism would demand. A more conventional way of reading this would be to suggest that we are diverse as individuals, but share qualities that supersede these differences. Yet, what this does is force our hand into assuming that the very meaning of freedom and rationality are independent of the very values, discourses, languages, and ways of life that comprise human difference in the first place. The issue for cosmopolitanism, as we shall see, is how to reconcile its attachments to global "universals," such as human rights, with its commitment to respect and value the "particulars" represented through diverse cultures and individuals. I turn now to the work of three theorists whose discussion of these difficulties raises important issues for rethinking cosmopolitanism and its relation to education.

BENHABIB AND THE TENSIONS OF BELONGING

In trying to chart the as-yet-emerging political forms of globalization with old maps, the political philosopher Seyla Benhabib (2004) remarks that "we are like travellers navigating an unknown terrain" (6). It is precisely this unknown landscape navigated by Benhabib in her promotion of cosmopolitanism. Hers is an attempt to offer a new political imaginary that, in my reading, takes issue with some aspects of universality, on the one hand, and grapples with the twin attachments of a cosmopolitan outlook (respect for rights and cultural diversity), on the other. However, as we will see below, her work also tells a cautionary tale of the limits of using old maps in new places.

Benhabib (2004; 2006) primarily addresses herself to the conditions of political community: how people come to belong and achieve political membership in the context of the current upheavals of the nation-state system and the vast migration and resettlement that is one of the hallmarks of the global era. She locates the boundaries of political membership within a dual context: First is that of the state's right to determine who and under what conditions citizenship can be held, as well as defining which political and civil rights that those who are not full citizens are entitled to. Those seeking asylum, for instance, rarely have any access to political forms of participation and their rights are severely curtailed, whereas some immigrants who are granted permanent residence might enjoy limited benefits.[9] Thus within liberal democracies, the lines of membership remain to a large degree nationally determined.

However, this is complicated somewhat by the second context: the transnational one. This is, in effect, a deterritorialized context, one with no geographic borders but one that nonetheless implicates nations in the regime of international human rights through various declarations, treaties, covenants, and laws that afford protection to individuals against states. Thus the issue for liberal democracies, in Benhabib's view, is how they can deal with the conflict between exercising their sovereignty in defining the terms under which persons will be considered as members, on the one hand, and upholding the idea that all human beings should enjoy the same right to be members of a democratic polity, on the other. She suggests that we see the complex negotiation between "context-transcending" rights claims and democratic life in terms of "democratic iterations" (2004, 176–183).

Drawing on Derrida's notion of iteration for inspiration, Benhabib sees that with every articulation, meaning is transformed, added on to, and enriched: there is no original meaning to which all iterations must conform (2004, 179). Every act of iteration is involved in making sense of an authoritative sign in a new and different context. This means that each act is a representation, or better, a translation, of an antecedent—a rearticulation that puts into circulation new forms of meaning. Through "complex processes of public argument, deliberation, and exchange" rights are contested, championed, and repealed. Such iterations occur in the "'strong' public bodies of legislatures, the judiciary, and the executive, as well as in the informal and 'weak' public of civil society associations and the media" (1994, 179). Democratic iteration allows Benhabib to keep the political conversation open to pluralism, seeing every robust democracy as embodying a diversity central to the functioning of that democracy.

Viewing the state as central to the flourishing of democracy which can ensure the political participation of individuals at a more local level, she is firmly entrenched in the idea that states still need to have a strong say as to how they grant citizenship rights to individuals within their borders. Nonetheless, she is committed to a cosmopolitan outlook in the sense of providing an overarching framework of rights to which states must be held accountable in pursuing their laws and regulations regarding political membership. Her navigation points, then, are positioned between the sovereignty of the state and international human rights, and she charts her response to her initial questions between them through the idea of a cosmopolitan federalism.

Cosmopolitan Federalism: Belonging as a Right

Benhabib's version of cosmopolitan federalism largely grows out of Kant's view of cosmopolitanism. As we have seen, Kant's third article for perpetual peace concerns cosmopolitan right as universal hospitality. Benhabib quite rightly makes much of this third article and of the fact that Kant proposes that the right to hospitality is a right of humanity—one that all possess by virtue of being human. Kant establishes a metaphysical justification for this right to hospitality. But this right is a long way off from being applied to the question of granting full membership to the foreigner. For Kant, it is only through the beneficence of the state that full rights of belonging are to be granted to the stranger. In other words the state is neither legally nor morally bound to confer such belonging—it is only morally bound to provide a hospitable environment to the stranger. For Benhabib, this does not go far enough. Her major difference with Kant is that she rereads the sovereignty of states as being *morally bound to extend full membership* to all residents (2004, 42). To make her case she must: (a) establish that membership rights are universal rights; and (b) clarify how democracies are to go about fulfilling this universal task without abrogating their self-rule, what she refers to as the "paradox of democratic legitimacy."

Benhabib explores Hannah Arendt's work in order to refine her views on the relation between membership rights and human rights. In the *Origins of Totalitarianism*, Arendt grapples with the difficulties of stateless persons and draws the conclusion that all people have the "right to have rights."[10] Benhabib's gloss on this phrase is particularly incisive in laying bare the two different aspects of rights implied here. Benhabib reads the first use of the term right as "*a moral claim to membership* and *a certain form of treatment compatible with the claim to membership*" (2004, 56). The second use refers to the rights already possessed by a member of a political community. Although the moral claim to be recognized as a rights-bearing person is universal (that is, it transcends all borders), Benhabib points out that in Arendt's case this was not due to some metaphysical properties of humanity (contra Kant). Arendt instead offers a political solution to recognition: it is only through political community where the right to have rights might be realized (2004, 59). At the end of the day, Benhabib sees Arendt's reliance upon political community as just as dissatisfying as Kant's failure to extend hospitality to include full membership, for it relies on the "historical arbitrariness of republican acts of founding whose ark of equality will always include some and exclude others" (2004, 66). So although Benhabib's view of cosmopolitan federalism incorporates the key terms "right of humanity" and the "right to have rights," what Kant and Arendt do not offer are solid justifications that avoid either the metaphysical claims of humanity or the total arbitrariness of putting one's faith into republican states. Benhabib proposes instead to offer a "postmetaphysical justification of the principle of right" (2004, esp. 131–134). For reasons I outline below, this is the weakest point of her project in that she slides all too willingly back into a universalist framework that leaves negotiation and iteration on the sidelines.

Beyond Discourse Ethics: "The Other Is Not Elsewhere"

Benhabib wants to secure a *universal moral obligation* for states to confer full membership on those who reside within their borders, without sacrificing the democratic ability of a political community to define for itself what it thinks best. The rights of others in this view must always occur within the paradox of democratic legitimacy—that is, the irresolvable conflict that arises when the sovereign of democracy ("we, the people") is legitimated by an act of constitution that itself conforms to universal human rights. Her attempt to universalize membership rights lies in her proposal of a discursive ethical position: "'I can justify to you with good grounds that you and I should respect each others' reciprocal claims to act in certain ways and not to act in others, and to enjoy certain resources and services'" (2004, 130). Here is where the universality of respect appears alongside egalitarian reciprocity as the metanorms that guide discursive practice in democracies (2004, 13). What she reveals here, though, is an unjustified appeal to these universal norms via discourse ethics that then serves as the justification for her claim that membership rights are universal. This position, however, fails to appreciate fully and bring to logical conclusion her otherwise compelling argument in favor of the rights of others and the notion of democratic iteration that, in my view, better support her cosmopolitan federalism. That is, democratic iteration has the potential to act as a model for the ongoing negotiation required between diverse world-views and the universal reach of rights.

Not that rules for communication are systematically unimportant, but it seems to me that not only does political discourse suffer if it becomes programmatic, it also fails to consider that communication with another human being is not simply procedural, nor can it always be about reciprocity and mutuality. What I would like to suggest is that returning to the other as the fulcrum for the communicative aspects of democracy would radicalize the potential for democratic practices to take alternative forms, ones that would truly take issue with the impossible task of seeking universal rules of justification as the only desirable means for our ability to listen to others. After all, as Benhabib suggests: "The Other is not elsewhere" (2004, 87). Others are a fundamental part of any society; "they are our neighbors, citizens, and ourselves" (ibid.). It seems to me, then, that I listen to my neighbor, not because I *wish* to follow a metanorm of reciprocity, but because without facing difference and alterity, there is no possibility for communication, for dialogue, for discourse. It is precisely this question of otherness, however, in which Kristeva locates the very idea of universality in a cosmopolitan frame.

KRISTEVA AND THE OTHERNESS OF BELONGING

Kristeva (1991; 1993; 2000), in a number of works focusing on the nation, citizenship, and the foreigner, explores the margins of cosmopolitanism through placing the notion of "otherness" as its core. Like Benhabib, she is concerned with rearticulating that space between universalism and pluralism in her advocacy of cosmopolitanism, but instead of turning to a universal normative theory that would guide our encounters across differences as Benhabib does, Kristeva locates universality in a reconception of humanity itself.

Kristeva's problem focuses on how to think about the relation between the human being and the citizen in order to work toward an idea of a cosmopolitan nation without racism. Thus, she is concerned with how to promote forms of political association that take into account the cultural differences within the state without reducing these differences into a "common identity" or conversely into an object of hatred. Her response, in this regard, is to speak from a position of cosmopolitanism: "this means that I have, against origins and starting from them, chosen a transnational or international position situated at the crossing of boundaries" (1993, 16). On Kristeva's terms, this cosmopolitanism represents a blurring of borders and invokes a sense of belonging that is not about being bound to a nation-state, but is something worldlier, more detached from the bonds of national identity and ethnicity. For Kristeva, cosmopolitanism emerges from a particular conceptual history that despite its effect of loosening up identities, nonetheless needs to be challenged.

> It would seem to me that to uphold a universal, transnational principle of Humanity that is distinct from the historical realities of nation and citizenship constitutes, on the one hand, a continuation of the Stoic and Augustinian legacy, of that ancient Christian cosmopolitanism that finds its place among the most valuable assets of our civilization and that we henceforth must go back to and bring up to date. But above all and on the other hand, such upholding of a universality, of a symbolic dignity for the whole of humankind, appears to me as a rampart against a nationalist, regionalist, and religious fragmentation whose integrative contractions are only too visible today. Yes, let us have universality for the rights of man, provided that we integrate in that universality not only the smug principle according to which 'all men are brothers' but also that portion of conflict, hatred, violence, and destructiveness that for two centuries since the [1789 French] *Declaration* [of the Rights of Man] has ceaselessly been unloaded upon the realities of wars and fratricidal closeness and that the Freudian discovery of the unconscious tells us is a surely modifiable but yet constituent portion of the human psyche. (1993, 26–27)

What Kristeva seeks to make plain here is that although there is something in the tradition of cosmopolitanism and its appeal to an idea of humanity which can offset the crassest aspects of nationalism (racism, xenophobia, self-aggrandizement), it nonetheless also poses its own set of problems so long as it continues to blanket over the (unconscious) violent aspects of social interaction, what Kristeva refers to as our "unsociable sociability" (1991, 171). That is, if cosmopolitanism is to have any meaning in the sphere of politics and rights, it must come to grips with the exclusionary practices that are carried on under the sign of humanity itself.

Kristeva's cosmopolitan project, then, is to recast—not reject—humanity on different terms than the normative ideal that so often serves to forget the difficult aspects of the human condition and the difference that constitutes human pluralism. But this is a very fine to walk. Like Benhabib in this regard, Kristeva's task at hand is to take pluralism seriously while at the same time retaining some notion of universality to act, as she puts it above, "as a rampart against nationalist, regionalist and religious fragmentation." Moreover, in making clear the distinction between "human being" and "citizen," Kristeva's comments inevitably raise the point that these two aspects of human life do not easily coincide, so that even if one revamps one's understanding of humanity one is still left with the question of how this might affect commensurate notions of citizenship.

The Foreigner: Between Man and Citizen

As intimated earlier, it is Kristeva's turn to otherness that marks the space of a renewed cosmopolitan sensibility, located in the interstice between the human being and the citizen, as they previously have been conceived. "Between man and citizen there is a scar: the foreigner. Is he fully a man if he is not a citizen?" (1991, 98). Like Benhabib's focus on "aliens," the figure of the foreigner as the other for Kristeva indeed acts as the starting point for her investigations into contemporary problems around forms of belonging. She writes:

> In today's circumstances of unprecedented intermixing of foreigners on earth, two extreme solutions are taking shape. Either we are heading toward global united states of all former nation states: a process that could be contemplated in the long run and that the economic, scientific, and media-based development allows one to assume. Or else the humanistic cosmopolitanism shows itself to be utopic, and particularistic aspirations force one to believe that small political sets are the optimal structures to insure the survival of humanity. (1991, 98)

Kristeva navigates her own path through these conventional alternatives by proposing a renewed idea of humanity that takes foreigners and otherness into account. Thus Kristeva seeks to reinvest universalism with pluralism, offering a contingent, if elemental, depiction of humanity that attempts to resonate equally with cosmopolitanism as it does with the idea of the particular conditions of citizenship. "It is only by maintaining the *principle* of that universal dignity— without scattering it among new national, religious, or private regionalisms— that one might consider modifying its *content*, taking into consideration what the behavior of human beings reveals as to their humanity" (1991, 152). In examining the nature of human rights, particularly in light of the French Declaration of the Rights of Man, as one of the hallmarks both of cosmopolitanism (humanity) and of modern state systems (citizenship), Kristeva outlines two conditions in order for them to be realized.

> It thus appears that while the *Declaration* is destined to remain untouchable, the practical fulfilment of human rights that will remain faithful to its spirit— and not to its letter—must presuppose two considerations.
> First, a progressive and reasonable adjustment of rights and duties of citizens with respect to non-citizens shall attempt to balance in the best possible manner the status of the former and the latter ...
> Second ... there must be an ethics, the fulfilment of which shall depend upon education and psychoanalysis. Such an ethics should reveal, discuss, and spread a concept of human dignity, wrested from the euphoria of classic humanists and laden with the alienations, dramas, and dead ends of our condition as speaking beings. Individual particularistic tendencies, the desire to set oneself up as a private value, the attack against the other, identification with or rejection of the group are inherent in human dignity, if one acknowledges that such dignity includes strangeness. That being the case, as social as that strangeness might be, it can be modulated—with the possibility of achieving a polytopic and supple society ... (1991, 153).

Thus Kristeva's two-pronged approach to the question of rights reflects her concerns both for cosmopolitan thought and for psychoanalytic approaches to subjectivity. With respect to the former, she draws inspiration from Montesquieu and sees in him a welcomed "rejection of unified society for the sake of coordinated diversity" (1991, 133). Through his notion of *ésprit general*, Kristeva proposes that the nation-state can be a reflection of the totality of *human beings* expressing the very diversity of its populace—even those who are *not formal citizens*. It is this "general spirit" which must be continually redefined even as it acts as placeholder for the universal in social and political organization. In this, every nation-state is a "cosmo-policy" (1991, 131). Yet, it is with respect to the latter, psychoanalytic views of subjectivity that Kristeva makes her true mark upon cosmopolitanism by claiming otherness as itself a universal.

Otherness Is Universal

In seeking to infuse universalism with the particularities and diversity of human lives, Kristeva gives expression to the notion of a subject as stranger, as other. As we have seen, this figure of the stranger is rendered in terms of the foreigner—as one who exposes the limits of the universal attachment to humanity as a condition for conferring rights upon citizens. This enables Kristeva to question the degree to which traditional conceptions of cosmopolitanism, insofar as they embrace this condition, actually account for the stranger in our midst. However, the truly radical turn in Kristeva's thought is her psychoanalytic insistence that otherness gives shape to each one of us as the very condition of human existence. Otherness, therefore, does not merely signal the "stranger" or "foreigner" as a political outsider, but also refers to the very unconscious dimensions of human experience that condition each individual's existence.

Thus the very singularity of our own individual otherness is precisely that which must inform the universality of humanity for Kristeva. The idea of humanity would therefore be concerned with the way human dignity is attached to each one of us through the fact that we are inherently not completely knowable to ourselves. Under a chapter entitled "Might not Universality be Our Own Foreignness?" Kristeva locates an "uncanny strangeness" *within* the human and from this she is led to question how this unconscious aspect of human existence—the unruly, wayward, destructive, and untamable aspect—can actually give rise to a remapping of the terms of cosmopolitan coexistence.

> With Freud indeed, foreignness, an uncanny one, creeps into the tranquility of reason itself, and, without being restricted to madness, beauty, or faith anymore than to ethnicity or race, irrigates our very speaking-being, estranged by other logics, including the heterogeneity of biology.... Henceforth, we know that we are foreigners to ourselves, and it is with the help of that sole support that we can attempt to live with others. (1991, 170, ellipses in original)

In calling forth the stranger within, Kristeva's line is that "we are all foreigners;" hence her paradoxical assertion that "if I am a foreigner, there are no foreigners" (1991, 192). Each of us insofar as we can make a relation to ourselves—to the stranger within—has the chance at resisting the impulse to impute to others an otherness that merely serves to justify exclusion, hatred, and discrimination. It is in this admission of our strangeness, this acceptance of the violence and passion that comes from we know not where, this recognition of human fallibility and limitation, through which a new cosmopolitan politics can be forged:

> The ethics of psychoanalysis implies a politics: it would involve a cosmopolitanism of a new sort that, cutting across governments, economies, and markets, might work for a mankind whose solidarity is founded on the consciousness of its unconscious—desiring, destructive, fearful, empty, impossible. (1991, 192)

Kristeva's reformulation of cosmopolitanism is thereby grounded in an idea of humanity that emphasizes the imperfectability of the human condition. In conceiving universality in terms of this imperfection, cosmopolitanism becomes a project of finding practices that enable us to discover paths of negotiation between our conscious selves and the unconscious dynamics that infuse our social and political relationships. As Kristeva notes, "To worry or to smile, such is the choice when we are assailed by the strange; our decision depends on how familiar we are with our own ghosts" (1991, 191).

Although in my view this familiarity is indeed crucial for developing insight into our dealings with others, my worry here is that the other *as* other slides out of the frame of Kristeva's picture. That is, Kristeva seems to suggest that the better I can face my own humanity, the better I can create the conditions necessary for more peaceful forms of coexistence. Yet, what is missing here is how those relations to others are not merely self-referential, or at least do not begin solely in the relation the self has to itself. Thus although I find compelling Kristeva's move to place strangeness—and all that that entails—at the heart of cosmopolitanism, what happens to those "strangers" who are not others to us the same way we are to ourselves? The question is particularly pertinent, it seems to me, if we are to take human pluralism (and the particularity this entails) as one of the starting points of the cosmopolitan project. Recasting universalism in terms of foreignness would also require, in my view, a serious consideration of how particular others factor into the terms of this new idea of humanity that Kristeva proposes. For if cosmopolitanism is essentially about the universality of otherness, it cannot be simply our relation to our own otherness that sets the terms of our encounters. This is why I think the issue that cosmopolitanism is most at pains to struggle with has to do with the very terms of engagement across diversity, and not merely the terms of engagement with the "other within" that then shapes, as it were, those external encounters. Thus I think turning to Derrida's recasting of cosmopolitanism as fundamentally about its legacy of hospitality lays bare for us the difficult—and impossible—kernel that lies at the core of cosmopolitanism itself. That is, its call for a universal right of humanity as hospitality and the attention to human pluralism together pose themselves as unending and irresolvable puzzles to be faced—ones to which Kristeva's theory only gives a partial answer.

DERRIDA AND THE IM/POSSIBILITY OF HOSPITALITY

Derrida begins his intervention into cosmopolitanism also through the concern for pluralism, particularly focusing on the nature and meaning of our encounters with others. So, like both Benhabib and Kristeva in this regard, Derrida is concerned with attending to those features of cosmopolitanism that center on the problematic staging of a universal right of humanity and respect for diversity and otherness. But there are some crucial differences between their views that are important to note from the beginning. Writing of the predicament of asylum seekers in his short essay "On Cosmopolitanism," Derrida comes close to Benhabib's concerns with how states might become more inclusive in granting rights to others. Yet, instead of appealing in the end to a normative cosmopolitanism (one based on the metanorms of discourse), Derrida focuses on the very problematic of how this other is—and can be—welcomed. Moreover, in writing of the "foreigner" who arrives and who must be greeted both as a human being and through the laws of the land, Derrida echoes Kristeva's identification of the problem of the foreigner as one who appears in the contradictory space between man and citizen. Unlike Kristeva, however, Derrida is less optimistic about overcoming that aporia through any reformulation of humanity or cosmopolitan hospitality. Instead, his project is one that seeks to expose the promises and limitations of hospitality itself in facing the other.

With respect to the legacy of what I have been calling a divided modernity, Derrida sharply identifies the divergence between the Kantian universal call for hospitality as a right of humanity and the immanent demands placed on states and individuals when faced with the otherness of the stranger or foreigner. In making a case for the creation and sustenance of "cities of refuge"—cities which are welcoming of asylum seekers and refugees—Derrida is "eager" to propose "an original concept of hospitality, of the duty (*devoir*) of hospitality, and of the right (*droit*) to hospitality. What then would such a concept be?" (2002, 5). Derrida's task here is to interrogate how these cities of refuge, as emblematic of a "new ethic or this new cosmo*politics*" (2002, 5), can confront the difficulties inherent in the promise that states have an obligation to provide hospitality at the same time that asylum seekers have the right to receive it. The tension here lies in the fact that states (as we have seen above) relate to foreigners as visitors or potential citizens—that is, in terms of a civic relation—whereas the right to receive hospitality is based on the fact that one is a human being. Thus there is a troubling—if by now familiar—split between the citizen and the human.

Not surprisingly, Derrida investigates the Kantian claims about hospitality and interrogates their potential to offer actual answers to the predicament of those seeking refuge. On the one hand, Derrida reads Kant's universal hospitality as one "without limit" (2002, 20); that is, one is based on natural law which recognizes all men who inhabit the earth. On the other hand, he recognizes in Kant two limitations of this law: the confining of hospitality to the right of visitation (not of residence) and the right of states to their own sovereignty. As we have already seen above with Benhabib, these two limitations have posed serious problems with respect to the treatment of foreigners and refugees. Where Derrida makes his mark, however, is in his assertion that these tensions within hospitality actually present us with an antimony from which cosmopolitanism itself cannot flee.

Two Laws of Hospitality

In a familiar double gesture, hospitality becomes in Derrida's hands both the possibility and impossibility of a universal right of humanity. That is, if we take hospitality as that which is due to all, hospitality is unconditional. And this is what Kant seems (at least at first) to be suggesting by claiming that it should be granted to all those who inhabit the earth. Unconditional hospitality thereby acts as *the* law, the one which signifies a welcoming of the other with no strings attached.

> To put it in different terms, absolute hospitality requires that I open up my home and that I give not only to the foreigner ... but to the absolute, unknown, anonymous other, and that I *give place* to them, that I let them come, that I let them arrive, and take place in the place I offer them, without asking of them either reciprocity (entering into a pact) or even their names. (Derrida 2000, 25).

Hospitality on these terms welcomes the other in all her singularity—it is a radically particular welcoming of the other into my home, into my territory—without expecting anything in return. It is a generosity that indeed exceeds expectations, a giving or offering attentive to the uniqueness of the subject, unsullied by neither wanting something from her in exchange nor demanding that she become someone different. Hospitality thereby acts as the universal law; but such a giving or offering of welcome cannot simply slide into a "right" without undergoing profound alteration. For as soon as one invokes a "right"—even a right of humanity—one is then caught up in the realm of laws, regulations, and political institutions of justice, according to Derrida. And, as soon as one moves into this realm, one can no longer exercise hospitality unconditionally. "The law of absolute hospitality commands a break with hospitality by right, with law or justice as rights" (2000, 25).

What Derrida means here is that this break signifies yet another kind of hospitality that emerges in this political-juridical realm. It is a hospitality that can no longer uphold fully the obligation of hospitality absolutely. That is, when we get into the sphere of laws and rights, hospitality necessarily becomes *conditional*. On this account, any promise to guarantee the cosmopolitan *right* of *humanity* actually becomes a highly suspect one. For if we speak of hospitality with respect to persons (humanity) we automatically invoke a sense of hospitality that is unconditional—*the* law of humanity—but if we also choose to call this a "right" then we invoke a different sense of hospitality altogether, one that is tethered to the laws (in the plural) that guide the entitlements and obligations one has in the eyes of the state or courts of justice. In Derrida's view, conditional hospitality is duty-bound whereas unconditional hospitality appears without plan or decision. Derrida draws the distinction thus:

> This unconditional law of hospitality, if such a thing is thinkable, would then be law without imperative, without order and without duty. A law without a law, in short. For if I practice hospitality *"out of* duty" [and only *"in conforming with* duty"], this hospitality of paying up is no longer an absolute hospitality, it is no longer graciously offered beyond debt and economy, offered to the other, a hospitality invented for the singularity of the new arrival, of the unexpected visitor. (2000, 83)

Thus conditional hospitality acts at the level of principle—the principle of duty, the principle of conforming to that duty—and as such it risks betraying the unconditional movement of a hospitality that is about being open to the other, without question. It is in this way that Derrida pronounces on the impossibility of unconditional hospitality itself:

> It is as though hospitality were the impossible: as though the law of hospitality defined this very impossibility, as if it were only possible to transgress it, as though *the* law of absolute, unconditional, hyperbolical hospitality, as though the categorical imperative of hospitality commanded that we transgress all the laws (in the plural) of hospitality, namely, the conditions, the norms, the rights and the duties that are imposed on hosts and hostesses, on the men or women who give a welcome as well as the men or women who receive it. And vice versa, it is as though the laws (plural) of hospitality, in marking limits, powers, rights, and duties, consisted in challenging and transgressing *the* law of hospitality, the one that would command the "new arrival" be offered an unconditional welcome. (2000, 75, 77)

Conditional hospitality, by never being able to live up to its "ideal," thereby always also includes a certain degree of hostility to the other (1999, 88). That is, the foreigner, stranger, other, must embody and live up to certain conditions imposed on her by her host—she must obey certain rules and become subject to the laws of the land (laws which in turn can claim to protect her rights). Thus Kant's plea for the "right of the stranger not to be treated with hostility" becomes impossible, on Derrida's terms, because this very "right" always places limits on hospitality since it introduces a certain degree of hostility that prevents the welcoming of her fully and completely. The host who supposedly enacts a gesture of hospitable welcome actually also is in the paradoxical position of enacting a violence. As Bonnie Honig notes, "the mutual implication of host/hostility ... illustrates the persistent trace even in our own most cherished ideals of that which we seek to overcome" (2006, 106).

Most importantly, for Derrida, it is not that these "two regimes of hospitality" (2000, 135) are mutually exclusive, nor can we simply decide to choose between them. It is, rather, that the cosmopolitan appeal to the universal right of humanity can never be fully universal since it must, by its appeal to "right," be incarnated through civil, political, and juridical laws, which, in turn, betray the very ideal they are based upon.

the unconditional law of hospitality needs the laws, it *requires* them. This demand is constitutive. It wouldn't be effectively unconditional, the law, if it didn't *have to become* effective, concrete, determined, if that were not its being as having-to-be. It would risk being abstract, utopian, illusory, and so turning over into its opposite. In order to be what it is, *the* law thus needs the laws, which however, deny it, or at any rate threaten it, sometimes corrupt or pervert it. And must always be able to do this.

For this pervertibility is essential, irreducible, necessary too. The perfectibility of laws is at this cost. And therefore their historicity. And vice versa, conditional laws would cease to be laws of hospitality if they were not guided, given inspiration, given aspiration, required, even, by the law of unconditional hospitality. These two regimes of law, of *the* law and the laws are both contradictory, antinomic, *and* inseparable. They both imply and exclude each other simultaneously ... they show that they are both more and less hospitable, hospitable and inhospitable, hospitable *inasmuch as* inhospitable. (2000, 79, 81)

What does all this mean for cosmopolitanism? How does Derrida's reframing of the problem of universalism in light of the pluralistic (and therefore singular) nature of hospitality open up new questions for cosmopolitan politics? First, in my view, Derrida exposes the split that lies at the core of Kant's claim of "cosmopolitan right as a right of humanity." Hospitality, instead of being the unified, solid ground upon which we respect and welcome persons from other cultures, becomes instead an image of our own imperfection. Imperfect because it cannot be "achieved" but must remain a reminder of a future that can never truly come into being. As Derrida points out, our ideals of hospitality as unconditional can never be "implemented" entirely, or completely, in the social, political, or juridical sphere. In this sense, it is an impossible stance to hold. At the same time, though, it is precisely this ideal which indeed has made possible the creation of laws, rights, duties, and cities of refuge (Derrida 2002).

Secondly, it is not as if Derrida is giving up on the idea of cosmopolitanism altogether. It is rather a question of how we continually work toward improving relations to the other through the contradictory and paradoxical space of hospitality. Thus Derrida troubles the way the idea of humanity is used as a justification for the cosmopolitan project, for, as he points out, if we take this idea seriously, we are necessarily speaking another language than rights; indeed, we are speaking a language of human diversity, pluralism, otherness that commands our attention to singularity and which cannot thereby be ferried across to the shores of politics. Cosmopolitanism thus becomes a project that cannot simply embrace universalism for the very universalism it claims to be embracing is one already laced with the threads of human diversity, which reveals itself to us in singular instances of otherness.

Yet, when it comes to rethinking the complexities of cosmopolitanism through the fault lines of universalism and pluralism, Derrida offers no easy solutions. His work remains in the realm of critique, without giving content to alternatives. Some might see this as real limitation to his work on cosmopolitanism, which is, after all, not only a set of abstract ideas, but has informed a way of doing politics. However, what his discussion on hospitality offers is a way of thinking through the tensions and gaps of promoting an idea of humanity. With this said, his work does seem to provide some bones upon which we can flesh out an alternative vision of an idea of humanity that is itself contingent upon those aporetic spaces of hospitality. In my view, his own assumptions about the centrality of the relation to the other—however contradictory that relation is—can help us to reclaim a language of humanity that is not based solely on individual reason and moral capacity. In this sense, his critique can give us a place from which to begin a reconstruction of cosmopolitanism and the idea of humanity upon which it traditionally so shakily rests.

RETHINKING COSMOPOLITANISM

As we can see from exploring what I have termed the fault lines of cosmopolitanism, upon which rest a series of paradoxes, ambivalences, and tensions, therein lay very serious challenges as to the meaning and practice of cosmopolitanism as a project, theory, and practice. What I see here as being of prime importance are the terms upon which these fault lines are expressive of a modernist heritage, concerned with, on the one hand, the universal appeal to humanity and the cosmopolitan right of hospitality this gives rise to and, on the other hand, the commitment to human pluralism and diversity which this very right of humanity is supposed to fulfill. My point here has been to highlight the problems to be faced, beyond whether or not one's approach is more in line with new or classic articulations of cosmopolitanism. In outlining these fault lines first through the work of Kant, my intent has been to show the difficulties inherent to the cosmopolitan promise of universal rights as they intersect with notions of humanity and the citizen. Indeed, my turning to Benhabib, Kristeva, and Derrida has been to reveal some contemporary ways in which these fault lines have been discussed, retheorized, and criticized with the aim not simply of abandoning cosmopolitanism as a potential model for making rights meaningful to those who have been traditionally been excluded from them (foreigners, strangers, asylum seekers), but of reformulating the conditions under which we can speak of cosmopolitanism as a meaningful project in the first place. Moreover, in the critiques discussed above, one of the key issues is how might we make a relation to the other, and to alterity more generally, in ways that do not fall back into the traps of modernist assumptions of humanity—which, as Kristeva in particular shows, has merely repressed or forgotten the most unsavory aspects of history and has underestimated our capacities for violence and destruction.

Thus my task throughout subsequent chapters is to expose those limits and possibilities of cosmopolitanism, offering critiques of certain related notions of human rights, democracy, citizenship, and the problematic assumptions of humanity upon which these rest. For now, I wish to state more clearly how the critiques of Benhabib, Kristeva, and Derrida bear upon my goal of rethinking cosmopolitanism and how I take this goal up in the chapters that follow.

First, what each of them focuses on is the question of *imperfection*. Benhabib tackles the paradox liberal democratic states find themselves in vis-à-vis their upholding of the rights of others and their own right to self-rule. That is, her point is to highlight that imperfection of the modern state system to secure for all its "members" (even those who are not citizens) the rights due to them through their belonging to a human community. Through this, she is concerned to articulate what states' obligations "ought" to be in facing otherness as a condition of the cosmopolitan project. What this suggests to me is that education as a state institution, mirrors, to a certain degree, this very paradox insofar as its policies are determined by this tension around attitudes to who belongs, on what grounds, and what securities or guarantees are made in the name of education itself—a point I discuss in chapters 3 and 5. Kristeva also emphasizes imperfection in her call for the need to come to terms with the "stranger within" as part of a cosmopolitan politics. Directly eschewing a narrow view of humanity in terms of reason and moral capacity (elements of the potential perfectibility of the human subject), Kristeva instead argues that it is the very imperfectability of humanity which binds us together—it is indeed otherness, our own foreignness, which paradoxically constitutes our humanity, as divided and split. This view poses a direct challenge to the frequent calls to direct our educational attention to a notion of a "shared humanity" based upon the goodness of the subject; instead, the task at hand is to introduce strangeness as a condition of educating beyond narrow nationalisms. I discuss this further in relation to citizenship and sexual difference in chapter 7. Derrida also draws our attention to imperfection in staging the call for hospitality as an im/possibility. Through Derrida, we can pose the question as to the extent to which we can educate for a cosmopolitan ideal when that very ideal can only be betrayed in our actual encounters with other people. How can we live and educate in the aporetic space of cosmopolitanism when we are confronted with real others who can only be met through a conditional hospitality? I discuss some aspects of this in relation to radical democracy in chapter 6.

A second, ongoing theme that these theorists bring to a rethinking of cosmopolitanism is the way in which the universal-pluralism divide can be *renegotiated*. Indeed, in calling for the need for democratic societies to extend forms of belonging more inclusively to all, Benhabib suggests practices of negotiation through which the voices of aliens, asylum seekers, and foreigners actually take part in the process of reformulating laws, civil regulations, and the like. Although I think she ends up uncritically—and unnecessarily—returning to a rigid form of universalism, for reasons I outlined above, her work nonetheless opens up important questions for rethinking education's role in contributing to such inclusion. My analysis of Muslim schoolgirls' predicament in France—and elsewhere—takes up this task more concretely in chapter 5. Kristeva's reformulation of universality as one that takes otherness into account, echoes to some degree Mignolo's calls for "diversality," discussed earlier in this chapter. With her attention placed on critically mobilizing an idea of humanity that recognizes its own otherness, Kristeva calls for a renewed attention to the subject as split—

as containing a difference to itself. Constructing a universality on this split means having to rethink the way we negotiate between three levels of experience: abstract principles and ideas; the way we relate to ourselves; and the meeting of actual people in time and space. Although not discussing directly the work of Kristeva in this context, her ideas nonetheless inform my approach to the issue of negotiation in making judgments in chapter 8. Derrida, too, compels us to look closely at what we are invoking in a cosmopolitan appeal to the universal right of humanity in light of what is possible in encountering real others. That is, his work focuses our attention on the way in which universality poses both limits and possibilities for thought and practice. As I read him, the space opened up by universal rights through unconditional hospitality, on the one hand, and the necessarily parsimonious nature of conditional hospitality in dealing with diverse others through institutions such as education, on the other hand, raises crucial questions for how education can negotiate between these two poles. I take up this aspect of negotiation in chapters 3, 4, 5, and 6.

My purpose in opening the terms of cosmopolitanism to some serious rethinking is to promote a critical awareness of the ways in which our "talk" about humanity, rights, citizenship, and belonging can mask the complexity of human pluralism. In seeking to rethink cosmopolitanism, my point is to make it more responsive—as an educational theory and practice—to the difficult task of facing humanity, outlined in the previous chapter. Thus my intent is not simply to dismiss or reject outright a long conceptual history, but to engage it in a way that can point us in new directions—directions which perhaps can no longer call themselves "cosmopolitan" in any classical sense. Be that as it may, the point is to expose those ambivalences, paradoxes, and tensions that mark our continual immersion in a divided modernity—so that, in echoing Kristeva, we can better come to terms with our own ghosts.

NOTES

1. Social theorist Zygmunt Bauman (1999) has suggested that globalization "means, among other things a separation of power from politics." Capital, he claims, is "no longer bound by the limitations of space and distance, while politics stays as before local and territorial. The flow is increasingly beyond the reach of political institutions" (120). Thus one of the issues that Bauman identifies is how local political agency might be remobilized as a response to global forms of power. Cosmopolitanism, in general, attempts to rethink this issue through appeals to cosmopolitan citizenship and a notion of responsibility beyond community.

2. Cosmopolitanism has been the theme of a number of edited collections. For example, Vertovec and Cohen (2002) critically focus on the theory and practice of cosmopolitanism; the essays in Breckenridge et al. (2002) take up the specific questions of culture; Bohmann and Lutz-Bachmann's (1997) volume centers on the bicentenary of the publication of Kant's essay, "Perpetual Peace." See also the special double issue of

Theory, Culture and Society, vol. 19: 1-2 (2002) whose essays cut across a wide range of issues in social and political theory.

3. One notable exception is the volume of essays edited by Vertovec and Cohen (2002).

4. Craig Calhoun raises criticisms with "cosmopolitan democracy" in that it needs to be far more concerned with pluralism: "It needs to approach both cross cultural relations and the construction of social solidarities with deeper recognition of the significance of diverse starting points and potential outcomes. It needs more discursive engagement across lines of difference, more commitment to reduction of material inequality, and more openness to radical change. Like many liberals of the past, advocates of cosmopolitan democracy often offer a vision of political reform attractive to élites partly because it fspromises to find virtue without radical redistribution of wealth or power" (2003, 111–112).

5. Ulrich Beck refers to the sense of actually existing cosmopolitanisms as "banal cosmopolitanism" (Beck 2006, 40).

6. David Hansen (2008) is one of the few to discuss "actually existing cosmopolitanisms" in education while also embracing a general appeal to humanity.

7. There is some discussion over how to translate the German *recht*, which refers both to law and to right. In this context, it is clear that to our modern English ears, law seems more appropriate here.

8. Note here that this passage is quoted from Ted Humphrey's translation of Kant's essay (2003), which offers a much smoother text in this instance compared to that which appears in Reiss's edited collection.

9. Benhabib (2004) has assembled comparative information on rights and benefits available to residents with varying status within EU countries. See pages 157–161.

10. I discuss Arendt's notion of the "right to have rights" more extensively in chapter 3.

3

Not Just for Myself:
Questioning the Subject of
Human Rights

The right to have rights, or the right of every individual to belong to humanity, should be guaranteed by humanity itself. It is by no means certain whether this is possible.

Hannah Arendt, *The Origins of Totalitarianism*

For pure suffering, which is intrinsically senseless and condemned to itself with no way out, a beyond appears in the form of the interhuman.

Emmanuel Levinas, "Useless Suffering"

Human rights as that project of securing an individual's freedom—historically from the persecution of the state, and more recently from social, cultural, and economic disadvantage—have become paramount in discussions of cosmopolitan politics, and to more general discussions about the betterment of the human condition around the globe. Belief both in their powers to assure that universal features of human life are protected and in their depiction of those features (usually rendered in terms of freedom, dignity, and equality) has fuelled major efforts in education in the recent past. Particularly in the wake of the United Nations Decade for Human Rights Education (1995–2004),[1] increasing pressure has been placed on governments around the globe to pay some (although, in actuality, fairly minimal) attention to defining education's role in furthering the human rights agenda.[2] Furthermore, with respect to the emphasis on globalization, cosmopolitanism, and world citizenship, educating for human rights is seen as both a moral and political necessity to the establishment of peaceful terms for coexistence.

One of the issues I consistently faced in reflecting on the status of rights as I delved into reams of educational material on the subject (e.g., teaching manuals, curriculum guidelines, action plans) was the uncomplicated manner in which rights themselves were treated.[3] Indeed, rights are not merely taken as a given, or seen as a fundament for educational values, but are often extolled in a way that is uncommon in other teaching subjects: they are more often than not considered to be inviolable. It is as though to think about human rights critically

51

would be tantamount to rejecting not only the possibility for justice in this world, but the very idea of humanity they aim to protect. But as Michael Ignatieff (2001) asks: "If human rights is a set of beliefs, what does it mean to believe in it? Is it a belief like a faith? Is it a belief like a hope? Or is it something else entirely?" (53). These are important educational questions. For if rights are to be taken seriously (as I think they should be) then educating for the betterment of human condition in all its plurality can only come about through a thorough analysis of rights and our belief in them—an analysis that isn't afraid of posing questions about the underlying principles upon which rights are based. To believe in rights unquestioningly, in my view, elides the very issue of their historical formation and puts at risk our ability to engage fully with what rights attempt to rectify—that is, human injustice.

The belief in the idea of humanity underpinning rights has been understood, since the American and French Revolutions, in terms of the qualities each one of us possesses by virtue of the fact of our being born human: life, liberty, and the pursuit of happiness; *liberté, egalité, fraternité*. These 18th-century words continue to resonate deeply in the western imagination, capturing the emancipatory flavor of political possibility. There is a slight irony here in that rights have historically been enshrined to protect individuals from external forces which threaten to erode our supposedly "natural" human claim to pursue these qualities to the fullest. They have become necessary mediators between, on the one hand, the entitlement of the individual citizen to pursue his birthright (and, of course, it was a specifically masculine citizen to which these early documents referred) and, on the other hand, those others (the state, fellow citizens, persons in political power) who could thwart the actualization of such qualities. What early rights declarations made so plain in their rhetoric was that each human being is entitled to the expression of their freedom and autonomy without worry from undue interference. Rights, in short, would ensure the empowerment of the individual in the face of wanton acts of power which could destroy one's very humanity. The belief in universal freedom and autonomy as signs of that empowerment were carried into the more modern declarations, particularly the United Nations Declaration of 1948, as a mark of the inherent equality, dignity, and worth of each human being.

The Flemish philosopher Roger Burggraeve (2002), however, comments that human rights "depart not from the empowered ego but from the disenfranchised (oppressed) Other" (104). On the face of it, this rather provocative statement would seem to champion a commonly held belief that rights are indeed an attempt to protect the freedom of those who are most in need of security and that they function as a preventative measure against precisely the kind of disenfranchisement and suffering we in fact are witness to around the globe. In claiming that human rights emanate from the other, though, Burggraeve actually proposes a far more radical challenge to conventional thinking on human rights, which borders, I think, on the heretical. For if our belief in human rights has rested largely on the notion that individuals are entitled to the expression of autonomous freedom, then what does it mean to our understanding of rights to assert that they emanate from the powerless other? Does not this focus on the other, as someone who is absolutely different from myself, actually undermine the very meaning of rights as emanating from the idea of humanity—that is, the dignity, worth, and equality that we share by virtue of being born human?

Although I do not wish to question the obvious necessity of recognizing and preventing abuses against individuals, and the even more obvious central role that educating for human rights can play in such a project, I do explore a number of themes here that problematize our naïve acceptance of human rights in education and suggest an alternative reading that actually takes up Burggraeve's challenge—a challenge which has been informed by an understanding of human rights offered in particular by Derrida and Levinas. As I have suggested in previous chapters, it is precisely in not coming to terms with the sheer inhuman element of human experience that has enabled an uncritical acceptance of rights as part of the cosmopolitan agenda. Ignatieff (2001) in fact warns against the veneration of rights as such, and proposes that we should resist the worship of the human being as sacred (83). My purpose here, then, is to infuse discussions on rights in education with a more complex picture of what rights entail, focusing on three themes in particular: the ambiguity of the state in promoting rights; the suffering of others which they attempt to alleviate; and the difficulties of negotiating the space between the particularities of the other's lived realities and the universality that lies in the claims to humanity.[4]

To begin this work, I first address the way this chapter's critique of some foundational thinking with respect to rights can actually be seen not as a denigration of rights themselves, but as an affirmation of the possibility for their continual renewal. I then turn to a discussion of Arendt's analysis of the problems and possibilities of human rights in order to amplify the themes under study. Following this, the chapter examines how these themes are addressed in the human rights education literature; and, finally, I return to the question of the subject of human rights for education as a question preeminently concerned with the other's right to be.

AFFIRMATION THROUGH CRITIQUE

The French "Rights of Man" (Droits de l'Homme et du Citoyen) and the American Bill of Rights not only inaugurated a new set of concerns for how to think about the relationship between humanity and the political formation of republican values, but also gave birth to a particular conception of human subjectivity. The human subject, as rooted in an idea of humanity, was to give legitimation to the new forms of political relations emerging in the 18th century. Despite the incompleteness and naked omissions of who counted as a subject in these documents (an important contemporary question for women, the poor, immigrants, and slaves), we nonetheless continue to live in the shadow of its legacy. This new subjectivity that emerged, this putting into discourse, text, and common parlance the very idea that certain qualities of humanity ought to be conferred on each individual by virtue of one being human is a truly revolutionary moment; and not because the idea expressed in these declarations could be actualized for one and all, but because the inscription of subjectivity took an overtly political—and secular—turn. The idea of humanity this new subjectivity was based on was an expression of the historical changes taking place in the aftermath of the "death of God"—that is, the authority for man's future lay within man himself.

As a number of theorists have pointed out, human rights themselves, as a series of articulations, are not reflections of any essence of humanity, but are historically-situated locutions that carry a great deal of moral, political, and ontological force. Ignatieff (2001), for one, warns against construing rights on metaphysical terms: "All that can be said about human rights is that they are necessary to protect individuals from violence and abuse, and if it is asked why, the only possible answer is historical" (83). As a self-proclaimed liberal, Ignatieff writes of his frustration with the way human rights and their portrayal of humanity are often presented as "moral trump cards" (21) that exist above and beyond politics, beyond the concrete disputes that rights are frequently invoked to solve. As such, they risk merely becoming the fetish of a humanism that holds itself up as the object of its own idolatry. Treating rights as sacred, for Ignatieff, neglects the ways in which rights are not all of kind and actually compete with another when it comes to practical issues. Without an historical and political understanding of rights, then, one does not have the tools necessary to make adequate judgments when actual civil struggles are at stake.

On the point of the historicity of rights, Derrida offers a similar comment in his Oxford Amnesty International lecture (2001): "what we call human rights is a set of concepts, laws, requirements which were not given in nature, from the beginning. It has been a long, long conquest, a long battle, to formulate what the human rights are or should be" (178). What Derrida makes so plain here is that not only are rights constructed at particular moments in history but they also have been forged through the sheer force of political struggle. Yet, unlike Ignatieff who sees rights on pragmatic terms—as embodying the bare minimum standards which enable us to resolve political violence and conflict—Derrida pushes the envelope further: the very declaration of human rights, in his view, including defining and redefining them, codifying them, and putting them into law, needs to be interrogated. He is adamant that we need to question rights in order to "improve upon the concept of the human subject" (Derrida 2001, 179). And this, for the simple reason that rights are by their very nature incomplete and thus need to be continually questioned for the exclusions they commit in the name of humanity itself—exclusions which have dire political and ethical consequences. It is worth quoting Derrida at length on the topic:

> We must (*il faut*) more than ever stand on the side of human rights. We need (*il faut*) human rights. We are in need of them and they are in need, for there is always a lack, a shortfall, a falling short, an insufficiency; human rights are never sufficient. Which alone suffices to remind us that they are not natural. They have a history—one that is recent, complex, and unfinished. From the

French Revolution and the first Declarations right up through the declaration following World War II, human rights have been continually enriched, refined, clarified, and defined (women's rights, children's rights, the right to work, rights to education, human rights beyond 'human rights and citizens' rights,' and so on). To take this historicity and this perfectibility into account in an affirmative way we must never prohibit the most radical questioning possible of all the concepts at work here: the humanity of man (the 'proper of man' or of the human, which raises the whole question of nonhuman living beings, as well as the question of the history of recent juridical concepts or performatives such as a 'crime against humanity') ... (Derrida 2003, 132–133)

In analyzing the historical, textual, and conceptual trajectory of human rights, the aim is not to dismiss the project of rights altogether, but to recognize in it the contours of its own limits with respect to what it decrees for the subject. That is, rights documents make certain assertions about humanity in the context of particular historical and political necessities. It is for this reason that rights need to be seen in more fluid terms, which can possibly offer new ways of conceiving humanity without disavowing rights themselves in the process. Treating rights in this way reveals the inherent ethical and political character of rights. Far from providing the universal grounding of politics (the "moral trump card"), rights actually expose the struggle that is required in expanding, rewriting, and refining our views of subjectivity. Moreover, rights reveal themselves not to be morally unassailable on the grounds of their universality; the very exclusions various rights declarations have produced (and will continue to produce) stand testament to this. Thus, if rights are going to be refined and rewritten, their universality must be put into question. Instead, as I develop more thoroughly below, such a critical commitment to rights emanates from a concern for particular others that are excluded in the name of this universality. By this I mean that rights are the effect rather than the cause of our political and ethical attention to the human condition. Rights, in Derrida's terms, are to be affirmed through our very questioning of their limits. As we shall see below with Arendt, it was the plight of stateless people that revealed to her the limitations of rights as they were then conceived. The universal appeal to humanity, then, cannot be accepted naïvely, but must be constantly rendered meaningful to the specific contexts in which we find ourselves. It is in such a relentless pursuit for furthering justice that the affirmation of rights can find its most loyal advocate in the critic.

What this affirmation through critique suggests to me is that human rights education is caught up in making claims about subjectivity that are historically and politically situated, and thereby incomplete. To my mind, its only options are to choose to ignore the claims it is basing its pedagogy upon or to interrogate its own practices and beliefs in order to provide some "improvement" on our understanding of the subject. My task here is to unpack a few of themes in the human rights literature in the spirit of working toward precisely such improvement. Reflecting on the incomplete nature of rights actually allows us to explore the extent to which an ethical and political concern for others can inform the way we teach. It is not that rights are incomplete now, only to be perfectly inclusive later. Rather, rights are by their nature incomplete because they cannot foresee the particular realities of human life in the future. Thus the question of who is excluded is not one we can find an answer to once and for all. Instead, it is to direct our attention to the different others whose lives have been made invisible through the appeal to a common ideal. How does the subject of rights in terms of *actual persons* intersect with the subject of humanity in terms of *abstract statements* about freedom, equality, and dignity?

THE RIGHT TO HAVE RIGHTS

Hannah Arendt, perhaps more than any other commentator on human rights, has addressed the question of what meaning abstract rights can hold for particular groups of people. She takes a critical position both with respect to the origins of rights and with respect to their enforcement, and elaborates upon what she sees as an even more fundamental necessity: the right to have rights. Her critique appears in the monumental work, *The Origins of Totalitarianism*, which was written in the early postwar years and originally published in 1951. In a tone at times redolent with bitterness and resignation, Arendt (2004) shows how both the origins and enforcement of rights are not unconnected. Writing of the predicament of stateless people in the ruined aftermath of the two 20th-century world wars, Arendt sharply analyzes their hopeless condition and the failure of rights to assuage it. Indeed, she sees a number of paradoxes in the very promotion of rights, and through examining who is excluded from their rhetorical dream, she pointedly reveals the fragility that lies at their heart:

> The conception of human rights, based upon the assumed existence of a human being as such, broke down at the very moment when those who professed to believe in it were for the first time confronted with people who had indeed lost all other qualities and specific relationships—except that they were still human. The world found nothing sacred in the abstract nakedness of being human. And in view of objective political conditions, it is hard to say how the concepts of man upon which human rights are based—that he is created in the image of God (in the American formula), or that he is the representative of mankind, or that he harbors within himself the sacred demands of natural law (in the French formula)—could have helped to find a solution to the problem. (380)

She traces this inability to assure rights to stateless people as growing from the paradoxical assertion that although rights supposedly emerged from the nature of man, man himself became subsumed under the rubric of a new collective. That is, in the revolutionary articulations of rights of the 18th century, which were said to be inalienable, based on birthright and not on God, they also served the "right of the people to sovereign self-government" (2004, 369). Arendt describes the paradox thus:

> In other words, man had hardly appeared as a completely emancipated, completely isolated being who carried his dignity within himself without reference

to some larger encompassing order, when he disappeared again into a member of a people. From the beginning the paradox involved in the declaration of inalienable human rights was that it reckoned with an 'abstract' human being who seemed to exist nowhere ... (2004, 369–370)

Hence the whole point of the inalienability of rights ended up not turning on man's belonging to a human community at all, but to a nation-state: the state became the guarantor of rights to its people. The tragedy of this situation, for Arendt, was brought into sharp focus with the coming into being of stateless persons, whose existence and fate challenged the limits of rights. For her, this is when the rights of man became a truly practical, political issue. She observed that the enforcement of human rights proved impossible as soon as people who lacked membership in a sovereign state appeared on the scene (2004, 372). Without a state to guarantee the rights conferred only on citizens, their so-called "human" rights seemed to be mere rhetoric. Adding further complication to this, Arendt states that even in postwar attempts to draft new human rights "no one seems able to define with any assurance what these general human rights, as distinguished from rights of citizens, really are" (372). Thus from the beginning of both the 18th- and 20th-century declarations, human rights have posed a particular problem when they come into contact with the concrete realities of actual persons.[5]

What Arendt's analysis of this situation reveals is that the idea of humanity casts an abstract sense of the human being (a "human being who seemed to exist nowhere") in natural terms and this masked the way rights actually functioned on two levels. The first is at the level of the rights of citizens; these rights require states in order to provide the conditions necessary for the actualization of human freedom and autonomy. They are, Arendt claims, ones which an individual can lose without becoming absolutely "rightless": such as the soldier who loses his life; the prisoner who loses his freedom. These rights are rights that hold within communities. The second level, by comparison, exists in what Arendt coins as the "right to have rights." Arendt uses her analysis of those who have become "rightless" through their non-belonging to a state to show that not even human rights can secure this prior right: "The calamity of the rightless is not that they are deprived of life, liberty, and the pursuit of happiness, or of equality before the law and freedom of opinion ... but that they no longer belong to any community whatsoever..." (2004, 375). Arendt depicts the true horror of this situation:

> But neither their physical safety—being fed by some state or private welfare agency—nor freedom of opinion changes in the least their fundamental situation of rightlessness. The prolongation of their lives is due to charity and not to right, for no law exists which could force the nations to feed them; their freedom of movement, if they have it at all, gives them no right to residence which even the jailed criminal enjoys as a matter of course; and their freedom of opinion is a fool's freedom, for nothing they think matters anyhow. (376)

The sad irony is, at this second level, one becomes rightless because one is not recognized as part of the common humanity that the rights declaration themselves supposedly enshrine. To exist in the "abstract nakedness of being nothing but human" (Arendt 2004, 380) was precisely the difficulty—and the downfall—faced by stateless people. She continues: "If a human being loses his political status, he should, according to the implications of the inborn and inalienable rights of man, come under exactly the situation for which the declarations of such general rights provided. Actually the opposite is the case" (2004, 381). Thus the right to have rights does not lie in conforming to a fuller picture of humanity, nor in a particular version of humanness, for what is at stake is nothing other than these persons' expulsion from humanity altogether. Instead, this right to be a rights-bearing individual should be read as both a moral and political claim: all should have the right to "expression within and action upon a common world" (383). Yet, it is a claim without foundation in any metaphysical sense of what is good or sacred, or in any Kantian ideal of humanity.

As can be seen in the opening quote of this chapter, Arendt is thoroughly pessimistic about the possibility that "humanity" can itself guarantee the right for individuals to belong to the human community. She takes no comfort in the apparent goodness inherent in such an idea, finding metaphysical justification for rights to be an inadequate ground for securing this right to have rights. Indeed Arendt goes so far as to warn of the risk of seeing rights as the "equivalent to being good" (2004, 379). Right is right; it should be neither confused with what it might be "good" for, nor seen as a reflection of the "goodness" of humanity; it simply must exist as an unconditional, nonfoundational feature of political life—a life that is, in her eyes, rife with potential for acting upon the world. Without this warranty, rights risk merely becoming a hollow promise.

What Arendt reveals through her discussion of the right to have rights are the precarious ways human rights, both in their conception and in their enforcement, are able to respond adequately to the needs of particular others—even when they lay claim to a universal humanity. Her analyses give good reasons as to why it is dangerous to treat rights as sacred, as divorced from the unsightly contexts of their own history, as though our belief in them is enough to automatically assure their intrinsic potential. Moreover, as Arendt demonstrates, it is not that the idea of rights is correct and we've merely got our implementation strategies wrong. It is, rather, that the very imperfection of rights needs to be attended to, knowing there is no hope for ultimate perfection. With constant vigilance, and a heightened sense of unconditional right, Arendt asks us to consider human rights as something more, perhaps, than they had heretofore been conceived. Akin to Derrida in this regard, Arendt seems to be saying that it is the interrogation of rights that can lead to an improvement of them. What Arendt's questioning of rights revealed was a gap between the stated human rights with their ideal of humanity, and the actual suffering of humanity, which rights were powerless to address. In locating this gap, she advances a nonfoundational "right"—a right that has nothing to do with a perfect conception of the human subject, but everything to do with recognizing human pluralism. That is, it is about living with the imperfection of the human condition, which one cannot justify through metaphysical notions of humanity. The abstract human being "who seemed to live nowhere" gets in the way of providing the proper political response to people whose right of human belonging vanished almost overnight. This image of the human being was based on "natural" claims from which could be deduced a set of rights seemingly independent of history and human plurality; they were supposedly "true" even if only one man existed on earth (Arendt 2004, 378).

What I see in Arendt's analysis is how the awakening to the plight of the stateless could not have arisen within an appeal to human rights themselves. Although this "right" to have rights leaves us with some very troubling questions, particularly for those who are searching for a stable ground of justification for human rights, Arendt's unabashed directness in asserting this right lays claim to the suffering of stateless people, of individuals who seem to exist outside the law, outside of rights themselves. Her attentiveness to their fate lies beyond a faith in rights and suggests to me that human rights cannot provide the moral anchoring point for acting against human injustice; rather they are complex articulations that must be seen in light of their exclusions and limitations so that we are in a better position to work with them. Moreover, insofar as Arendt's critique and affirmation of the right to have rights grew out of concern for those who seemed to be abandoned by human rights—a concern for others who are not like myself—I contend here that any ethical justification for human rights emerges precisely out of such concern, and not out of any prior definition of humanity that rights declarations pronounce. That is, it is the concern for others who are not like myself rather than an idea of a shared humanity that mobilizes a justification of rights. In order to put forth this view more thoroughly in relation to education, it is necessary first to examine some critical challenges that have been mounted within the human rights education literature—challenges which reflect the Arendtian themes discussed above: the relation of rights to the state; the universality of rights in relation to particular contexts; and the relation between rights and the suffering of others.

SUBJECT TO THE STATE

As we saw in Arendt's discussion, rights have a particular historical and political relation to the state, which can, at times, pose particular problems for the individuals they aim to be protecting.[6] Within the human rights education literature, there is an admitted paradox to be faced between the state as guarantor of human freedom and human freedom as in need of protection from the wretched whims of the state. States thereby become at once a powerful authority that simultaneously through their rights agendas must seek to limit their own powers over individuals. Lingering within our current "Age of Rights," then, is a reliance upon the laws of states to uphold the ideals of justice even as those states are the ones most threatening to individual liberty. Upendra Baxi (1997) claims that there is a need for limiting the overwhelming power of state operators and hegemonies; nonetheless, state action and intervention seem to offer the "most reassuring promise of providing chemotherapy to the cancerous growth of culturally rooted, economically derived forms of human rights violations; this new dialectic, the rights discourse, must both disempower and empower the state" (143).

Embedded in Baxi's observations is the sense in which education must occupy this space in between the state's impulse to socialize individuals into conformity (in which education has long had a central role to play) and its capacity to ensure social security for all its members through a rational and detached legal system which can enshrine human rights law. Thus although the appeal to education in the human rights education literature is largely preoccupied with encouraging students to "know" about rights (often as they are inscribed in civil codes, laws, and charters) and thus to encourage moral action based on this knowledge, what is largely missing is a sense of how the state occupies a precarious—indeed ambiguous—place—in establishing freedoms or even sustaining freedoms already achieved. In short, the state's role in safeguarding personal freedoms is one that undermines the power of the state itself. A failure to recognize this from an educational point of view runs the risk of depoliticizing, and I would argue dehistoricizing, human rights.

However, the very appeal to rights is precisely a denouncement of the state's capacity to regulate human life. Rights, then, are held up to indicate what is possible, what ought to be, and not what is, nor what the state has claimed. Unlike democracy and citizenship education, which is often tied to a notion of what a good citizen will be, human rights education, according to one author, "takes as its sole premise the individual as a member of the human race. Human rights education has as its moral authority not the legitimacy of any particular state, but the inherent dignity and potential of each person" (Tibbits 1994, 366). Thus within the acknowledged overt political reliance on state law to enshrine rights, human rights education also largely sees itself as embracing a universal view of subjectivity that exists paradoxically outside the laws that legitimate rights in the first place. How might one work in and through such a paradox in proposing, through education, that rights are simultaneously inscripted by the state and yet exist prior to any state intervention? This "existing prior to state intervention" expresses the second theme that I want to address, namely that of universality.

ISSUES OF UNIVERSALITY

In the education literature, the appeal to universality often works through a call for a universal normative framework (Andreopoulos 1997) that would both counteract any state's attempt to restrict individual freedom to the degree that loss of dignity is a result, on the one hand, and offer support for enshrining rights in a global context, on the other hand. Human dignity thus becomes one of the cornerstones of the universal argument, appearing as it does in the UN Declaration of 1948, and quoted repeatedly in virtually all human rights education sources I've read. The moral authority sought through an appeal to human dignity that is applicable to everyone largely has to do with the double threat perceived as being posed both by the state itself and by a pluralistic society. Thus with respect to the state, a claim to universality works against a nation-state education agenda (Tibbits 1994), and this is particularly the case in Europe (more so than in North America) where, as Sissel Føyn (1994) notes, the advancement of human rights education has to do with an engagement with local histories of totalitarianism. Also, as Aaron Rhodes (1994) claims, national European initiatives in human rights education were based on complying with international commitments while, in contrast, the US in particular advocates human rights education to combat a range of abuses and discriminatory social practices.

With respect to the perceived problem of pluralism, this is where the thorny issue of difference arises. Universalism will ostensibly solve the difficulties posed by cultural relativity. Some authors suggest that a uniform normative framework will bypass complications of ethics in considerations of cultural differences (Andreopoulos and Claude 1997). Difference is seen to be a problem in need of a remedy since it threatens to undermine the universal quality of what counts as a "human" right, and therefore what counts as subjectivity. If cultural differences do matter in ascertaining what assurances are necessary to ensure justice in particular times and spaces, then how could human rights ever be upheld against political conflict between groups, between individuals, and between states and their citizens? Indeed the idea that humanity could be something else than sameness threatens to open the floodgates of violations which is why what Betty Reardon (1995) calls the "core generative principle of human dignity" is seen to exist above and beyond the law. The instantiation of rights in terms of a universal principle, however, effectively ignores otherness as opposed to attempting to engage with it differently. For as soon as rights become law-bound, otherness has a strange way of disappearing, of slipping through the cracks. Thus how might one keep alive difference, enshrining what Derrida (1978) refers to as a "letting-be" of the other, unless one engages the other as part of the very project of human rights? With respect to education, it seems to me that establishing a principle that has at its very heart a denial of difference does little to elucidate the very real problems that face oppressed (disenfranchised) groups, for the very quality of human dignity (or any other concept for the matter) surely needs to account for the fundamental reason of why rights matter in the first place and why it matters to teach and learn human rights: that the unjust suffering of others, and not only of myself, is lessened.

RIGHTS AND SUFFERING

Such suffering is a key element in the third theme I wish to address: the relation between rights and perceived injustice. Marked by the stamp of Enlightenment virtues of liberty and equality, human rights declarations have become preeminent symbols of hope in a world where suffering shows no signs of retreat and seems in fact to continue to assail with a vengeance. Although the inauguration of rights declarations themselves has long been associated with the project of freedom, rights have also from the outset been formulated in light of perceived injustices. As stated earlier, whether we think of the US Bill of Rights, the French Droits de l'Homme et du Citoyen, or the more modern UN Declaration, each has taken on the task of historically responding to the distress of nameless others (colonialism, the *ancien régime*, and the Holocaust, respectively). Rights are cast, then, on the border between human freedom and human suffering, between what I have called in previous chapters, the "human" and the "inhuman." That is, inalienable rights are conferred on individuals by virtue of the fact of their humanity, yet they offer an idea of humanity as the very ground of their constitution—an idea that counteracts the very inhumanity seeming to be suffered.

Derek Heater (1991) brings to our attention the ways in which, pedagogically speaking, human rights education is often concerned with teaching about violations as much as it is with teaching about rights themselves. Echoing the very early history of the establishment of various human rights declarations, human rights education puts human rights into relief against a background of a history of harm. Most human rights advocates claim that knowledge about human rights leads to the combating of injustices and that teaching about abuses, repressions, and genocide enables fundamental freedoms to be exposed (Reardon 1995). This inverse correlation strategy, however, only highlights for some authors how human rights education is often "goal rich and content poor," as Ian Lister puts it (1991, 246). Indeed, for Lister, human rights education initiatives in the UK often forget justice altogether, so concerned as they are with teaching codes bereft of any sophisticated theoretical underpinning. Such teaching becomes devoid of a sense of a larger moral and political project of which human rights are a fundamental part. In terms of their relation to justice, what becomes remarkably clear is that the possibility of rights, and especially of entrenching rights into law, always lies in the impossibility of justice itself. From the ruins of its absence is erected a magnificent monument to the potentialities of human life free from suffering. In other words, at the very moment justice has failed to be present, it ironically makes justice and rights conceivable.

Thus human rights sit uncomfortably on the proverbial fence, at once a testament to the human potential for dignity and freedom and a witness to its torturous persecution. In educational terms, acknowledging the impossibility of justice would seem either to fall into a despairing hopelessness or, conversely, an overly optimistic view that learning about suffering automatically leads to a concern for justice. As Lister (1991) remarks of human rights education (and as I have remarked elsewhere [Todd 2003]), attempts to empower students can lead to feelings of guilt and powerlessness and actually thwart the best of educational intentions. The question that I think is more important to ask is how education might teach human rights not so that there is a "balance" between discussions of violations, on the one hand, and those of human rights, on the other, as if establishing some middle ground were all that was required, but so that justice is revealed as a potentiality, a promise one makes to an other that must be striven for beyond the letter of the law. Thus I propose that if our concern lies with the amelioration of suffering in local and global contexts, then how might human rights education be reconceived along the lines of response to this suffering?

RIGHTS, RESPONSIBILITY, AND SUFFERING

Levinas (1994) offers some useful ways to think about the dilemmas posed by the state, by universalism, and by injustice. He proposes that rights do not begin with myself but that they are rooted in a sense of an original right that has no origin, but lies in the proximity between a self and absolutely other (124). In claiming an original right that has no origin, Levinas gestures to the idea that rights are born in this proximal encounter instead of being located in a conception of my own autonomous freedom. It is here in this relation of fraternity that Levinas claims responsibility emerges and thus coupled with the birth of rights is the notion of concern for the other. Rights, then, are from the very beginning of human fraternity a responsibility rather than an entitlement. For Levinas, freedom then takes on another meaning than that usually understood by the Kantian emphasis on the free individual as a sign of humanity. Freedom, which is so central to rights, instead exists in the I's capacity to respond to the Other; the I escapes the entrapment of its own limitations by encountering and welcoming the other as other. My freedom, in other words, lies in freedom from my own immanence. To transcend the ego and to extend ourselves beyond self-interest requires that I attend to others around me. Our capacity to exceed ourselves—therein lies our capacity for freedom. Thus the question of whether justice is enacted or served by putting rights into law is not the whole question. Rather, justice is about securing the other's freedom to be and through this my own is then secured. In this sense, Levinas writes: "There also remains the question of determining whether the limitations of rights by justice is not already a way of treating the person as an object by submitting him or her (the unique, the incomparable) to comparison, to thought, to being placed on the famous scales of justice, and thus to calculation" (1994, 122). Here Levinas cautions against a view that laws offer us the refuge we need from suffering. Rights as they are entrenched in law necessarily must play the game of the state, paradoxically enforcing that which cannot/ought not to be enforced (if the word right is to have any meaning). For Levinas, the "defense of the rights of man corresponds to a vocation outside the state ... a vigilance totally different from political intelligence, a lucidity not limited to yielding before the formalism of universality" (1994, 123).

Thus where justice lies is not in the rights themselves but in defending the inalienable freedom of the other to be, which at times requires acting beyond the letter of the law. Thus to defend rights means to attend to the other in her singularity. This absolute difference from the other does not logically lead to indifference; rather, by claiming that one's own freedom is ultimately tied to an attentiveness to difference and singularity within the plurality of our social life, Levinas suggests that rights are always a responsibility conferred on me. But if attending to difference is the condition for justice, as opposed to attending to rights in and of themselves, then what does this mean for human rights education? How do we think about justice in the context of our teaching practices?

EDUCATING FOR THE OTHER'S RIGHT TO BE

What I am suggesting is that teaching students to follow codes even when they are encouraged to fight on behalf of others in ensuring that those codes apply to everyone equally does little to promote justice as an ongoing quest that requires sustained analysis and reconceptualizations of rights in order to, drawing on Derrida's words once again, "improve the concept of the subject." Such improvement it seems to me is not simply an academic exercise divorced from the realities of suffering; rather the very process of engaging in a constant renewal of rights to promote better and more just conditions under which subjectivity can flourish is very much an ethico-politico project, one that involves concern for others beyond my own ego investments and entitlements. My worry is that if human rights are taught as though obeying and upholding their legal incarnation is reflective of justice itself, then the possibility for justice remains foreclosed. And this is the case, particularly if we are to make the distinction, following Levinas, that the law is not to be equated with justice. That is, even as the exercise of justice requires laws, such as human rights codes, justice cannot be collapsed into them. Justice, like rights, necessarily always must remain in an exterior, albeit elusive, relation to such legislation. With this said, focusing on the other's right to be as a condition for human rights education leads us to ask serious questions as to the nature of our teaching and the dilemmas we face as educators in opening up a space for freedom and justice. This is the subject of the next chapter.

NOTES

1. This has now been continued with the UN's World Programme for Human Rights Education which is seen to be an ongoing project. The first phase of the program ended in 2007.

2. See Rosemann's (2003) comments on the disappointing numbers and quality of governmental response.

3. Between 2001 and 2004 I was head of a project that involved investigating notions of justice as they were portrayed in Human Rights Education policy and curricula in both Canada and Sweden.

4. As I intend to make clear, there is a distinction to be made between the kind of universality that presents rights as applying to one and all equally and the claim that universality resides in a trans-historical understanding of humanity itself.

5. Jacques Rancière (2004) in his reading of Arendt on this point suggests that what she was critiquing was nothing less than modern democracy itself (298).

6. See chapter 5 for a discussion of the 2004 French law prohibiting the wearing of religious symbols to school as a specific case of this type of conflict

4

Promoting a Just Education: Dilemmas of Rights, Freedom, and Justice

Hannah Arendt (1965), in her essay, "The Crisis in Education," points to the power granted, however misguidedly, to education in political projects. She writes, "The role played by education in all political utopias from ancient times onward shows how natural it seems to start a new world with those who are by birth and nature new" (176).[1] Indeed, this observation has become a sort of truism in how we think about education with respect to human rights in particular, admitting, it would seem, that the culture of rights needs education for its future security. The idea is that through institutionalized practices of knowledge, children will come to form habits of thought, attitude, and spirit which are conducive to promoting and creating landscapes of living with others that embrace a commitment to democratic and rights-based principles. There is a large dose of common sense—and indeed consensus, at least in the west—in this hope we grant to education, and in this trust we place in youth to be able to make a "new world," better than the old one we were born into. And not simply better, but more just. In the west, human rights education initiatives have been developed in an attempt to ensure that youth can well take on the demands of democratic citizenship, both locally and globally. Thus such initiatives would therefore appear to be excellent starting points for the pursuit of justice, understood in terms of creating forms of living that serve to nourish the very freedoms that allow dignity in human life.

Thus it is with some discomfort that I approach writing about the *dilemmas* of human rights education, for it does indeed appear to be a luxury to write of dilemmas in times of such global want. Nonetheless, I address in this chapter the fundamental fictions that rights are based on and how those fictions are nonetheless useful for opening up the ethical terms of human rights education. In the previous chapter, I outlined some of the challenges to be faced with respect to teaching for rights and discussed rights as a responsibility conferred on me by the other. Here, I focus on the idea that part of the difficulty inherent to human rights education initiatives lies in the ways in which value has been historically conferred upon particular notions such as freedom and justice. A just education, it seems to me, must grapple directly with the conceptual dilemmas that have been inherited, especially with respect to freedom, and refuse to shy away from the implications of these dilemmas. If the UN Declaration is to be treated with the respect it deserves, it must be engaged as a living document which has the capacity under the weight of its own convictions to demand something more of us than simply learning *about* it. Rather, the questions addressed here are: how might we bring into focus those underlying conceptions of freedom, justice, and responsibility in ways that enhance our living arrangements, and that do not leave us totally subject to an authoritarian reading of the declaration? How might we think beyond an education that merely seeks to inculcate knowledge toward a *just* education that provokes insight into the conditions of freedom, justice, and responsibility themselves?

I have intimated above that education is perceived to be instrumental to the purpose of human rights, yet the issue at stake is how education can be something more than mere transmission in enhancing the cause of justice through human rights. In previous chapters, I have examined the limitations of education with respect to the call of educating *for* humanity and have presented the difficulties inherent to the status of education in such a call. It is not that education has no role to play (in fact I think it has a very important role) in familiarizing students with basic rights, but even the best intentions of teachers and technologies of education cannot guarantee the expected outcomes, particularly one so grand as justice. Indeed I think it is wise to return to the observations of Jean-François Lyotard (1991), who considers that the very humanity of young persons reveals to adults (who are supposedly "in the know") precisely what we lack. As discussed in chapter 1, it is children's nascent humanness that "manifests to this community [of adults] the lack of humanity it is suffering from, and which calls on it to be more human" (3–4).

Responding to this call to be more human means that both human rights and education need to come together in ways that assume responsibility for children, which cannot be done solely through the content of what we adults teach. Part of a rethinking of human rights education, in my view, needs to take into account that the freedom, for instance, upon which it is based, is not simply "content," a concept to be apprehended, used, and ultimately applied to daily life. It seems to me that knowledge about rights is the bare minimum required and that the real potential of education lies in its capacities to provoke insights that help youth live well with ambiguity and dilemma, where freedom, justice, and responsibility cannot be dictated *at* them, but are tough decisions that must be made in everyday living. For, to my mind, this is a significant aspect of the project of facing humanity itself.

FREEDOM IN RIGHTS: FICTION AND ACTION

Article 1 in the UN Declaration states: "All human beings are born free and equal in dignity and rights." Add to this Rousseau's (1974) comment that "man is born free and everywhere is in chains" and what floats inevitably to the surface is the tension created when one mobilizes the idea of "natural" freedom to counteract the actual bonds of servitude humans continue to endure around the world. Thus freedom here is a fiction, a device we use to measure as unjust the very existence of people in chains. It is therefore not a description of the conditions under which people live. It is an ideal, or horizon that has little basis in the actuality of most people's lives. But, as Agnes Heller (1992) writes, "statements such as 'all men are born free' need not be unmasked as fictions, because they are meant to be fictions (or metaphors). Their ontological character is illusory. *They are ethical and political principles.* they [sic] are *not theoretical,* but rather pure practical principles" (351). Thus the question of what to do with the fiction, in practice, is of utmost importance—for it is not to say that freedom has no meaning if rights, and the freedom that is asserted in them, "means to claim something that is due, which is justice" (354).

Freedom here is needed for practical reasons, in order to take action, to leap into lively human activity and to decide what is just. But it is a freedom not based on the volition of an individual to direct itself to take action. Rather, as Arendt (1965) claims, freedom is something that can only be experienced in practice. It is thus not an "absolute" freedom, but is conditional upon a social and political reality. It is a concept, though, that has been distorted by its turn inward, as though freedom were a phenomenon of the will, an expression of an inner life (147–151).

Arendt instead proposes a double movement: that freedom can only emerge through political organization, and that freedom is the very reason why we have need of politics in the first place (1965, 146).

> Without a politically guaranteed public realm, freedom lacks the worldly space to make its appearance. To be sure it may still dwell in men's hearts as desire or will or hope or yearning; but the human heart, as we all know, is a very dark place, and whatever goes on in its obscurity can hardly be called a demonstrable fact. Freedom as a demonstrable fact and politics coincide and are related to each other like two sides of the same matter. (Arendt 1965, 149)

For Arendt, simply claiming that freedom belongs to the will puts us in a very precarious position indeed. The "dark place" of the human heart cannot guarantee that freedom can be willed into existence. What she stresses instead is that freedom emerges out of the political communication we participate in with one another. She writes that "a state, moreover, in which there is no communication between the citizens and where each man thinks only his own thoughts is by definition a tyranny" (1965, 164). The capacity for freedom to be realized demands, then, a presence of political community. For it is only upon the scales of public life where freedom's possibilities can be weighed. Freedom as a practice must always live in the shadow of its opposite; the threat to freedom comes not from a failure to exert one's will, but from certain arrangements of public life that threaten to dissolve its possibility. I read Arendt here as suggesting that it is the very human capacity for acts of inhumanity that requires constant political vigilance. That is, we need to *face* the possibility that freedom can indeed be foreclosed by acts of human interest in order to build a robust public space that can contribute to bringing freedom into presence.

As for the declaration "all men are born free," Arendt's views underline the nature of it as a necessary fiction, for if freedom is to mean anything at all it must participate in a practical realm, where social and political organization allow not for its expression, as if it existed prior to action and communication, but for its very inception. What Arendt captures is the interdependent nature of freedom, a freedom built on intersubjectivity, on communication, on public life.

Working within the dilemmas of freedom (as both fiction and practice) demands, then, attending vigilantly to the possibilities that the fiction of freedom grants us. With respect to education, it seems especially pertinent to read the connection between freedom and rights less in terms of having a definitive content, and more in terms of how freedom is *performed* in acting with others. Freedom is not about telling others how they should live, but engaging in a communicative process that focuses attention on the many faces of freedom within rights-based societies. Thus when Heller (1992) suggests that "rights are the institutionalized forms of the concretization of universal values (both the value of freedom and of life)" (93), she seems to sidestep the question as to how rights themselves and the freedom they represent are possibly contestable in the actual concrete communicative practices humans engage in. While the fiction of freedom in the statement "all human beings are born free" allows us to entertain, and helps to regulate, justice, the idea that all have a right to life as well as liberty leads to the very difficult work of building a new public realm while simultaneously aiming to secure individual needs. This double project means that political projects, such as those concerned with human rights, work on two fronts simultaneously. The question for human rights education, in particular, is how might it live well in the space between creating environments that support human life while creating possibilities for the active, practical condition of freedom.

JUST RESPONSIBILITY

In wanting to extend the importance Arendt places on the public, communicative quality of freedom, I also want to introduce here, through the work of Lyotard and Levinas, the idea that justice and responsibility are based neither on criteria nor content, and that this shifts our model of human rights education from one that is deducible from principles to one that emphasizes communicative practice. In my reading below, I draw out how this latter model is linked to a particular ethical conception of rights. This, I suggest, is what allows human rights education to work simultaneously in the two directions mentioned above: toward both the support of human life and the active conditions of freedom.

Seeing modernity as that which "comprises in itself an impulse to exceed itself into a state other than itself" (Lyotard 1991, 25), Lyotard notes that pluralities that mark life in modernity impel us to reflect upon the universality of principles, like freedom and justice, which frequently have been used as means of

oppression. To loosen up these modernist commitments, Lyotard discusses justice in relation to pluralism through an analysis of language games and the ways
certain statements perform certain functions. As we have already seen, the
statement that "humans are born free" is not a descriptive statement, even
though it is stated as fact. Instead, it poses as a descriptive phrase that implores
one to act *as though* each human were indeed free. Conceived as a fiction for
Heller, Lyotard posits freedom as the Idea that regulates justice (Lyotard and
Thébaud 1985, 84). Relying heavily on Kant's (1997) second critique, he proposes that freedom is not determinate; that is, it does not establish the content of
laws, nor can it determine its own content (Lyotard and Thébaud 1985, 84).
"Freedom is regulatory; it appears in the statement of the law only as that which
must be respected; but one must always reflect in order to know if in repaying a
loan or in refusing to give away a friend, etc., one is actually acting, *in every
single instance*, in such a way as to maintain the Idea of a society of free beings"
(84–85). Under this view, freedom cannot tell us how to judge, how to decide; it
cannot be concretized, for it is an Idea that one uses reflexively, as opposed to
obeying it as though it held the answers for combating injustice. As a specifically *regulative* Idea, moreover, it is used in such a way so that it acts as a horizon against which we can assess, weigh, and consider our action in the world.

  Now this carries significant meaning for justice. Freedom (even in the guise
of a descriptive statement) cannot determine for us how we are to judge, or why
we ought to judge. Descriptive statements cannot logically give rise to prescriptive ones (Lyotard and Thébaud 1985, 21–22). Thus, the statement that there is
massive suffering in the world, while speaking a truth, does not *logically* lead to
the statement that I ought to do something about it, which speaks a command to
be just. "In other words, in so far as justice is prescriptive it cannot be derived
from theorizing 'the true'" (Smart 1998, 52). There is no justification possible
for being just, or for the command to be just; "it is proper to prescription to be
left hanging in midair" (Lyotard and Thébaud 1985, 45). A prescriptive phrase
neither denotes nor describes the human condition as it actually is, nor does it
derive its ethical force from a factual depiction of the world. As prescription, it
exists beyond the boundaries of what we can see, what we can know, what we
can report. But it is far from "empty."

  For Lyotard, a judge decides, case-by-case, without definitive criteria. Justice comes about through the exercise of prudence, not through the application
of rigid criteria or principles (Lyotard and Thébaud 1985, 26).[2] Lyotard is em-
phatic that "any attempt to state the law, for example, to place oneself in the
position of the enunciator of the universal prescription is obviously infatuation
itself and absolute injustice, in point of fact" (Lyotard and Thébaud 1985, 99). It
is, instead, an idea of justice that guides the judge in her decision. Moreover, this
idea is in turn regulated by, if you will, an imaginative faculty that seeks to bring
the law in line with the individual circumstances of each case. In this regard
adherence to principles alone brings us up short in actually analyzing what takes
place in the practices of judgment (a topic I take up in more detail in chapter 8).
That is to say, what Lyotard focuses on here are the ways in which decisions of

justice are made always in relation to a specific activity, a specific case. So although one might believe in the universality of a principle like justice, its enactment is only possible in the encounter with concrete reality. Like Arendt in this respect (and perhaps in this respect alone), Lyotard asserts that judgment occurs in action.

The language game, then, of justice is one of prescription, and has no basis in fact or truth. Justice problematically rests within a language game that can have no grounding on the concrete content of freedom. Rather, it is situated within a set of, what Lyotard refers to as, "pragmatics;" there are certain pragmatic rules that define each language game, and each of us participates in several (Lyotard and Thébaud 1985, 93). The pragmatics of justice lie, for him, in the obligation we have to others to decide and to make that decision among competing language games. Most importantly, these pragmatics force us to continually hold open the question of justice itself, where we can return to it again and again. That is, each time I come into contact with a situation where individuals speak to me, they not only speak to me through different language games, but also command from me an obligation by virtue of the fact they address me. They require a response. And that response can only live up to its name of response when I refuse to impose upon them a set of criteria or to hear their words only through a filter of laws, regulations, and such. Instead, the response that is commanded is a listening to the other knowing that my judgment must come through a reflexivity in which I continually ask myself—is this a just decision? This is the language game of justice. And although we can never know with complete certainty whether we have been just, Lyotard states that

> absolute injustice would occur if the pragmatics of obligation, that is, the possibility of continuing to play the game of the just, were excluded. That is what is unjust. Not the opposite of the just, but that which prohibits that the question of the just and the unjust be, and remain, raised. Thus, obviously, all terror, annihilation, massacre, etc. or their threat, are, by definition, unjust. (Lyotard and Thébaud 1985, 66–67)

We can see here that Lyotard is concerned to get away from the relativism that appears to be implied in any language game. What is to be underscored here is that it is not that "anything goes," but that justice is held together both through obligation to the other and the Kantian idea of a society of reasonable, free beings. This latter idea, he is insistent on pointing out, does not in any way determine our action. Indeed, if it were to do so, it would constitute a terror (Lyotard and Thébaud 1985, 92), and make it impossible to keep open the question of justice. Instead, the idea guides our decisions *in the context* of the obligation that itself knows no language game, that only arises in our encounter with the other. To keep open the language game of justice requires regarding our decisions in terms of how well the decision that I have made actually has been responsive to the specific situation of the other.

Obligation to others, in conjunction with the regulatory ideas of freedom and justice, informs the pragmatics of justice. As a practice, justice then does not solely rest on how well laws, or rights, are articulated, but on how individuals are responded to, which requires not treating those laws as though the contents of them were transparent. Instead, it requires an attentiveness directed toward the particularity of each case in relation to the law at hand. Thus seeking to promote the right to freedom among women in Afghanistan or Guatemala or Ireland or France, cannot be judged in the abstract—as if justice had little to do with the differences that matter to these women's life situations. It is not that there is a plurality of justices, but that there is a justice of plurality.[3] It is only sensitivity and flexibility that keeps the self-questioning—am I being just?—at the forefront of one's decision. Justice, then, is to be seen "against the horizon of a multiplicity or diversity" (Lyotard and Thébaud 1985, 87). Interestingly, Lyotard attributes this refusal to see judgment simply through the means of obeying predefined prescriptives to the teachings of Judaism. He writes:

> The refinement that Judaism brings to the notion of obligation is precisely that one has to watch out for prescriptions that appear to be just or authorized; they are not always to be taken literally, and they may result in the most extreme injustice. They must always be taken as much as traps as obligatory prescriptions. And thus they always refer one back to responsibility, to the responsibility of listening, of lending oneself to obligation. (Lyotard and Thébaud 1985, 66)

In this way, justice carries within its practice notions of responsibility and obligation. Levinas, upon whom Lyotard also draws, proposes that this obligation, which amounts to a command from the other, cannot be justified. Not only am I subject to the other as soon as she addresses me for no *logical* reason, I am commanded by her to respond *beyond* all reason. Thus, my commitment to her does not arise from the freedom of my will—i.e., that I choose to be responsible; it is instead a *"responsibility that is justified by no prior commitment"* (Levinas 1998a, 102). This non-justifiable responsibility is something that grips me unawares; just by encountering another's face an obligation to that other wells up in me. Levinas (1998a) writes, "There is a paradox in responsibility, in that I am obliged without this obligation having begun in me, as though an order slipped into my consciousness like a thief, smuggled itself in...." (13). This paradox is precisely what underlies our commitments to justice—and to rights. My ability to decide, to make decisions that keep open the question of justice, is, therefore, not a result of exercising my freedom. Quite the contrary. It lies instead in my capacity to be the receptacle for smuggled goods.

> The responsibility for the other can not have begun in my commitment, in my decision. The unlimited responsibility in which I find myself comes from the hither side of my freedom, from a 'prior to every memory,' an 'ulterior to every accomplishment,' from the non-present par excellence, the non-original, the anarchical, prior to or beyond essence. (Levinas 1998a, 10)

As that which cannot be concretized (that is, that freedom exists in a particular condition), freedom can only be experienced as I exceed myself, take the other's command into me, and thereby enable the freedom of the other to emerge.

In terms of justice, I decide, evaluate, compare, and prioritize on the basis of my obligations to others, not upon the basis of predefined principles, laws, or rights. And, of course, the practice of justice then requires that I live in concert with those others. "The one respected is not the one to whom, but the one with whom one renders justice. Respect is a relationship between equals. Justice presupposes this original equality" (Levinas 1987, 43–44). Naturally, justice requires something more than simply my own judgment. And Levinas is adamant, of course, as a Jewish philosopher writing in the wake of the Holocaust, that we be able to judge that which is unjust; but nowhere does he describe the content of what that justice looks like. Thus, the capacity to judge totalitarian states such as Nazi Germany as unjust, rests precisely on what Lyotard refers to as subjecting ourselves to a prescriptive. We exercise rational thought only after the command from the other has been heeded, and that command rests on our capacity to be moved by others' suffering—or more specifically on *my* singular capacity to allow it to enter me as difference. Thus it is not suffering in and of itself that gives us the reason to act, but our sensitivity to the plight of others initiates a command to respond responsibly.

Recognizing that justice simply does not lie within the judgments you and I make, but within forms of sociality that bring to mind Arendt's public sphere, Levinas reveals a necessary paradox: that the state is necessary for justice at the same time that it cannot enact a responsibility for each individual in its care.

> But it is very important, in my view, that justice should flow from, issue from, the preeminence of the other. The institutions that justice requires must be subject to the oversight of the charity from which justice issued. Justice, inseparable from institutions, and hence from politics, risks preventing the face of the other man from being recognized. (Levinas 1999b, 176)

In this sense, laws, rights, or institutions such as education, must constantly keep vigilance over the inevitable and necessary failure of justice to be realized. Embedded within this is a plea for laws to change constantly in order to improve upon the possibilities for justice, or as we might say along with Lyotard, upon the pragmatics of the justice language game.

What I have discussed thus far has enormous bearing upon how rights might be rethought. In an essay entitled "The Rights of Man and the Rights of the Other," Levinas proposes that rights begin with the Other, rather than with one's own freedom (Levinas 1994, 124). Justice can indeed come to the defense of rights, but if, and only if, it is not based on a notion of an autonomous freedom, or free will. He writes, "in defending the rights of man, the latter should no longer be considered exclusively from the point of view of a conception of freedom that would already be the potential negation of every other freedom and in which, among freedoms, the just arrangement could only come from reciprocal limitation" (123). This means that my own freedom is not the arbiter of the other's freedom. The defense of rights is not about limiting, in Hobbesian fashion, my freedom as against your freedom, as though freedom were something that each one of us possessed internally and that each of our individual freedoms is in competition for superiority. The point for Levinas is that the other's freedom always takes precedence over my own, for it is in such a defense of the other's freedom that my own makes its appearance. A "just arrangement" in defense of rights suggests itself when freedom becomes linked to this responsibility:

> One's duty regarding the other who makes appeal to one's responsibility is an investing of one's own freedom.... My freedom and my rights, before manifesting themselves in my opposition to the freedom and rights of the other person, will manifest themselves precisely in the form of responsibility, in human fraternity. (Levinas 1994, 125)

In another essay on the same topic, Levinas writes that while the universal character of freedom needs to be granted in defending rights, he also concedes that even "consenting to the rationality of the universal [i.e., that all humans are free]" does not (and cannot) guarantee that any good will result (Levinas 1999a, 148). As we have seen in chapter 1, the point that he makes here is that goodness neither arises out my "inner" nature nor in my adherence to a universal principle. The Good only makes its appearance as a quality of relation that requires putting the other before oneself.

> Unless a pre-eminent excellence were granted to the other *out of goodness*: unless *good will were will*, not just out of respect for the universality of a maxim of action, but out of the feeling of goodness. A simple feeling that we speak to children about, but that can have less innocent names, such as mercy or charity or love. An attachment to the other in his alterity to the point of granting him a priority over oneself. (1999a, 149)

Levinas brings to our attention here that the justice that we grant to human rights is thereby not based on an idea of humanity that is in itself good, nor on an idea of respect for moral law (and for others as rational subjects), but on an attachment to the other—a susceptibility to the other's condition, a concern for the other's suffering—that puts responsibility at the heart of human rights. The turn that Levinas makes is to view human rights as an ethical project, not a project of rationality or knowledge alone. Like Lyotard's, such a project cannot be grounded in rational arguments; it is rather a practice constructed around a recognition both of the idea of freedom and that of justice, based on a command to respond to the other. This command, moreover, is something prescribed to me before any freedom. Freedom, on this view, is not the ground of rights; rather responsibility is.

HUMAN RIGHTS EDUCATION: TOWARD RESPONSIBILITY AND JUSTICE?

Documents and policies dealing with human rights education place great emphasis on how best to instill and inculcate among children the values inherent in the

UN Declaration as well as various Human Rights Codes. The calls for education to transmit the contents of the Declaration and to help students engage in an understanding of human rights that are found within the UN documents themselves, smooth over the very dilemmas that students face in coming to grips with how abstract and apparently universal principles speak to the particularities of their own and others' life situations. And this is especially true when those students come from societies, cultures, and languages where freedom and individuality signify something quite different than they suggest in the schools in which they are being educated. Moreover, there is no single content that one can give to freedom across languages (a point which I develop in more detail in the following chapter). For instance, the French term *liberté* and the English freedom do not encompass the same nuances of meaning.[4] Furthermore, calls for individual freedom cannot be easily imported into cultures with a deep sense of duty to community.[5] Moreover, if pursuing justice, which is the stated aim of the development of the UN Declaration in the first place, cannot be secured through recourse to knowledge alone, then it would seem that the goal of disseminating knowledge as fixed and transportable to practice is simply not adequate. What I am offering here, by way of conclusion, are points that suggest possibilities for rethinking education's role in the project of human rights by working with, as opposed to smoothing over, the dilemmas of freedom and justice.

First, following the above thinkers, but particularly Arendt, education can be deeply involved in constructing public spaces for students to experience human rights. With respect to the right to education (Article 26 of the UN Declaration), UN special rapporteur Katarina Tomaševski (2001) proposes that human rights be integrated into all aspects of education, as opposed to treating human rights as a separate topic in social studies. In particular, she is concerned with focusing on the process of education itself. With respect to process, I earlier raised a question: how might education participate in creating spaces that nourish human life as it creates possibilities for the active, practical condition of freedom? If public life is to be invigorated, then how might any systemic practice, including education, attend to the needs of individuals? There are no clear, prescriptive answers to these questions, least of all ones that rely on an idea of humanity that leaves out of the equation the potentially inhuman elements of our actions. Indeed the very *fiction* of freedom seems to underline the very real inhuman conditions that continue to exist. Listing a series of tasks that would bring about the attentiveness to specific individuals seems to rub against the grain of the kind of everyday judgments that go on in schools, where dealing with many different individuals precludes the possibility that each one's needs can be responded to all of the time. Yet, it is not enough to say nothing. Understanding first of all that pedagogies, even when promoting conditions for social justice, cannot rely on curriculum alone to create an atmosphere of equality and respect is a step in the right direction. The authority granted to teachers suggests that they are in a position to create conditions where students begin to exercise their faculties of communication in order to produce lively social and intellectual communities. Differential treatment of individuals can indeed be an important place to begin, but seen in the service of enabling students to live also with the difficulties of pluralism; to have opportunities to listen to one another and to speak with responsibility is certainly something that any human rights education can be concerned with, not just in terms of the classroom, but in terms of community organizations with which schools are connected.

Secondly, the difficulties posed by freedom and justice (both of which always remain on a horizon of possibility, as opposed to something one achieves through certain behavior), demand a rethinking of education's role in promoting human rights. Even in familiarizing students with the actual articles of the Declaration, or using case studies to encourage them to apply certain rights and codes in order to make judgments, the tasks are set up too often to reflect the ease with which judgment can be made. It seems to me we do a disservice to children to present judgment in this light. Although we are not educating children to be Human Rights Commission judges, we are educating them to participate in society (of which school is undoubtedly a part) reflectively, prudently, and critically. How students make meaning of human rights, how they fathom freedom and justice, and how they perceive their own rights in relation to others can be given expression through engaging with the *dilemmas* of rights and judgments as opposed to pretending they do not exist. To have students be creative with language that gives them some space for indeterminacy, and that allows them to ask questions and ponder the very dilemmas that rights present to individuals and states, does not denigrate the project of human rights. I think some human rights educators are afraid that once uncertainty is allowed in, rights will be thrown out the window and an anything-goes attitude will run rampant. Although I acknowledge this as a real concern, I do think that discussions with youth on how critique might be constructed on the basis of an affirmation of rights can be crucial. Further, as we have seen in chapter 3, the educational documentation that exists often proposes teaching about rights through violations, with no adequate language for teachers (and students themselves) to think about the strong expressions of guilt, powerlessness, and apathy that often accompany the reception of these stories. Thus, an important task for human rights education is to begin to construct a language that allows youth to question their responses in ways that makes obvious their own implication in the lives of others.

Finally, a note on responsibility. If freedom is found in responsibility, one might be tempted to state that the role of education in human rights initiatives is to educate responsibility in students. But my discussion of Levinas suggests that the obligation we have toward others is not something one learns as a piece of knowledge. Responsibility is a response to the command of the other; it is a prescriptive to a prescriptive. In no way can responsibility be instilled or inculcated in a direct fashion and thus it cannot be systemized into any curricula or teacher manual. But this is not to say that it has no bearing upon education. In fact, viewing rights in terms of responsibility rather than entitlement (the latter making up much of the educational literature), suggests a reorientation to the actual teaching of human rights. Moving away from didactic materials that only seek to ensure students have learned what their rights are, a renewed education would need to discover ways of creating a pedagogy of implication. That is, a pedagogy whereby we are continually vigilant in attending to the needs of others in a way that takes responsibility for our own responses. Such vigilance does not come easy, but if human rights education is to have any hope of creating a just education, paying attention to how we judge and why we judge seems to demand just such measures.

NOTES

1. Arendt is, of course, critical of this view; but it is the seeming naturalness of the link between education and political projects that continues to be operative, in my mind, to human rights education initiatives.

2. See also his comments in Lyotard (1988, section 44: 31; 1991, 5–6). The problem with Human Rights declarations is that of course they have attempted to state the law, and thus to a large degree Lyotard sees them as closing off possibilities for justice.

3. Lyotard asks: "Can there be a plurality of justices? Or is the idea of justice the idea of a plurality? That is not the same question. I truly believe that the question we face now is that of a plurality, the idea of a justice that would at the same time be that of a plurality, and it would be a plurality of language games" (Lyotard and Thébaud 1985, 95).

4. One can also see even greater difficulties when looking at translations. For instance, the beginning of Article 4 of the Rights of Man reads: "*La liberté consiste à pouvoir faire tout ce que ne nuit pas à autrui....*" In English, *liberté* is, as usual, translated as liberty, while *pouvoir faire*, which means, literally, power to make, is translated as freedom.

5. See, in particular, Wang (2002) and Pollis and Schwab (1979).

5

Whose Rights? Whose Freedom?

Man and *citizen* do not designate collections of individuals. Man and citizen are political subjects. Political subjects are not definite collectivities. They are sur-plus names, names that set out a question or a dispute (*litige*) about who is in-cluded in their count. Correspondingly, *freedom* and *equality* are not predicates belonging to definite subjects. Political predicates are open predicates: they open up a dispute about what they exactly entail and whom they concern in which cases.

Jacques Rancière, "Who is the Subject of the Rights of Man?"

The historical call of modern justice, heard through the demand for rights, free-dom, and equality, seems ineradicably etched on modern consciousness. Its echo reverberates through contemporary struggles to articulate paths of peaceful co-existence, and western institutions such as human rights organizations, schools, and national development agencies are particularly susceptible to the demands of justice placed on them. Indeed, the voice of our modern inheritance, whose tenor of liberalism resounds throughout the world, has been challenged by those who wish to sing something other than its praise. Voices which raise themselves over the din of this inheritance seek to alter the rhythm of justice: how it is pro-nounced, decided upon, and regulated, particularly where human rights are con-cerned.

These voices, of course, are not all of a kind, and they make themselves heard most often in contexts where rights are perceived as "impositions" from the west, within lands whose communal traditions are seen to be at odds with the individualism embedded in human rights themselves (see Pollis and Schwab 1979; Wang 2002). What the presence of these voices raises is the question of pluralism within human rights agendas. Yet, it is not only the exportation of western-style universalism to non-western countries in which a tension is felt, for how universal rights are invoked *within* western societies reveals an equally difficult dilemma around questions of pluralism. That is, through appeals to cer-tain principles (such as secularity and self-determination), western nations are pursuing an increasingly aggressive campaign to delimit certain civil freedoms, particularly with regard to education. Nowhere is this perhaps most clearly evi-dent than in the recent rash of regulations and legislation compelling girls and women to refrain from wearing headscarves and other religious dress in educa-tional settings; acts which disregard any particularity as to religious and/or cul-tural practices.[1] But what makes these regulations particularly pernicious is that they are legislated (or seek to be legislated) in the name of rights, equality, and freedom: specifically, the right of the state to self-determination; the protection of gender equality; and freedom from religious influence in the public sphere. In Sweden, schools are now given the right to expel students who wear the *burqa* on the grounds that it does not promote equal treatment of all in the classroom. In France, it is now illegal to wear a headscarf, or other "ostentatious" religious symbols, in schools on the grounds of the state's right to secularity.[2] And across Europe, in Belgium, Germany, and the UK, there have been cases concerning girls and women wearing *hijab, niqab,* and *jilbab* to schools appearing before the human rights courts (most of which have supported the community's or state's right to restrictions).

In previous chapters I have myself raised a critical voice with respect to the ways in which rights are conceived and enforced and how through exploring these critiques, education needs to shift its pedagogical practices. Here, I delve further into the question of rights as they intersect with cultural and sexual difference. What is on the table here are a series of tensions that speak to the inherent ambiguities to be faced by cosmopolitanism. As discussed in chapter 2, cosmopolitanism upholds universalism and supports the framework of human rights, on the one hand, while also appreciating and respecting cultural diversity, on the other hand. What I focus on in this chapter are the specific tensions that surround human rights themselves when the respect for cultural difference comes into conflict with the state's right to self-determination and when education as an institution is put into the service of this state right.[3] Moreover, I seek to address the particularly gendered nature that such conflict has taken with respect to the French law prohibiting religious symbols in schools, which was passed in 2004. Although much has been written about this law, most authors focus on the tensions it raises for liberal democratic states and do not address directly the gendered aspects of this legislation (see Gereluk 2008; Benhabib 2002, 2004). My point is that it is not simply *Muslim* sartorial practices that are at stake here; it is, rather, specifically Muslim *girls' and women's* sartorial practices that are singled out. Part of the reasoning employed in this chapter's argument builds on feminist criticisms of human rights and the way women have been positioned historically within them. Specifically I outline how cultural and sexual difference[4] have particular salience in reframing our relation to freedom, equality, and dignity and how this contributes to rethinking education's role as institutionalized bearer of human rights.

RIGHTS FOR WHOM?

Challenges to the globalizing tendencies of human rights have opened up considerable debate around the universalism of those very rights. And the question that has been raised is: whose rights and whose freedom are being advanced in this universalism? Bryan S. Turner (2002) notes three main criticisms: (1) that rights are saturated in western values of liberal individualism and are incompatible with non-western societies; (2) that they are not enforceable, particularly those rights that have a cultural component; and (3) that rights imply obligations which have not been fully given adequate attention (46–47). The first, "cultural-ist" argument, carries perhaps the most weight in terms of levying critique against the way rights discourse appears to turn a deaf ear to cultural difference, and it is this upon which I focus my attention here. More particularly, principles of freedom, equality, and justice are often seen to be in tension with specific linguistic, social, and cultural contexts. The charge is that universalism pays inadequate attention to the local complexity of how such principles are under-stood and practiced. For instance, the language of freedom carries with it spe-cific meanings marked by its long conceptual history in the west—and even within the west, the French *liberté*, for example, does not have the same cultural associations as "liberty" does, particularly in the US context. The importance of this lies in the relatively simple fact that such meanings cannot be translated directly and imposed on local contexts as though they carry the same conse-quences for subjectivity. Indeed, this culturalist argument revolves around the idea that rights have turned into a symbol of western imperialism (particularly as it is exported through developmental aid), and that under the rubric of universal-ism they, in effect, serve only to exclude those cultural practices which do not "fit" easily with the individualism inherent in the Enlightenment conceptions of freedom, equality, and dignity. That is, it is not as though freedom, for instance, has no meaning, merely that the content of that meaning does not jibe with western expressions of it. The major tenet here is that human rights need to be flexible enough to recognize the legitimacy of other cultures to define freedom, equality, and dignity on their own terms.

What is notably absent from Turner's list, though, are the feminist critiques that have also highlighted the ways in which rights fail to protect the interests of girls and women around the globe. They charge that rights which actually apply most directly to women (social, economic, and cultural rights as opposed to po-litical and civil ones) are not adequately enforced by local governments. The upshot is that for some feminists, rights are universal neither in principle nor in practice. Now, one could easily make the claim, as some feminists have, that women experience a similar disaffection as the culturalists claim in fact they do. Not necessarily in terms of western prejudice, but in terms of patriarchal privi-lege. Feminist analyses of human rights treaties and practices have paved the way for understanding how documents such as the UN Declaration as well as national and international enforcement policies both create and sustain the sys-temic exclusion of women. There are two reasons generally given for this exclu-sion based on two distinct feminist critiques, what I call the access and specific-ity critiques.[5]

The first focuses on the lack of women's equal access to rights protections; that is, this view asserts that women face enormous difficulties in accessing and achieving the same rights protection afforded to men, through legal procedures and institutional support. This view is largely entrenched in a recognizably lib-eral feminist position. The second charges that women's specificity is absent from rights; that is, how the actual concerns of women, based on their particular lived experiences, have failed to be reflected in various rights declarations and treaties. On this account, women's specificity is not fully recognized in rights documents, which thereby render women as "other" to masculinist notions of freedom and equality. And this is particularly the case with those rights that protect civil and political freedoms. What is particularly masculinist has also to do with, on the one hand, the privileging of freedom in civil and political rights in the public sphere, which leaves patriarchal dominance largely intact in all other forms of life and, on the other hand, the paucity of attention given to economic, social, and cultural rights, which are largely reflective of the private sphere (O'Hare 1999; Gallagher 1997).

But where things get interesting, of course, is in the intersection between the feminist and cultural critiques, particularly with respect to women's specificity. As Eva Brems (1997) puts it, "each wants to make the 'human' in 'human rights' a little less abstract by returning its gender or its culture" (154). The access critique, since it does not challenge directly the universal aspect of human rights, can easily claim their distance from charges of cultural bias. When alluding to women's specificity, however, the point that some feminist critics make is that one cannot talk about sexual difference meaningfully without understanding the importance of culture in creating and sustaining practices of femininity, sexuality, motherhood, and reproduction. Yet, in introducing women's specificity, we need to be careful about how we are invoking a particular take on women's relation to culture. As Gayatri Spivak (2004) expresses it, "the name of 'man' in 'human' rights (or the name of 'woman' in 'women's rights are human rights') will continue to trouble me" (564), for the simple reason that the name of "woman" risks the elision of the differences between women, particularly as these differences are inflected through culture. What is at issue, then, are the tensions that women as a *collective* face in terms of various expressions of patriarchal power and that *each* woman faces in terms of her self-worth and self-understanding within a specific set of cultural dynamics. Keeping alive this doubleness, I think, is important for reflecting on the kind of obligations that a commitment to rights necessarily entails. Although the culturalist and feminist specificity critiques do not always enjoy an easy alliance (a point which I return to below), attending to the complexity of gender is nonetheless important for analyzing how sexual difference intersects with the dual cosmopolitan demand of respect for other cultures and of adhering to universal human rights. Since making divisions along the lines of sexual difference is a focus of all cultures (Irigaray 1996; Okin 1999), it is important to keep in mind how the interworkings of sexual difference and culture open up possibilities for rethinking priorities within human rights.

Discussions, then, about the effects of cultural differences in society cannot ignore the centrality given to gender roles, to expressions of masculinity and femininity, or to how the private-public distinction is defined in relation to sexual difference. What this suggests to me is that culture creates sexed conditions for human rights, including the right to education, and this cannot easily be "overcome" through appeals to universalism or a shared humanity. Moreover, the singling out of Muslim girls in the European educational context indicates the way sex is located differently in concerns about cultural diversity in western democracies. As Benhabib (2002) asks, "How can we account for the preponderance of cultural practices concerning the status of women, girls, marriage, and sexuality that lead to intercultural conflict?" (84). Thus, discussions about rights need to confront head-on the implicit and explicit ways sexual difference factors into the tensions between the nation-state and its diverse populations, even when that difference is rendered largely invisible. For to my mind, it is not only a question of religion that is at stake here, but a question of the right for women and girls to participate freely in the public sphere. This obviously raises serious questions about who has rights and under what conditions.

HUMAN RIGHTS AND THE SEX-CULTURE DIVIDE

Two of the most influential documents in terms of the feminist and culturalist critiques have been the UN Universal Declaration of Human Rights of 1948 and the Covenant on Economic, Social and Cultural Rights of 1966. The UN Declaration focuses almost exclusively on what is generally known as first generation rights, that is, civil and political rights. Such rights mainly seek to protect individuals from the reach of state power and, through entrenchment in national legislation and international law, to protect an individual's right to be a free and active agent. Its articles are largely characterized by a notion of "negative liberty"—that is, a notion of freedom *from* coercive power (see Berlin 1997; Ignatieff 2001). Developed in the shadow of European genocide, the document largely sought to articulate a preventative strategy against state violence and abuse. In order to gain widespread approval from as many states as possible, it embraced a secular orientation and avoided any religious or metaphysical justifications for its foundational principles of freedom, equality, and dignity. In other words, from its very inception, the document attempted to embody minimal standards, what one might call the lowest common denominator, in articulating its vision.

The Covenant on Economic, Social and Cultural Rights addresses what are generally known as second generation rights, which focus more on an individual's basic needs and less explicitly on civil and political agency. It develops in further detail some very basic claims made in the first Declaration: the right to food, clothing, and shelter; the right to participate equally in economic production for fair wages; the right to free education; the right to social security, particularly for mothers; the right of all to take part in cultural life; and the right to the highest standard of health care. Explicitly stated in Article 3 is the state's responsibility "to ensure the equal right of men and women to the enjoyment of all economic, social and cultural rights set forth in the present Covenant." By focusing on basic needs, the underlying thrust is that individual agency is meaningless if the requirements for elementary survival cannot be met. Thus what marks this document as different from the UN Declaration is its attempt to expand beyond the minimalist conception of "negative liberty" and to push for standards of treatment that empower people to assume an equal place in social, economic, and cultural life. It indicates a shift from a notion of "freedom from" to a notion of "freedom to."

What many critics point out, however, is that these rights do not enjoy as much protection through international law or national legislation. These rights, in the eyes of many, remain terribly neglected in terms of international pressure on states to comply with their basic message, and are often seen more in terms of charity than in terms of a right to a basic need. As one of the main critics of how these rights have failed to be enforced, feminists have been instrumental in championing them as crucial to the empowerment and advancement of women across national and cultural boundaries.

The International Conference on Human Rights in Vienna in 1993, was seen to represent a major victory for bringing these issues to the table. Both the access and specificity arguments were used to convince conference members that the universality of second generation rights, and not only civil and political rights, needed to be upheld. This reassertion was felt to be needed in the face of signatory nations who seemed to be lax in living up to their obligations. Indeed the Vienna Conference resulted in a renewed unanimous commitment to the universality of both first and second generation rights, largely due to feminist pressure (Binion 1995). But this meeting was also important in other ways. What feminists essentially achieved here was a linking of women's rights with human rights and they saw those rights as largely belonging to the economic, social, and cultural sphere. Thus, in some ways, both the focus on women's specificity and the focus on issues of access came together to promote the idea that rights are indeed both a source of protection and empowerment for women.

Yet, most importantly for my purposes here, in achieving a renewed commitment to universality, they also served to silence the culturalist position which claimed that the universalism of human rights served to deny the right of collectives to live according to their own cultural precepts. Feminist response to the culturalist argument hinged on the fact that "culture" has often been used as the rationale to sustain oppression and abuse of women within various communities and the examples most prominently given were (and continue to be) the practices of sati, purdah, female genital mutilation, and forced marriage.[6] The culturalist argument was seen by feminists to be protecting patriarchy against the proposed transformation of the status of women through the universal applicability of human rights. Thus what happened was that in appealing to rights for all women irrespective of cultural context, both liberal and radical feminists seemed to acknowledge the importance of appealing to universalism in their arguments.

So this seeming polarization between feminist and culturalist positions raises some interesting issues with respect to how feminisms construe rights, and how cultural practices come to shape both collective and individual self-understanding for women. Taken in broad brushstrokes, liberal feminists have much less difficulty in defending the universalism of women's rights for the simple reason that the universalism of human rights in general is largely not an issue for them. But can those who advocate for rights on the grounds of women's specificity argue equally strongly for universalism if an important aspect of their critique involves the claim that human rights are not universal in the first place? One could of course claim, from this point of view, that first generation rights are not universal in the sense that they do not reflect women's experience adequately, but that second generation rights are universal insofar as they do offer protections to both women and men equally. And this is largely the argument that won the day in Vienna. However, if we take seriously the issue that women are not all of a kind, and expressions of sexual difference are indeed culturally inflected, then how does one think about rights as universal without rescinding the claim to women's specificity? That is, if the idea of humanity that underwrites claims to universalism is an incomplete one, often relegating women to the margins, then what kind of protections can be made to women universally that respect their right to be different and to decide for themselves how they express their own being in the world?

UNIVERSALISM AT THE INTERSECTION OF SEXUAL/CULTURAL DIFFERENCE

One of the problems in addressing questions of universalism in human rights lies in not wanting to appear to suggest an anything-goes relativism whereby rights are rendered completely insignificant. There is simply too much suffering and violence and too little protection against them for the majority of people around the world to take this line of argument seriously. Yet, there is a significant problem if we dispense with the importance of difference entirely, for we end up merely reasserting an idea of humanity that diminishes the reality of human pluralism, including the different ways women live their lives. This latter danger is made plain by a commitment to what I view as a strong universalism, one that sees rights as defining a universal set of standards for both moral and political action based on a metaphysical or religious justification of dignity and/or the sacredness of human life. As we saw in chapter 3, this view risks turning rights into a form of idolatry, into a worshipful enterprise. That is, it fails to take account of how rights cannot correspond to any eternal truths about what humans are, but are constructed and written by humans themselves in an attempt to contain the extreme violence and inequity humans have shown toward each other through history. Moreover, they can be seen as attempts to enshrine a certain emancipatory ideal of human subjectivity. Ironically, in its call for the autonomous freedom of the individual, the consequences of taking a strong universalist position is that it cannot exact the same critical and autonomous reflection over its own grounding principles.[7]

Yet, not all forms of universalism take such a hardened view. What I see as a more contingent version of universalism involves viewing rights as agreed-upon minimal standards that optimally aim to enable humans to live well together. In this view, documents such as the UN Declaration are pragmatic in orientation and their universalism does not lie in a prior definition of what is good for all. They do not "reflect" some essence of humanity, but represent a contractual obligation of what is right that must be held universally for them to work. They define, in other words, a starting point for political discussion. Universalism is understood on this account in terms of the universal power of rights to protect each individual from harm and the right of every individual to assume agency over his or her life. They are historical constructs that serve a political purpose and can only do so on the basis of their universal appeal.

If we return for the moment to the two feminist critiques, the kind of universalism that is often at work in the women's access argument is the strong claim. Liberal feminists generally assume that rights are by their nature reflective of both men and women equally; that the real problem does not lie in rights themselves, or in the assumptions about dignity or sacredness of human life, but mainly in the mechanisms of access to due process. They largely stay within the framework, logic, and language of human rights, and do not challenge the legitimacy of universality within them. The problem with this view of universalism, from the point of view of sexual difference, is that it fails to challenge the ways in which women's experience of violence, for instance, is often simply not reflected in specific articles of rights themselves. As Luce Irigaray (2001a) has put it with respect to rape:

> National civil codes as well as constitutions, and the *Universal Declaration of Human Rights* all lack the terms relating to specific rights which would enable such crimes to be judged. Thus rape is defined as a crime and not as rape, which fails to protect the woman as such and leaves the ordinary citizen unaware of the felony he commits when he rapes someone. (71)

Now, the second critique based on women's specificity, depends to a greater extent on the recognition of women's differences. It seeks to transform the system of rights and challenge claims to universality which are largely seen to be based on masculinist notions of autonomy and a robust individualism. Instead, women's central role in the family and roles that highlight cooperation with other community members are emphasized. This position would seem to put these critics out of the universalism ballpark altogether; yet in also seeing that new rights need to be developed in order to transform the inherent exclusion of women and better reflect their life experiences, they nonetheless still hold onto the idea that these rights ought to enjoy universal appeal. By this I mean that their universalism is contingent upon the *universal acceptance* of rights that promote gender equality even when it means that currently existing rights do not necessarily do so. The universalism here is more in keeping with a desire to expand rights in a way that gives greater priority to economic, social, and cultural rights and that extends the rights framework to include relations between private persons and not just between individuals and the state. They argue that what explicitly should be mentioned in rights treaties are such things as rape and physical abuse as these occur both within and outside the family. Thus, the UN Declaration and the laws which are based on it are not all-encompassing; rather the universality of rights needs to come about through expansion and extension of the Declaration and other Covenants themselves.

This more nuanced version of universalism would seem to dovetail nicely with the idea that I expressed in chapter 3, that rights need to be subject to critique in order for them to be affirmed anew. In thus including a notion of transformation, this position of specificity raises some very productive ways of thinking about universality that fully recognizes the importance of the contingency of rights: they are contingent upon social actors to shape and reshape them. By seeking to expand and extend already existing rights, the political nature of what rights can do—their pragmatic nature—becomes highlighted. As Eva Brems (1997) writes, "the argument in favor of increased specificity of human rights precisely aims at improving their reach, at making human rights meaningful for the greatest possible number of people" (156). That is, by adopting a contingent universalism, one can acknowledge that women have collective interests and basic needs which second generation rights largely can protect.

Yet, it does not entirely solve the problem of women's ambiguous predicament in terms of rights. The whole idea that a group can be collectively represented in rights poses a serious problem when we look at the lives of individual women qua individuals; that is, rights protections and violations do take on particular contours in light of how women live their lives in the everyday. How an individual woman understands herself within the terms of the culture in which she lives cannot be swept away under the collective banner of women's rights. As we shall see with the French law banning religious symbols, women's right to equality was indeed invoked as one of the reasons for restricting Muslim girls' and women's wearing of *hijab*. The problem with this, as I explore below, is that this cannot adequately account for the plurality of reasons as to why *hijab* (or *niqab, jilbab, burqa*) is worn and what meaning it carries for the individuals who wear it. In other words, when we look at individuals as unique others, and not simply as tokens of their respective cultures, religions, or sex, women's specificity begins to take on another kind of significance. If rights are going to have any meaning in everyday lives, they cannot do so without taking into consideration the lives of the individual women they are aiming to protect and empower.

One way of troubling and pushing at the limits of this contingent universalism is to work with the complexity of culture and promote a *perspective of negotiation and translation in appeals to universality*. As Ann-Belinda Preis (1996) observes, "a more dynamic approach to culture is needed in order to capture the various ways in which human rights give meaning to, and are attributed with meaning in, the ongoing life experiences of men and women" (290). While feminists should indeed be wary of cultural arguments that are used to justify women's oppression, we should not fail to take notice of how cultural practices themselves shape and are expressive of individual women's self-understanding. The need to feel that one belongs, the risk of ostracism, and feelings of self-worth must necessarily feature into any attempt to apply universal standards to individual situations. "When the debate on the universalism or relativism of human rights is so radically removed from the cultural 'realities' it alleges to speak about, it hardly creates anything but its own impasse" (Preis 1996, 293). So while the "goal" of sexual equality and freedom is not in question at the abstract level, in practice the response to local context needs to be an essential feature of implementation—that is, if rights are not going to become new tools of oppression. Preis (1996) further notes that human rights conventions might set a goal, but "they are only intelligible in situated contexts" (311). For feminists, looking at "situated contexts" might at first appear to slide into the kind of culturalist argument that can work against women's equality and sustain patriarchal authority. But to consider justice from the position of the intersection of sexual and cultural difference, "situated contexts" means viewing rights—their implementation and interpretation—as a cultural practice of translation.

One of the most cogent theorists to take up this space of negotiation is Judith Butler (2000), who reclaims universality in the name of cultural translation. Butler's focus on translation begins in her critical analysis of the formal aspects of universality (not simply the content of its claims). She sees that no claim to universality can be made from outside language, which means it is necessarily situated within a set of linguistic and cultural practices which cannot be entirely divorced from the claim itself. "The claim to universality always takes place in a given syntax, through a certain set of cultural conventions in a recognizable venue" (2000, 35). This would, on the face of it, seem to be leading us down the royal road of relativism indeed; yet, Butler's point is that the cultural embeddedness of universality is reflective of the way cultures themselves are constituted. "Cultures are not bounded entities; the mode of their exchange is, in fact, constitutive of their identity...." (2000, 20). In thus ceasing to talk of culture as a unified entity, Butler enables us to question the ways in which universality is already part of a process of the constitution of culture itself and thus already involved in processes of cultural translation and exchange. "No notion of universality can rest easily within the notion of a single 'culture', since the very concept of universality compels an understanding of culture as a relation of exchange and a task of translation" (2000, 24–25). That is, there is no givenness to or intelligibility of universality without an ongoing struggle to translate its meaning and significance into those very particular situations it claims to be accounting for. This has a significant bearing upon how we think about the work to be done on the global stage, where universal appeals to rights and justice are often assumed to be transparently applicable to local contexts. Butler (2000) writes, however, and I quote her at length:

> there is no cultural consensus on an international level about what ought and ought not to be a claim to universality, who may make it, and what form it ought to take. Thus, for the claim to work, for it to compel consensus, and for the claim, performatively, to enact the very universality it enunciates, it must undergo a series of translations into the various rhetorical and cultural contexts in which the meaning and force of universal claims are made. Significantly, this

means that no assertion of universality takes place apart from a cultural norm, and, given the array of contesting norms that constitute the international field, no assertion can be made without at once requiring a cultural translation. Without translation, the very concept of universality cannot cross the linguistic borders it claims, in principle, to be able to cross. Or we might put it another way: without translation, the only way the assertion of universality can cross a border is through a colonial and expansionist logic. (35)

In obviously seeking to avoid the imperialist tendencies of universality, Butler focuses on the task of translation that is incumbent on all of us who promote universal claims to rights and justice. Introducing the importance of cultural translation into the field of our philosophical and political endeavors does not mean that we can abandon universality altogether. Indeed, universality is a necessary aspect of political life. Nor is the point simply to rid universality of its colonialist or masculinist assumptions, "purifying" it as it were, for the very act of purification promotes an abstraction at odds with the cultural embeddedness of our claims. No universality, by virtue of its formal qualities, can be all-encompassing. The question is, rather, to rethink universality itself as an open-ended struggle which involves a qualitatively different approach to our search—and longing—for overarching universals. The task of translation, then, on Butler's account, turns universality into a struggle for intelligibility as opposed to a standard or home base from which we can measure and justify our condition in the world. Our deployment of terms such as justice, and the commitments to recognition, redistribution, and representation that this may entail, needs always to acknowledge the insufficiency of its own claims. This is, then, a universality forever dissatisfied with itself, forever restless in its search for meaning, and it lives only at the very limits of its own articulation. "To claim that the universal has not yet been articulated is to insist that the 'not yet' is proper to an understanding of the universal itself: that which remains 'unrealized' by the universal constitutes it essentially. The universal announces, as it were, its non-place" (2000, 39).

The very difficult question that is raised, of course, is how to develop equality between the sexes and at the same time be sensitive to how women think about the kinds of cultural practices that perhaps, at first, do not appear to allow for women's empowerment or protection. For example, the no-fault divorce law that was proposed in Sri Lanka in 1991 to the acclaim of human rights and women's rights activists, was met with the abject disapproval of many women who believed strongly in the unity of the family. This group, which was led by mostly prominent women lawyers (who in other issues were active in supporting "women's" rights), interpreted the proposed law as working to diminish the image of women within the family, a traditional site of some power (Coomaraswamy 1994, 51). Thus, it also must be recognized that paying attention to "situated contexts" and the "struggle for intelligibility" also means having to reframe one's attention to what gets counted as freedom, equality, and dignity, and accept—however difficult that may be in terms of one's personal beliefs—that decisions made by women for themselves can have consequences which "appear" to work against one's own preconceptions. Such difficulties underscore, for me, the idea that human rights themselves (their articulation, implementation, and enforcement) constitute a complex cultural practice through which abstract notions, universal principles, and philosophical assumptions come into conversation with the concrete desires, attachments, and consciences of embodied individuals and are thereby translated and retranslated.

To advocate for human rights requires, on this view, navigating a course that both promotes and protects the agency of individual women and recognizes when that agency has been so limited that it requires more aggressive forms of intervention. There are no easy answers to the very real moral dilemmas to be faced here. And I think it is in this particular struggle that the question of the universalism of rights becomes most acute. The question on the line here is *how* we judge when the right to equality is being violated. Merely appealing to the universality of equality says little about what the content of that equality should be. If we take a strong universalist position, it is not just the abstract principle which is being invoked, but also a certain concrete image of what counts as equality . For example, claiming that Muslim women who wear *hijab* are subservient to men or embody *in*equality between the sexes is not reflective of the principle of equality *per se*; it is reflective rather of a very particular, culturally inflected image of it. My point is that even in appeals to strong universalism one's judgment is not based on any "pure" or uncontaminated ideal of equality, but is already laden with one's understandings of what it supposedly *is*; that is, it is a result already of cultural translation, in Butler's (2000) sense. Thus I don't find this form of universalism to be the answer to difficult questions of judgment; indeed, as I address in detail in chapter 8, it is the attention to the particularities of situations with an eye to the suffering of others that must factor into our decisions. This is not to take a nihilistic stance with respect to judgment; rather it is to allow for the flexibility that is required when dealing with individual women and it is to allow for the possibility that we actually might be moved and transformed by our encounters with others who are different from "us." Human rights, as many activists know, involve contradictory and complex processes of negotiation and translation in making them meaningful to individual lives.

To return more specifically to the question of education as a bearer of both human rights and state agendas, what becomes important to keep in mind is how sexual and culture difference intersect to give shape and meaning to human rights. The shoring up of the nation-state, of course, partly falls on the shoulders of schools and so it should not be surprising that they are expected to enforce the specific content of those rights.[8] But the issue of whose rights and freedoms are being advocated for in the educational arena becomes especially difficult to ferret out when we look at the competing claims between state rights and individual rights. And it is precisely this difficulty which is encapsulated in the French law banning religious symbols in schools. Taking a position of strong universalism does not help us here, for the point is not only do the rights themselves conflict, but also the *content* of what those rights seem to entail poses a conflict, inscribed as they are through particular histories and cultural practices. As we will see, what counts as the right to gender equality, to freedom of religious expression, and to self-determination (along the principle of secularity), cannot be adjudicated through an appeal to universalism alone. Thus, my own analysis of this law below is informed by the perspective of translation outlined above, one that champions a view of rights as necessarily always being in conversation with concrete others.

Yet, rather than despair over the sheer complexity of taking culture and sexual difference into account in an already ambiguous and messy "tension between universal human rights claims, and particularistic cultural and national identities" (Benhabib 2004, 44), we might actually instead view such tension as part and parcel of what it means to advocate for rights in pluralistic societies. The point is not to do away with such tensions, but to find ways of learning to live better within them. To view the French *hijab* ban from the point of intersection between cultural and sexual difference not only requires a loosening up of the universal grip rights have in the hands of the state, but an acknowledgement of the dilemmas to be faced in making rights more expansive through cultural translation.

THE "*HIJAB* BAN"

Having its roots in the "*l'affaire du foulard*" (the headscarf affair) of 1989, the French law on Secularity and Conspicuous Religious Symbols in Schools was voted in overwhelmingly by the legislature on February 10, 2004 (494 for, 36 against, 31 abstentions), and signed by the President on March 15 of that same year.[9] Coming into effect on September 2, 2004, the law has created a lively and divisive debate around the nature of the right of the state to uphold its constitutional commitment to *laïcité* (secularity) and the right of individuals to freedom of religious expression.

The headscarf affair began with the expulsion of three girls from their school in Creil for observing *hijab*. It galvanized focus on the republic's educational system and the constitutional principle of *laïcité*. More than simply embracing secularization, the French term *laïcité* refers to a complex and deeply-held set of cultural meanings about the necessity of having all public institutions free from any signs of religious expression. But it also has at its center the freedom of conscience to choose one's spiritual and religious beliefs. Largely based on the autonomous and rational subject that informed the French Revolution and Enlightenment, *laïcité* is very much concerned with creating a state that respects personal liberties. It serves as the principal means to assure the common good in civil society.[10] As Benhabib (2004) notes, *laïcité*

> can be understood as the public and manifest neutrality of the state toward all kinds of religious practice, institutionalized through the vigilant removal of sectarian religious symbols, signs, icons, and items of clothing from official public spheres. Yet within the French republic the balance between respecting the in-

dividual's right to freedom of conscience and religion, on the one hand, and maintaining a public sphere devoid of all religious symbolisms, on the other, was so fragile that it only took a handful of teenagers to expose this fragility. The ensuing debate went far beyond the original dispute and touched upon the self-understanding of French republicanism for the left as well as the right, on the meaning of social and sexual equality, and liberalism vs republicanism vs multiculturalism in French life. (186)

Benhabib's observations focus on those elements in the debate which have served as a powerful precursor to the existing French law. Although, in France, the law that restricts all students from wearing "conspicuous" (*ostensiblement*) religious symbols in schools affects Jewish and Sikh boys (as well as anyone wearing a large Christian cross), it is not difficult to see in demographic terms the overwhelming affect this law has on a substantial portion of Muslim girls. Indeed, taken within the context of the debates around the "headscarf" which have raged in France for 15 years, and in the aftermath of September 11, 2001, the French law was indeed drafted against a background of fear of Muslim militantism (Stasi 2003, 14, 35). The original lawmakers admitted, for instance, that they failed to consider the implications of the law for the 5000 members of the Sikh community in France.

Elsewhere, I have argued that this obsession with headcovering reveals much about the views of how a society seeks to define itself as an "us" against a "them" and very little about what wearing *hijab* actually means to those who do so (Todd 1997). Although my focus was an incident of school expulsion in Montréal, Québec, the internal debate which ensued (which in that case divided opinion along cultural-linguistic lines) is to some degree echoed in the current questions being asked of the nature of French society. In defining who ought not to belong in certain segments of the public sphere, who ought, that is, not to participate in institutional life, the state recenters an idea of citizenship that is firmly rooted in an idea of unity and sameness. It is, we might say, a "negative" citizenship, for the prohibition of certain articles of clothing from public institutions such as schools does not offer a productive view of belonging in civil society; it merely confirms who does not belong, who is not welcomed. It also raises questions regarding the relations between the state and its own citizens, given that some citizens are deemed to be outsiders to the perceived unity of the state. What is so compelling about the French case is that unity is thus not simply accomplished through the sharing of a common principle (the principle of *laïcité*, for example), but is demanding a public identity based on what not to be. The failure to comply with this outward identity carries with it serious consequences in terms of the protection of one's individual rights.

Of course, this question of citizenship raises the issue of the nature of freedom of religious expression and the degree to which states can impinge upon that right with democratic legitimacy. The Stasi Commission, set up by the French government in order to report on the application of the principle of *läicité* within the Republic and to make recommendations of future actions to be taken, acknowledged the importance of upholding freedom of religious expression. However, in citing various cases presided over by the European Court in Strasbourg, the Commission dismissed any foreseeable problems with placing restrictions on religious dress in schools; indeed it saw any intervention on the part of the European Court as remote. According to the report, the European Court "protects *laïcité* when it is a fundamental value of the State. It allows limits to the freedom of expression in public services, especially when it is a matter of protecting minors against external pressures" (Stasi 2003, 59, my translation).[11]

Aside from the problems contained in the use of the term "external pressures," which I discuss below, what also concerns me is how education is treated here. Surely not merely a public service, access to education is a *right* that enjoys protection under the European Convention as well as the UN Declaration. The French law makes access to education conditional upon the forfeiture, to some degree, of yet another right, freedom of religious expression. Moreover, its target is primarily, although not exclusively, Muslim girls. But of course this is not merely an issue of access. It is in failing to address the specificity of some women and girls from Muslim backgrounds that the right to education is so seriously put into question. Comparatively speaking, with respect to Sikh boys some French schools have ruled that the Sikh turban and *kirpan* are expressions of culture and not religion, which puts into relief how the practice of "veiling" is solely seen as an expression of religion, not culture.[12] This law is very much about circumscribing the freedoms of others, expressions of which fundamentally cut across the cultural meanings of sexual difference and gendered experiences of culture.

For example, one of the main rallying cries in promoting the law was that French society stood for sexual equality, and that *hijab* was seen to be a serious obstacle to women's full empowerment. Thus, the logic of the argument implies that if everyone refrains from "conspicuous" religious symbols, the furthering of equity will be served. The point is that this connection between lack of equality and the wearing of religious symbols is only ever made in light of Muslim practices. The argument is, of course, never marshalled to defend Jewish or Sikh boys' equality. This is not to say that enforcement of Muslim dress by fundamentalist groups is not an issue of equity (it is in all cases of enforcement, not only those of a religious or Muslim character), it is merely that this argument lacks proper nuance with respect to the conditions under which *hijab* is worn when it is not required by the laws of the land.

This emphasis on equality, reveals, I think, a mendacious picture of how nations (not only France) currently deal with issues of sexual difference. Whilst Muslim girls are under attack for representing an "unacceptable inequality" based on sex, using the nation to defend sexual equality is problematic in terms of how women are usually positioned in discourses of nation, as agents of biological reproduction (Yuval-Davis 1997, 26–38), or as "carriers of tradition", particularly though times of change (ibid., 61). Moreover, underpinning this charge of inequality is the view that Muslim religious practices are in and of themselves denigrating to women.

Benhabib (2004) notes a paradox in relation to *l'affaire du foulard*, which is pertinent to the contemporary issues resulting from the French law:

We seem to have a paradoxical situation here, in which the French state intervenes *to dictate* more autonomy and egalitarianism in the public sphere than the girls themselves wearing headscarves seem to wish for.... although there was genuine public discourse in the French public sphere and a soul-searching on the questions of democracy and difference in a multicultural society ... the girls' own perspectives were hardly listened to. (190–191)

Although I challenge Benhabib's assertion that the French state wants more autonomy and equality than "the girls themselves seem to wish for" (this seems to be only possible if we think that those girls' decision to choose to wear *hijab* is not an aspect of their autonomy), the point I wish to make here is how difference based on sex is produced through such western fixations with the "headscarf" to the exclusion of hearing the voices of those who are most affected. To consider that one can speak in the name of a universal right of equality on behalf of others who are quite capable of speaking for themselves, means that the state does not simply deny the wearing of headscarves but is defining the public sphere without the express involvement of all of its members, namely its sexual and cultural "others." For to my mind, it is not only a question of religion that is at stake here, but a question of how women and girls may be systemically excluded from participating freely in the public sphere, to the point of risking their right to education. Moreover, there is an odd tension promoted between the public and the private spheres that, I think, exacerbates this risk. Freedom of religious expression is fundamentally not a private matter, particularly for those religions whose very practices are about public modesty. The very idea of head or body covering for these girls arises precisely in the context of the public sphere. Thus, to claim that students and teachers can practice whichever religion they wish after school hours, makes little sense in the context of these practices. In putting the schooling of girls at stake by prohibiting religious expression in public fora, we must ask ourselves is this risk really worthy of a liberal-democratic state—and is it truly defensible?

When we look to the French law as an example, it is evident that what is being advocated is a principle—the right to a religious-free education—and it is a principle defined by a particular state in a particular context. This means that it is not a human right, with the same kind of legitimacy as the right to education, freedom of religion, and gender equality, enshrined as they are in the UN Declaration and Covenant on Economic, Social and Cultural Rights. So the question not only has to do with whose rights are being advocated for here in this law but on what grounds is such advocacy taking place?

On the one hand, there is, more generally speaking, a paternalistic element evident in laws which attempt to enforce and protect national traditions (be these of a political, economic, or cultural nature), and not actual persons. The paternalism resides in telling the other that the state knows what is best in looking out for the interests of the collective. The French law is no exception here. It was enacted on the grounds of promoting greater unity in the reassertion of the republic's defining principle of *laïcité*. On the other hand, advocating for a principle, of course, risks treating certain citizens with great indifference. And, in

particular, the national struggle for rights has to examine carefully how sexual and cultural difference is constructed in a story about national unity. In this case, advocating for a principle took precedence over the protection of basic rights and in so doing the state left out of the equation those citizens it deemed to be more expendable than others.

It is not that states can do away with institutions, their histories, and their national identities (indeed institutions, such as education, to a large degree constitute their very character). But the question of how to navigate a passage between the shores of national unity and the plurality of difference hinges on how well institutions can negotiate principles in relation to the concrete needs of different groups. Diminishing women's and girls' right to religious expression in the name of a basic right to a state's self-determination—a right which appears to conflict with yet another: a right to a basic education, no matter what religion one holds—simply does not recognize difference sufficiently in providing possibilities for just practices.

It seems to me, then, that one of the issues to be addressed is how to evaluate and prioritize competing rights, particularly as those rights are poised between universalism and the particularities of cultural and sexual difference. No one wants to claim that states should not have the right to uphold their constitutional provisions through legitimate democratic procedures. But at what cost? What kind of obligation to cultural and sexual difference do nations have with respect to their right for self-determination? For what the *hijab* ban has shown, beyond all arguments for or against, is that difference is not perceived to be as equally important to protect as is the right to define a nation in unifying terms; and this in spite of the apparent universal protection of the right to freedom of religious expression and the right to education. Moreover, the positioning of the principle of sexual equality in this mix reveals, to me, more about the myopic vision embedded in the content of that principle than it does about the many reasons why girls and women wear *hijab* in the first place.

WHOSE VOICE COUNTS?

What I wish to suggest, by way of conclusion, is first that the failure to appreciate the ambiguities, contestations, and diversity *within* cultural communities has led to assumptions about the cultural meanings of *hijab* for the women and girls who wear it. Secondly, that such views position educational institutions such as schools as merely being defenders of state interests instead of being involved in ongoing negotiation between the principles of the state and the members of the community they are responsible for educating.

With respect to the first point, the idea that sexual equality should (literally) look the same for all women, independent of faith, family, and community, leads to narrow assumptions about what freedom ought to mean for women. At stake is the nation's right to define for itself the constitutional pillars that support the common good in political, social, and cultural life. Without denying this right, I question the ways in which its defensive reassertion has actually been based on an ideal of sexual equality and the way it expresses a view of culture that cannot accommodate difference. Seeing *hijab, jilbab, burqa,* or *niqab* as already embedded in patriarchal relations that oppress women means viewing cultural communities as homogeneous with respect to expressions of sexual identity. Despite what one might think about these varied practices personally, the point is that these women are being defined by a universal image of their freedom. Although I take the issue up in more detail in chapter 7, suffice for now to say that such a move also suggests that women's freedom is encapsulated to a large degree in what they are or are not "permitted" to do. What is needed, I think, is a more careful and considered examination of the specific contexts and conditions under which *hijab*, for instance, is worn. As Bonnie Honig (1999) notes,

> veiling might be a sign of sexist, enforced female subservience ... or it can also be one of a broader complex of efforts aimed at both sexes in order to manage a community's sexual and other relations. We need to know something about how veiling functions, what it signifies, in a particular context before we can decide that it means for everyone what it means for us. (37)

In other words, the reasons for wearing *hijab* are wide-ranging, from fervent religious observance to comfort in dealing with a new social life in the west; from enforced veiling to freely chosen expression of modesty. The "us" that Honig refers to here is, in the case of the *hijab* ban, precisely the imagined "us" constituted as French, as if there were no differences within the body politic itself. As we have seen, this "us" explicitly excludes a portion of the citizenry—and not on grounds of violence, crime, or treason, but on the grounds of wearing headscarves in public institutions such as schools. This leads me to my second point.

Such a perception of who belongs, moreover, raises the very crucial question of whose rights and whose freedom are being protected through state policy, particularly when it comes to education. What is evident in the case of the French law, and the *l'affaire du foulard* which preceded it, was precisely the inability of authorities, including the Stasi Commission, to speak with those who were most affected by it. Although response to *l'affaire du foulard* was, of course, not all of a kind, Bhikhu Parekh (2000) also notes that "the dominant view was firmly committed to the practice of *laïcité* and hostile to any kind of compromise with the Muslim girls" (250). That is, Muslim girls were never fully consulted as to the various meanings *hijab* held for them, a point also echoed by Benhabib (2004).

When we think, then, of prioritizing rights, especially those that affect education, does the state hold all the trump cards, or is there room for some acknowledgement of sexual and cultural difference? Is there room, in other words, for hearing those voices that challenge the *content and the principle* behind certain rights? This is a particularly important question for education, given its position as both an institution of the state and its role as a bearer of human rights. From the point of view of the French law, schools were seen to be public services, serving state interests of *laïcité*. Yet, citizens invest schools with a trust that their rights will indeed be respected. When it comes to the question of prioritizing rights, it seems to me there needs to be some attention paid to how those rights are negotiated in concert with the concrete realities that Muslim women and girls live in the everyday. Such negotiation requires taking cultural translation seriously by seeking out practices in which their particular voices play a part in formulating the meaning of rights and their function in the state. What this case revealed was that it was precisely those voices that were drowned out in the state's univocal insistence on the abstract principle of *laïcité*. The real tragedy of the situation is not that the decision to ban *hijab* was taken, but that the voices of Muslim women and girls were neither heard nor counted. Listening to these voices means listening to a translation of what freedom and rights mean in specific contexts; and acknowledging the dilemmas, tensions, and contestations of rights claims needs, in my view, to be the focus for new terms of democratic engagement across cultural and sexual differences, terms which are taken up more fully in the chapters that follow.

NOTES

1. There are a number of different kinds of Muslim dress that fall under these restrictions. For example, the *burqa* generally refers to a veil that covers the face with holes for the eyes. The *niqab* covers the lower part of the face, up to the eyes. Full *burqa* or *chador* covers the entire body and face with nets for the eyes. *Jilbab* is a long dress and headscarf that allows the hands and face to be exposed. *Hijab* is generally used to describe the wearing of a headscarf, but it can also refer to a modest form of attire as well. See Ruitenberg (2007b) for a discussion of the importance of not subsuming all practices under the banner "veiling."

2. Although the situation for Muslim girls is not as dire in the North American context, it is not as though they have escaped all form of persecution. For instance, in 1994, a Montréal student was expelled from a high school (see my analysis of this case in Todd [1997]) and more recently in Québec a soccer player was kicked off the pitch for wearing *hijab* during the game. Nonetheless, laws regulating the wearing of *hijab* are far more pronounced in the European context by comparison.

[3] In viewing the wearing of *hijab* as a cultural practice my point is not to diminish the religious significance that this practice carries for some Muslim women, but to stress that the meaning it carries for western societies also places this practice within the sphere of cultural intelligibility.

[4] I primarily use the term sexual difference instead of gender in this chapter. While a more thorough discussion of sexual difference will be taken up in chapter 7 from the perspective of Luce Irigaray's philosophy, for now I simply want to indicate that I see the use of the term sexual difference to be exposing a gap in educational, social, and political practices in a way that gender does not.

[5] See Brems (1997) for an extensive discussion of the many faces of feminist and cultural critiques.

[6] The Shah Bano case in India is a case in point, and illustrates the tensions between gender and culture. According to Coomaraswamy (1994) Shah Bano was a Muslim woman whose husband kicked her out of the house after 25 years of marriage. After a few months of receiving no support (he was a prominent and well-off lawyer), she filed a prevention of destitution provision against her husband (a provision that is well-entrenched in Indian law). Under Muslim personal law he was only required to return the *mehr*, or dowry, he had received upon marriage, which he did. He argued that Muslim personal law took precedent over Indian legislation regarding family matters, and so he was not required to pay support. The Supreme Court ruled, however, that the provision against destitution in no way conflicted with Muslim personal law. However, in a number of months, Rajiv Gandhi, seeking to appease Muslim rioters, passed legislation that over-turned the Supreme Court decision: Muslim personal law was held up to be superior. The cultural argument was used to trump this woman's civil rights and prevent her dissent from the community (even though moderate Muslims initially supported her).

[7] See Perry's (1997) analysis of the sacredness of human rights and his defence of the universalism of rights based on basic needs of all humans.

[8] See Todd (forthcoming) for a discussion on the relation between nationalism and school policies affecting Muslim girls.

[9] The official name of the law is "*loi encadrant, en application du principe de laïcité, le port de signes ou de tenues manifestant une appartenance religieuse dans les écoles, collèges et lycées publics.*" Although the term conspicuous or ostentatious (*ostensiblement*) is not used in the title of the law, it appears in its first article. See Assemblée Nationale (2004).

[10] See Bernard Stasi,"Commission de reflexion sur l'application du principe de laïcité dans la republique: Rapport au Président." (2003), 9–18. See also Benhabib's discussion (2002, 95–100).

[11] The original paragraph reads: "*L'obstacle juridique de l'incompatibilité d'une loi avec la Convention européenne de sauvegarde des droits de l'homme et des libertés fondamentales, qui était fréquemment avancé peut, à l'issue des travaux de la commission, être écarté. La Cour européenne de Strasbourg protège la laïcité quand elle est une valeur fondamentale de l'Etat. Elle admet que soient apportées des limites à la liberté d'expression dans les services publics, surtout lorsqu'il s'agit de protéger des mineurs contre des pressions extérieures*" (Stasi 2003, 59).

[12] See Leila Ahmed's (1992) thoughtful comments on the cultural practices of veiling which predated Islam, noting that both before and after Islam, veiling was associated with class and sexuality (14–15). She also writes scathingly of the attention it has received in terms of women's equality: "As item of clothing, however, the veil itself and whether it is worn are about as relevant to substantive matters of women's rights as the social prescription of one or another item of clothing is to Western women's struggles over substantive issues.... That so much energy has been expended by Muslim men and then Muslim women to remove the veil and by others to affirm or restore it is frustrating and ludicrous" (166, 167, respectively).

6

Educating Beyond Consensus:
Facing Cross-Cultural Conflict as
Radical Democratic Possibility

> The folly of the times is the wish to use consensus to cure the diseases of consensus. What we must do instead is repoliticize conflicts so that they can be addressed, restore names to the people and give politics back its former visibility in the handling of problems and resources.
>
> Jacques Rancière, *On the Shores of Politics*

The question of how to "handle" conflict, particularly that emanating from within cross-cultural encounters, is undeniably high on both the political and educational agendas in western liberal democratic societies. With respect to the cultural practices of some Muslim communities, in particular, such antagonisms have been fuelled by the high-handed rhetoric of the clash of civilizations and the hyperbolic equation of Islam with terror. As we have seen in chapter 5, the debate about what Muslim girls and women are allowed to wear in public settings such as schools has raised crucial questions around whose freedom and whose rights count. Moreover, populist expressions of anti-immigrant sentiment and racism have created an ever-more urgent need to rethink the role of education in creating democratic forms of coexistence.

Although democratic projects focusing on civic or citizenship education are not new, there has been increasing attention paid to broadening our self-understanding as members not only of democratic states but also of a world community. As discussed earlier, this cosmopolitan direction in education can be understood as a political and philosophical call to secure harmonious global relations, to promote a dual commitment to universal human rights and cross-cultural understanding, and to advocate for a notion of "world citizenship." Moreover, in its appeals to a sense of "shared humanity" as a condition for building enduring links across cultural communities around the globe, cosmopolitanism frequently expresses an underlying commitment to certain features of dialogue as a way of promoting relations across cultural differences. Nussbaum (1997), for one, states that "awareness of cultural difference is essential in order to promote the respect for another that is the essential underpinning for dialogue" (68). Moreover, this dialogue, in turn, becomes the means through which to address these very differences democratically, primarily since dialogue builds our capacity to reason with one another: "This demand [for reasons] now begins to seem not an idle luxury in the midst of struggles for power, but an urgent practical necessity, if political deliberation is ever to have a dignity and consistency that make it more than a marketplace of competing interests, that make it a genuine search for the common good" (Nussbaum 1997a, 25).

Seyla Benhabib (2006) also ties the cosmopolitan project to democracy in her development of a deliberative democratic framework, informed by discourse ethics.[1] Here, dialogue, or what she calls the "moral conversation," is expanded to take into account global diversity and is not limited "to those who reside within nationally recognized boundaries; it views the moral conversation as potentially including all of *humanity*" (18). She continues, "I have a moral obligation to *justify my actions with reasons* to this individual or to the representatives of this being. I respect the moral worth of the other by recognizing that I must provide him or her with a justification for my actions" (18). On this account, dialogue takes the form of rational deliberation across a community of diverse interlocutors. It seeks to arrive at some kind of shared meaning based on the normative adherence to the universal, rational rules of argumentation. Derek Heater (2002) remarks that there is a close relationship between discourse ethics and world citizenship: "The concept provides for a set of arrangements based upon communication and collaboration, not domination or tight integration" (81).

Although these represent different models of cosmopolitan dialogue, they nonetheless share a view of democracy that is based on the idea of consensus; that is, we can come to mutual decisions about the "common good" and work toward "common meaning and action."[2] The idea is that through forms of dialogue and deliberation, we can better understand others and reach reasonable agreement over conflicting perspectives. While it is not as though all who embrace the cosmopolitan project can be identified formally as deliberatists or promote democracy in terms of discourse ethics, there is nonetheless the oft-repeated assumption that dialogue is an important factor in mediating conflict or in averting conflict altogether. Dialogue and deliberation, it is assumed, can lead us, optimally, toward more peaceful forms of coexistence and, minimally, to a reduction of conflict and violence between cultural communities. In light, however, of the severity and seriousness with which cross-cultural conflict emerges, cosmopolitanists favoring some form of dialogue and deliberation are often left with only two options: resolve the conflict through mutual understanding via dialogue; or dismiss the conflict itself as being antithetical to the normative frame of deliberation itself.

Although the call for a reduction—and elimination—of conflict might seem on the surface to be an unquestionable good, politically speaking it has become a main source of critique in the work of theorists committed to what is generally referred to as radical democratic theory. In short, advocates of this theory (such

as Ernesto Laclau, Chantal Mouffe, and Jacques Rancière) challenge deliberative models of democracy on the grounds that they do not give conflict its proper
due in contributing toward the creation of democratic political spaces. The
charge is that insofar as dialogue promotes understanding as a way of moving
toward consensus, they miss the very nature of democratic politics, which requires opposition, dissent, and disagreement for its survival. Instead, these theorists suggest that certain forms of antagonism are essential to the very possibility
of democracy; if one seeks their erasure, one risks democracy itself. Democracy,
they insist, cannot be reduced to procedures of rational or disimpassioned deliberation, but is, rather, a contingent, unstable political relation. On this radical
democratic view, the two options left open to cosmopolitanists—resolving conflict or dismissing it as being unamenable to the norms of deliberation—simply
make little political sense. Instead, the question becomes how and what type of
conflict actually contributes to a project of democratization.

These specific aspects of radical democracy have not been taken up in any
significant way in the literature either on cosmopolitan education or on citizenship or democratic education.[3] This chapter, then, seeks to open up a conversation between education and radical democratic theory in the hope of offering a
corrective to what I see are naïve (and depoliticized) assumptions about conflict
in deliberative or dialogic models of democracy as they inform a cosmopolitan
project in education. My primary thesis is that so long as antagonism is seen to
be deleterious to democracy, we lack adequate means for *facing* cross-cultural
conflict in our educational endeavors, and thereby undermine the very possibility for recognizing pluralism. My intent is to develop the idea that a fundamental
aspect of working toward democracy requires facing conflict as opposed to doing away with it, either through understanding or sheer dismissal. To do this, I
first explore briefly the idea of consensus, through the work of Jürgen Habermas, and then turn to the radical democratic challenge to dialogic solutions of
conflict, particularly focusing on the work of Chantal Mouffe. I then outline
Mouffe's proposal for "agonistic pluralism" which theorizes conflict as a condition of democracy. Following this, I turn to a discussion of how democracy itself
can be rethought as an unstable political moment that always contains an element of conflict and dissent, drawing on the work of Jacques Rancière. The
chapter then argues that such a radical view of democracy requires a different
orientation to the other beyond the notion of respect. I conclude with some
thoughts on facing conflict as a way of promoting the promise of democracy in
and through education.

CONSENSUS, DELIBERATION, AND DIALOGUE

A major trend in educational thinking has been to place emphasis on a conception of deliberative democracy inspired by Jürgen Habermas. This view of democracy seems to have a lot to offer education in that it is based on formalized
and rationally motivated communication that seeks to resolve conflict through

promoting shared understanding. It, moreover, has been taken up by a number of scholars committed to the cosmopolitan project (Benhabib 2006; Linklater 1998). In Habermas's view, participants in dialogue come together to present their arguments, or truth claims in such a way that the justifications for the claim are subject to scrutiny. "A justified truth claim should allow its proponent to defend it with reasons against the objections of possible opponents; in the end she should be able to gain the rationally motivated agreement of the interpretation community as a whole" (Habermas 1996, 14). This model, moreover, attempts to deal with the pluralism of diverse opinions in order to establish the consensus necessary for coordinated action. That is, it is not only that participants need to scrutinize their discourse but they also must come to some collective decision about how to act in the world. As Habermas puts it, the assumption underlying this view of democracy is that participants "are ready to take on the obligations resulting from consensus and relevant for further interaction" (Habermas 1996, 4). What Habermas's theory promotes is a normative framework based on a respect of the rules of communicative engagement. Deliberative democracy in this light is seen to offer possibilities for overcoming those conflicts that can detract from consensus building and decision-making.

In a time of increasing fragmentization of the perspectives on offer in the classroom, this model at first appears to propose a productive way of dealing with the diversity of worldviews.[4] And one, of course, can see that dealing with such diversity dovetails nicely with one of the main commitments of cosmopolitanism. As promising as this can sound, however, there are still some serious flaws with such hope of a common, normative standard of communication for all. Not the least of which is that the rational deliberative framework seems to imply the impossibility of real disagreement in its promotion of consensus as a goal of liberal democracy. That is, it does not have a theory for promoting democracy when views are incommensurable, and its view of pluralism is rooted more in the diversity of views on offer than it is in some more fundamental aspect of the human condition.[5] The underlying assumption in importing deliberative democracy into education is that youth can learn to be democratic citizens insofar as they accept the normative rules of deliberative democratic communication to overcome their differences. This is problematic in at least two ways: first, it fails to engage rationality as itself a contested political concept; and secondly, it tends to narrow the scope of democracy to include only those who are willing (or able) to adjust to the stipulated understanding of rationality on offer here.

With respect to the first claim, the normative rules of rational dialogue set up by deliberative democracy are themselves representative of the particular ways in which the human subject has been historically constructed since the Enlightenment. They represent, in other words, how people through history have tried to make sense of who they are and it is important to see that they are historical constructions that do not reveal a single truth of what it means to be human. A rigid view of the rational subject excludes, for example, those who understand themselves in religious (or other metaphysical) terms, where rationality is not a defining aspect of their values in the first place. That is, there may be no way of providing rational justification for a truth claim (in the Habermasian sense) if that claim is grounded, for instance, in faith, as opposed to reason. In addition, what becomes particularly problematic with a concept of rational communication in the name of deliberative democracy is that if it claims to be an appropriate response to questions of disagreement, then it risks reducing the political itself to a form of procedural democracy where disagreement all but disappears (a point taken up in detail below).

The second point is that in claiming that rational forms of argumentation are needed for consensus (and indeed that the whole point of argumentation, as Habermas sees it, necessarily requires consensus for action), it further risks creating a situation in which the articulation of a point of view that does not "fit" or "accept" the normative standard of communication can be dismissed under the sign of "private interests" at best, or "irrationality" at worst. Thus, in principle, everything diverse and unique risks being contained within the same normative frame of reference: differences between us become less important than the goal to create a unified "we" that is already enclosed and defined by the discursive rules of liberal democracy itself. Dissent, therefore, is seen as something to be surmounted since it cannot be tolerated fully within the rules of rational communication. In this light, respect becomes conditional upon adherence to a normative framework, and therefore curiously detached from concrete others who hold different—and competing—points of view.

Thus in any taking up of either discourse ethics as formalized through Habermas and his followers, or dialogue as a general means for overcoming conflict, there is a risk of what happens to the legitimacy of conflict for democratic practices. It is not that these models have nothing to offer, at least some of the time, in terms of establishing discursive procedures for taking certain decisions, and potentially opening up spaces for communicating. But as a model for actually confronting competing "truth claims," values, and perspectives, it fails to sustain the diversity and necessary incommensurability upon which democracy itself rests. The set of problems discussed above all seem to follow from the incapacity of the deliberative view to acknowledge that world views may not be temporary or fleeting, but are, rather, expressions of pluralism as an ontological condition of our world. As Mouffe puts it, the central question for democratic politics is not about "how to negotiate a compromise among competing interests, nor is it how to reach a 'rational', i.e. fully inclusive, consensus, without any exclusion" (Mouffe 2005, 14.). Instead, what Mouffe suggests is a way of orienting ourselves to conflict that makes disagreement itself central for democratic possibility.

THE RADICAL DEMOCRATIC CHALLENGE

Chantal Mouffe (1993; 2000; 2005; and Laclau and Mouffe 2001) has been one of the most vocal critics of both cosmopolitanism and dialogical models of democracy. She sees that both these views hold certain assumptions about the ways in which democracy is conceived as a project for eradicating social antagonism and in so doing she charges that these views of democracy have become depoliticized. Mouffe's main critique largely centers on two interrelated themes. The first concerns the plural nature of human sociability; the second involves the nature of the political itself.

With respect to the first theme, Mouffe claims that:

> Democratic theory has long been informed by the belief that the inner goodness and original innocence of human beings was a necessary condition for asserting the viability of democracy. An idealized view of human sociability, as being essentially moved by empathy and reciprocity, has generally provided the basis of modern democratic political thinking. (2005, 2–3)

This idealized view, in her eyes, has prevented democratic theory from dealing with the "ambivalent character of human sociability" (2005, 3). Echoing the critique of the idea of humanity I have been promoting throughout this book, Mouffe seeks to disrupt the conception of the inherent goodness of humanity that has accompanied our theorizing of politics. Thus efforts to conceive of democracy along rationalist lines, for instance, actually fail to take account of the passionate commitments that factor into contesting and competing points of view and interests. Indeed, such efforts seek to sanitize democratic practices from all contamination of passion and focus on procedures that eliminate such undesirable elements. But it is not as if Mouffe merely counterposes a dire view of human sociability. Rather it is that she recognizes that contestation is an indelible part of social interaction by virtue of the fact that we live in a world of human pluralism and difference. For this reason, conflict must assume a place in any conception of democracy—that is, if pluralism is to have any real political meaning. For her, "democratic politics needs to have real purchase on people's desires and fantasies and that, instead of opposing interests to sentiments and reason to passions, it should offer forms of identification conducive to democratic practices" (2005, 28). What this means, then, is that pluralism, and the antagonism that is inherent to the expression of radically different worldviews cannot be done away with simply through an appeal to democratic rationalism, which is so often implicit in deliberative and dialogic models of democracy. Neither can the cosmopolitan dream of empathy and reciprocity across cultures provide us with an adequate model. Indeed, Mouffe charges that liberal forms of cosmopolitanism themselves embrace a "consensual model of politics" in their search for harmony and world citizenship and in their advocacy of human rights, which implies, to her mind, an "enforced universalization of the Western model" (2005, 86). Cosmopolitanism in general, she notes, particularly those that are democratically oriented (and not neoliberal), take up plurality, but avoid the agonistic dimension of social relations. Instead, political projects must deal directly with the conflictual demands posed by pluralism itself and offer diverse alternatives around which these differences can coalesce. As opposed to a cosmopolitan vision, in which people from different cultures and political alle-

giances come together under the auspices of world citizenship or global harmony, Mouffe proposes a "multi-polar" perspective that takes the consequences
of pluralism as the very starting point for a radical democratic project. As she
writes with Laclau, "we are confronted with the emergence of a *plurality of subjects*, whose forms of constitution and diversity it is only possible to think if we
relinquish the category of 'subject' as a unified and unifying essence" (Laclau
and Mouffe 2001, 181). Thus subjectivity itself is not simply a manifestation of
social diversity (marked by race, class, ethnicity, or gender) but is, rather, rooted
in an inescapable ontological condition whereby what it means to be a subject is
already understood in terms of its inherent multiplicity and its difference from
other (equally non-unified) subjects.

The second theme of her critique involves what she defines as the aban-
donment of the political in the turn to the ideas of consensus and harmony that
pervade dominant formulations of liberal rationalism in both democratic and
cosmopolitan theory. That is, while "politics" as a "set of practices and institutions through which an order is created" (2005, 9) is very much part of contemporary trends in these areas, Mouffe seeks to reinvigorate the democratic discussion with a focus on "the political." Based on her ontological views of human
sociability and human plurality, Mouffe defines the political as that "dimension
of antagonism ... constitutive of human societies" (2005, 9). But what makes the
political different from the social is that these different interests seek to establish
hegemony. Hegemony is the practice through which order is established and the
meanings of social institutions are "fixed," however incompletely. Hegemony
itself is a struggle over which views will hold sway over interpretations of what
is politically best for a community. This hegemonic aspect of the political establishes exclusions even as it seeks consensus on the signification of social institutions (2005, 18). It creates a "we" in contradistinction to a "they" and therefore
cannot promote the kind of harmony that cosmopolitanists hope to achieve.
Moreover, it is precisely through such articulations of exclusion that counter-
hegemonic practices can emerge. That is, those who challenge the signification
granted to social institutions seek, in turn, to establish their own meanings.
Rather than see this as a failure of consensus or compromise, Mouffe locates the
very possibility of democracy within this hegemonic struggle. Thus democratic
models that begin with the aim of eradicating conflict are seen by her to be
oddly antidemocratic since they, on the one hand, forfeit the very nature of political interest that lies behind articulations of dissent and, on the other hand, fail
to articulate their own consensual interests as themselves hegemonic. Moreover,
in her discussion of those political theorists who embrace a "post-political vision," which include cosmopolitanists such as Ulrich Beck, Mouffe criticizes the
tendency to transform properly political discussion into moral discourse (2005,
72–76). Although not directly attacking deliberative models here, she nonetheless sees a danger in positing consensus as a "universal good" in that dissent
then becomes placed on a moral instead of a political register (2005, 75). "Far
from creating the conditions for a more mature and consensual form of democracy [as these theorists claim], to proclaim the end of adversarial politics pro-

duces, then, exactly the opposite effect.... Indeed, when opponents are defined not in political but in moral terms, they cannot be envisaged as an 'adversary' but only as an 'enemy'" (2005, 76). Furthermore, in her critique of Habermas, Mouffe notes that "every opposition is automatically perceived as a sign of irrationality and moral backwardness and as being illegitimate" (2005, 84–85). What Mouffe means here is that insofar as democracy is built upon a normative model of dialogue and refuses to acknowledge its own hegemonic intentions, it shuts others out of the democratic conversation on purely moral grounds. Thus casting the opposing view in terms such as "evil" or "enemy" merely serves to refuse any legitimate claim to dissent. This substitution of ethical discourse for political engagement ironically leaves those committed to consensual democracy with no real *political* framework for handling conflict.

Whether or not one is in full agreement with the details of Mouffe's critique, the issue that is difficult to avoid is that the aims of consensus and harmony actually put at risk *political* solutions to questions of cross-cultural conflict. And this has a bearing, it seems to me, on how one approaches and reflects upon cross-conflict in the classroom: is there a way to forge political responses to the manifestations of conflict in education? But this does not of course mean that all conflict is beneficial to democracy, nor does it mean that any consensus around political issues is impossible. This is why Mouffe takes care in acknowledging that the real question for democracy is how to move toward an "agonistic" politics whereby enemies can become legitimate adversaries within the field of human plurality.

AGONISTIC PLURALISM AS A RESPONSE TO CONFLICT

As mentioned above, Mouffe recognizes that all democratic politics is a claim for hegemony and as such it creates those who ally themselves with a particular point of view as a "we" at the same time as it constructs its constitutive outside: a "they." For Mouffe, the point is not to do away with this distinction, which would simply mean an end to pluralism as such, but to ensure that such distinctions are played out within the horizon of democratic possibility. This means that disagreement is essential to the well-being of democratic societies.

> A democratic society requires a debate about possible alternatives and it must provide political forms of collective identification around clearly differentiated democratic positions. Consensus is no doubt necessary, but it must be accompanied by dissent. Consensus is needed on the institutions constitutive of democracy and on the 'ethico-political' values informing the political association—liberty and equality for all—but there will always disagreement concerning their meaning and the way they should be implemented. In a pluralist democracy such disagreements are not only legitimate but also necessary. They provide the stuff of democratic politics. (2005, 31)

What Mouffe suggests is that democracy as an ongoing struggle, marked by the delineation of a "we" and "they," does not occur on the moral register of good and evil; instead, in insisting on its political character, democracy creates what she calls an "agonistic politics" that moves beyond simple antagonism. This agonistic dimension of democracy can be seen in her advocacy of the idea of "conflictual consensus," whereby liberty and equality are shared ethico-political signs yet their meanings can be contested and are not "the expression of a universal morality" (2005, 121). Her model of agonism is one whereby I recognize my opponent not as an enemy but as a legitimate adversary. "Conflicting parties must recognize that while there is no rational solution to their conflict, they recognize the legitimacy of their opponents" (2005, 20). But how do "we" decide who is a legitimate adversary and who is simply seeking to destroy democratic possibility altogether?

For Mouffe, there must be a common bond across the parties in conflict—not one based on a synthesis of competing views, but on the idea that political association itself can continue. This requires, for Mouffe, the existence of a shared symbolic, defined in terms of the ethico-political values of liberty and equality; the point is that dissent about their interpretation is what creates agonistic political space (2005, 121). Thus it follows that Nazis cannot be legitimate adversaries since they seek to destroy the very basis of democratic institutions. In moving toward the idea of legitimate conflict, then, Mouffe's theory attempts to outline the conditions under which conflict can contribute to the project of democratization. It is clear that this does not mean that "anything goes" in facing one's opponents, nor does it venerate conflict in some perverse fashion. Instead, it asks us to consider the limits of certain models of democracy for handling conflict on political terms. Moreover, it compels us to see that democracy is an ongoing project of struggle, rooted in human pluralism, that actually can be undermined in calls for harmony and consensus. But most importantly, what Mouffe's agonistic politics allows is a rethinking of democracy beyond the implementation of new and improved procedures for handling conflict within liberal democratic states (through institutions such as schools), as though this will take care of the matter once and for all. Rather, it is the very movement, instability, and unpredictability in agonistic encounters that is at issue here.

THE INSTABILITY OF DEMOCRACY

Like Mouffe, Jacques Rancière situates democracy as a radical possibility that only arises at the moment disagreement and conflict make their appearance. In contradistinction to appeals for harmony and consensus, Rancière emphasizes that democracy itself is neither procedural nor is it a political ordering of society, but represents an unstable condition of political possibility. For Rancière, democracy is not "'just a word' or illusion. Rather, it is the disposition of the name and appearance of the people, a way of keeping the people present in their absence" (1995, 97). On the surface, this would seem to suggest that "the people" is a unified entity, such as citizens of a nation-state or even citizens of the world. However, for Rancière, "the people" is always a double assignation that names the divided nature of political community. He writes: "the name of the people is at one and the same time the name of the community and the name of a part of—or rather a split in—the community. The gap between the people as community and the people as division is the site of a fundamental grievance" (1995, 97). What Rancière signals here is that from the beginning the people do not represent a singular body politic, but suffer from an internal division: the people can never be one because there are always those who are not counted. Yet, paradoxically those who are not counted appear as included in the notion of the people. They are included *as* excluded and it is their absent presence that makes the political community a divided one.[6] There is thus what he calls a "wrong" that exists in all forms of political order that rely on the demos, the people, for their justification. Instead of locating democracy as a political order that reflects, or corresponds to, a singular people (as we find in appeals to national or world citizens), Rancière locates it in the moment where the "grievance" of a wrong inserts itself as an antagonism into the already existing social regime—even if that regime declares itself to be democratic. What this means is that the "grievance" forces itself into the existing shared symbolic space through altering the meaning of that space. It is a work of re-signification, whereby, if we may be permitted to use Mouffe's language here, the hegemonic interpretation of what liberty and equality mean in the social order are challenged and contested.

Thus, for Rancière, democracy is neither order nor procedure, but is the momentary disruption of stability that seeks to address a wrong; it is what he calls a "forced-entry" (1995, 51). But it is not just any forced assertion or act of aggression. It is, rather, a remobilization of the *terms of equality* that force themselves upon the political stage, creating a new space of shared meaning and visibility for those who have previously been unheard and invisible. He writes:

> the repetition of egalitarian words is a repetition of that forced-entry [in this case, of the French Revolution] which is why the space of shared meaning it opens up is not a space of consensus. Democracy is the community of sharing, in both senses of the term: a membership in a single world which can only be expressed in adversarial terms, and a coming together which can only occur in conflict. (1995, 49)

On this view, democracy is that volatile instant which allows the entry of equality into the social order *as* conflict. Let me explain what is meant by this.

According to Rancière, the social order is structured by inequality and yet in order for this inequality to work or to be effective, it actually presumes the equality of all subjects to understand one another. That is, in order for a worker to assume an unequal position in relation to her employer, or a student in relation to her teacher, they both must understand *equally* the discursive terms of that *inequality*: "in order to obey an order at least two things are required: you must understand the order and you must understand that you must obey it. And to do that, you must already be the equal of the person who is ordering you" (1998, 16). Thus although, like Mouffe, Rancière draws our attention to the way conflict is not antithetical to democracy, his agonistic vision begins in the notion of equality, while hers begins with the antagonistic features of human sociability. Yet both take issue with the idea that consensus can ever belong to democracy proper. Indeed, under a heading entitled "Racism: The Disease of Consensus," Rancière outlines the ways in which a project of consensus actually starts out from a position of inequality from which it cannot hope to rescue itself. On the consensus view, "grievance is simply the symptom of a problem, and no problem is anything more than the lack of means to solve it. Exposure of wrong must now give way to identification of the lack, followed by its remedy" (1995, 101). That is, in seeking consensus, deliberative projects build upon the assumption that the inequality that exists in society can be redressed if agreement can be reached on what to do about it. Consensus hence appears to suffer from a pragmatic delusion in Rancière's eyes. What Rancière's radical vision contends is that consensus can only ever repeat and reiterate inequality since it does not allow the (forced) entry of equality into the social order *as conflict*. Instead, in seeking harmony, consensus actually prevents equality from emerging. Consensus, he claims, denies the otherness that breaks through the system of unequal social relations. In a rather scathing portrayal of dialogue, he writes:

> Testimony to this is supplied us every day in the form of pathetically well-intentioned consensual roundtables aiming to solve the problems of which current outbreaks of racism are said to be just symptoms. The trouble is that racism is not the symptom but the disease—the disease, in fact, of consensus itself, the loss of any measure of otherness. (1995, 104)

Relying upon consensus as a goal for democratic dialogue would seem to suggest, therefore, that in erasing otherness, one erases the possibility for democracy itself.

What we can glean from Rancière's critique of dialogue is that it is built upon two false equations: that between equality and consensus; and that between equality and harmony. Furthermore, it is based upon the assumption that equality is a relation of agreement. Instead, what Rancière's work lays bare is that equality can never be achieved without conflict and disagreement since the very assertion of equality is an assertion of a difference into—as something totally "other" to—the established set of ordered social relations. Thinking that we only need to understand each other better in order to reduce violence, conflict, and antagonism assumes that we do not already understand the shared social meanings that legitimate inequalities in the first place. But Rancière's whole point is that we understand each other all too well. What we cannot seem to tolerate is difference and disagreement about the meanings we make of that social space. The real democratic task at hand is how to make equality visible and audible, knowing that it conflicts with others' commitment to the status quo. This is why "democracy is neither compromise between interests nor the formation of a common will. Its kind of dialogue is that of a divided community.... The political wrong does not get righted. It is addressed as something irreconcilable within a community that is always unstable and heterogeneous" (1995, 103).

The instability of democracy is thus coupled with the appearance of otherness—an otherness that seeks to assert an equality that has not been previously instituted in society. In insisting on equality as a destabilizing force within existing forms of social inequality, Rancière's point is to show (and he does this frequently through historical example) how social relations can be re-signified so that existing wrongs find new ways of articulating political subjectivity. Similarly, Mouffe sees that in transforming antagonistic into agonistic conflict there is an interruptive shift in the conditions under which I meet my opponent. That is, it is in the move from enemy to legitimate adversary where my relation to the other undergoes a profound change. In moving beyond consensus and harmony as worthy models of democracy, both Mouffe and Rancière root their radical democratic challenges in the very emergence of a plurality that cannot be subsumed into notions of the same. Democratic assertions of equality and liberty, for them, are only made possible in the difficult encounter with difference, and as such they intimate that the conflict so necessary for democracy requires different terms of engagement than that promoted by dialogue and deliberation. The repoliticization of conflict demands an acceptance of the turbulence and unpredictability of our encounters, particularly if they are to have any democratic meaning. But even more than this, I want to suggest, the terms of engagement that such repoliticization requires need to be thought of as interruptions in their own right.

DEMOCRACY, CONDITIONAL HOSPITALITY, AND ETHICAL INTERRUPTION

In a chapter entitled "The Ethics of Democracy," Mouffe (2000) herself points to the necessity of establishing different relations between ethics and politics—relations which refuse to turn the political imperative of power, hegemony, and conflict into a moral or ethical discourse of sameness—a charge which she levies against deliberative democrats as well as the postpolitical visionaries, as we have seen. Yet she also takes issue with what she refers to as the "postmodern" ethical discourse of otherness, for whilst proponents of this view acknowledge the centrality of difference, Mouffe considers them unable "to come to terms with 'the political' in its antagonistic dimension" (2000, 129). That is, in her eyes, even the attention to alterity can occlude the central moment of decision which enacts an element of force and violence that can never be eliminated from the field of the social (2000, 130). Responsibility for the other cannot assure the transition from antagonism to agonism. Ethics, insofar as it is conceived as a solution, a resolution, or an answer to conflict—even when it does so through the "recognition" of otherness—ultimately fails to acknowledge that the violence of human association does not disappear in turn. "This is to imagine that there could be a point where ethics and politics perfectly coincide, and this is precisely what I am denying because it means erasing the violence that is inherent in sociability" (2000, 134–135). So, the ethical cannot provide the political with its normative dimension, nor act as its complement. In short, it cannot ground politics, as if the political somehow grew organically from the seeds of the ethical relation to the other. Instead, Mouffe rightly calls for a "problematization of the notion of human sociability which underlies democratic thinking" as the basis for reframing the relation between ethics and politics (2000, 130). As discussed above, it requires seeing human sociability in all its abrasiveness and madness and not through a sublime possibility embodying the virtues of the good and the rational. Thus there is nothing about the ethical that can tell us how to judge, how to calculate one's actions, how to decide, given the messy terrain of human sociability. Her move, therefore, is to recognize the necessary *hiatus* between ethics and politics, which in Simon Critchley's (2004) terms, "opens onto a new experience of the political decision" (177). That is, the distance that separates ethics and politics needs to be thought anew.

Although I agree with this move to reformulate the relation between ethics and politics as hiatus, what remains underdeveloped in Mouffe's work is how to think the political move from antagonism to agonism as revealing simultaneously a renewed understanding of the ethical itself. That is, it is the transformation of conflict in the political sphere which suggests something about the need to invest ethics with language that moves beyond "respect for the adversary." Although there exists a common bond between parties in conflict in the agonistic model (Mouffe 2005, 20), how is the respect to be granted to the legitimate adversary any different from the rational Kantian model she claims to be criticizing?

Kantian respect is largely conceived on the premise of the moral law. Even though respect is directed to persons and not to things (Kant 1997, 66), the basis of that respect is the extent to which persons subject themselves to the moral law as that which guides the authorship of their actions (Kant 1997, 72). This means that only rational subjects are capable of receiving respect; "the subject thus respects not the other's singular and irreplaceable personality but rather that which makes him or her similar to itself: the other's humanity, that is, according to Kant, his or her capacity to be author of the moral law" (Chalier 2002, 65). Thus what we respect is in fact a commonality with the other, who, like us, is an autonomous subject, a finite and reasonable being. If, as Mouffe argues so forcefully, the very Kantian universalism which deliberative democrats have all too often embraced through their appeals to rationality fails to account for the conflictual nature of human sociality, then how does the political defense of respecting one's adversaries (insofar as they respect the ethico-political values of liberty and equality even while disagreeing on their content) get us any closer to what it takes to become agonistic? How might a rethinking of the ethical actually take into account the transformation she requires, without trying to erase conflict itself?

For instance, as Derrida (1997) has pointed out, it is only along with responsibility that respect marks the political virtue of friendship—a cornerstone of democratic thinking. On the one hand, friendship is reliant upon the separation and distance one has to another that only respect—unlike love—can give, and it is also caught up in the reciprocity and equality between subjects. Yet, on the other hand, respect is also coupled with responsibility for the singular other. This responsibility comes prior to reason, the reason which "makes the Idea of equality an obligation" (Derrida 1997, 276). In a deconstructive reading, Derrida unpacks the structure of democratic friendship as embodying both a *nonreasonable responsibility* and an eminently reasonable respect. Thus in wishing to disentangle democracy from rationality, since it fails to account adequately for dissent, Mouffe needs also to shift her seemingly ethical presumption of respect from a similarly rational bias. This is not to suggest that reason plays no role in the movement from antagonism to agonism, but neither can a language of respect without passion, without sensibility prior to reason, fully take into account the transformation between subjects that this move requires. Indeed, if democracy is going to be conceived as a never-ending process of transforming conflict without every doing away with it, then how might we think this transition beyond conventional notions of respect? And how might this reinform education's relation to democracy?

The ethical, for both Derrida and Levinas, is rooted in an unlimited responsibility to the other that finds its best expression in the figure of hospitality. With respect to responsibility specifically, Levinas (1969) locates its emergence in the response the singular I *gives* in *receiving* the other in all her alterity. The dual movement between giving and receiving is the place and time of hospitality—a welcoming of the other that is at once a gift and a reception of generosity (see Todd 2008). Respect, on this account, is not about treating the other as another rational subject like myself, but about *responding* to her specificity in a way that secures her right to be other. That is, as hospitality faces the other as other, she is welcomed without limits and without conditions. Indeed, the hospitable relation would appear to be the ethical relation par excellence: an inexhaustible responsibility to the other opens up in the time of this hospitality.

When discussing responsibility in this way, Levinas is all too aware of how this ethical dyadic relation cannot simply be mapped onto the political sphere. Politics by its very nature cannot be about a relation between a singular "I" and the "other" alone. But as Levinas maintains, it is nonetheless this responsibility for the other which informs our political life; that institutions and states, if they are to be just, ought to begin from the position of what one might call a "hospitable respect," not from a position of granting respect to a rational subject (Levinas 2001, 167). "The one respected is not the one to whom, but the one with whom one renders justice" (Levinas 1987, 43). Beginning with hospitality does not mean, for Levinas, that we merely "institutionalize" responsibility for the other (which simply is not possible), but instead marks the extent to which institutions can allow for hospitable respect to emerge—however momentary and fleeting such occurrences might be. Although the field of political conflict cannot be reduced to the ethical relation, ethical respect for the other can act as an interruptive moment to the otherwise rational decision-making, planning, and prioritizing that goes on in the name of democratic politics. As we have seen in chapter 2, this unconditional hospitality cannot be guaranteed by legislation or the state (Derrida 2003, 129); it merely "happens," erupting into the field of political experience.

In his discussion of tolerance, Derrida makes an important move that gives us yet another way of thinking about the relation between hospitality and democracy. In making a crucial distinction between *unconditional* and *conditional* hospitality, Derrida looks to how hospitality functions in the sphere of politics. He illustrates the conditional aspects of hospitality as that which we in fact live with day-to-day; for example, tolerance is a "conditional, circumspect, careful hospitality" (Derrida 2003, 128). Moreover, he details how unlike unconditional hospitality, conditional hospitality is necessarily parsimonious. It enacts instead a gesture of welcome to those who are invited into my home—with definite strings attached: "I invite you, I welcome you into *my home*, on the condition that you adapt to the laws and norms of my territory, according to my language, tradition, memory, and so on" (2003, 128). On this view, at the level of politics, the welcoming of the other is contained within certain parameters of acceptability. The one who hosts can because she has the power to do so. It is as if a certain hegemony watches over our invitation. Moreover, it is this conditional hospitality that is tied to the cosmopolitan project via Kant, through which the relation to the other is regulated.

On the one hand, all politics occurs at the level of conditional hospitality: at stake is the question of power and control, and it is always at risk of turning itself into something terribly nonhospitable. Yet, on the other hand, democratic politics, if we follow Levinas's and Derrida's logic, also embodies within it a possibility for ethical disruption. Although Mouffe is critical of an ethics of alterity on the grounds that it cannot deal with the violence of social relations (see above), conceived in terms of "interruption," such an ethics lies at the heart of the transformational moment through which antagonism becomes agonism, through which equality as conflict appears. Moreover, as I discussed in chapter 1, Levinas's conception of ethics does indeed take the possibility of violence into account. It is not merely a Kantian respect that is on offer on Levinas's and Derrrida's view, but a hospitality in which respect for the other as other has the potential to emerge and transform our existing relations of hostility. Thus while ethics does not ground politics, it nonetheless remains an anarchic presence that announces itself only through this surprising moment of transformation. This possibility of surprise suggests that democracy is founded on a memory of ethics, where the passage from antagonism to agonism, from raw conflict to the political formulation of legitimate conflict, is one in which pure (or unconditional) hospitality does not fully disappear, but must nevertheless remain unnamed. Such an ethics of democracy cannot sediment into appeals for a normative discourse ethics or rules of communicative engagement; instead, it emerges, is *revealed*, in the actual encounter between people holding different points of view. Although conditional hospitality is provisional, it nonetheless contains this trace of interruption upon which the *promise* of democratization rests. In my view, without this notion of interruption, the transformative moment from antagonism to agonism risks becoming the "result" of yet another procedural norm instead of becoming a truly disruptive political moment.

In this sense, the move from antagonism to agonism demands that we think conflict anew: neither as something to be feared nor controlled, and not even as something to be overcome, but as something that needs to be transformed into a relation that keeps open the possibility of further dissent. Because decisions are born out of indeterminacy and conflict, democracy is, therefore, not a "nice" relation, nor is it even a fixed form of political organization, but in Critchley's (2004) words, "a *deformation* of society from itself.... as the movement of democratisation" (183). And the place of the ethical is not, therefore, about a normative imperative of what we should do in order to reach consensus, but about how we live with the "endless betterment" of the state (Critchley 2004, 183) through the possibility of upheaval and disturbance that the ethical relation to the other brings.

FACING CONFLICT AS A PROMISE OF DEMOCRATIC EDUCATION

What theorists of radical democracy, such as Rancière and Mouffe, show is that conflict is an indelible feature of our political life. In educating for democracy within cosmopolitan projects, the question is not one so much concerned with implementing better strategies for dialogue and deliberation, but how to politicize democracy itself. Too often in education we teach either *about* democracy—exploring the rights and obligations of citizens, the rules and structures of government, and the nature of civic participation—or teach *as though* democracy were a pedagogical matter of collective decision-making and of establishing rules of discussion and discursive engagement. It is not that these aspects of teaching are unimportant, but my point in this chapter has been to caution against seeing democracy as a method or strategy for "handling" or "dealing with" conflict, which is particularly the case in appeals to deliberation and dialogue. In drawing on radical democratic theory for inspiration, my intent here has been to raise questions about the nature of putting the political back into educational concerns with democracy in order to think about the terms upon which we can *face* conflict, particularly that of a cross-cultural nature.

My reason for doing so, as I stated in the introduction, is that cross-cultural conflict presents educators with an exigent need to think about what they are doing in democracy's name. What radical democracy offers is a way of reflecting on the political nature of that conflict and as such it seeks not to silence those voices with which we might disagree, but calls attention to the difficulty of living in a world of human plurality, where the specter of inequality is an especially felt presence. The major issue that arises from both Mouffe and Rancière's work may be summed up as: how do we face conflict in ways that can promote democratic possibility, without either resolving disagreement or dismissing it?

In calling for a repoliticization of conflict, as Mouffe and Rancière do, I am quite aware that the conflict that arises on the political stage is not of the same stripe as the cross-cultural manifestations of conflict so common to classrooms. Yet, centering as these conflicts also do on expressions of racism, antireligious sentiment, and nationalism, I do think that many of them are indeed instantiations of broader political contestations in society at large. For this reason I think it behooves us to consider that the ways in which we face such conflicts can indeed contribute to a more nuanced pedagogical intervention, one that seeks not to silence voices in the name of our own discomfort, but seeks to recognize the "wrong" by opening up new contexts for shared meaning and continued contestation.

Facing conflict requires, it seems to me, two major moves. One is the difficult task of reframing conflict in political terms, which means moving away from seeing conflict as a moral transgression. Indeed, conflicts over whether pork should be included on the lunch menu, or prayer rooms provided for different religious faiths, or whether school dress codes should allow girls and women to wear a *niqab*, do not automatically signal some moral failing. What they signal might just be an attempt to address what some have perceived to be a "wrong," to put it in Rancière's words. Disallowing conflicting points of view on moral terms—or resolving them into oblivion—would actually risk the possible appearance of equality as it conflicts with the traditional practices of the school. It is not that we can "make" equality happen for others; it is rather to give students the opportunities for developing political spaces through which their own assertions of equality might become noticed and realized.

The second move requires introducing to students a political language in which to recognize the ways in which their passionate commitments to certain positions actually construct political, and not merely moral, exclusions. That is, the point here is to help turn antagonistic conflicts, where the exclusions risk descending into violence, into agonistic ones. This means helping students to reframe expressions of conflict as constituting we/they relations—relations which are continually shifting and contingent—and to help them recognize that the point is not to win the argument, or to eschew the passions of others, but to live in that fragile and unstable space of "conflictual consensus."

Such a process is best offered, in my view, through a conditional hospitality. On the one hand, such hospitality has obvious "strings attached;" that is, not all views will or can be entertained equally if they are expressed as direct threats to the ongoing project of working for democracy itself, that is, views which seek to prevent the equality and liberty of others to be asserted. Hence, offering conditional hospitality provides the limit situation in which students' views can seek and find legitimation. And, in this sense, what matters is not whether others are respected as rational moral agents themselves, but how teachers might take responsibility for creating the best possible limit situations through which passionate perspectives find legitimate outlets—after all, we, as teachers, have the power to host by virtue of our professional authority. On the other hand, this conditional hospitality also brings into the discussion the ethical dimension of democratization. It is not that one can teach or impart to students an unconditional respect for the other; rather it is a question of attentiveness to the ethical possibility that emerges both in the transformative movement from antagonism to agonism, and in the appearance of the other through the assertion of equality. What this means for teachers is becoming attentive to the moments in which responsibility for the other breaks through classroom convention; for it is here that the other's point of view is accepted as different and legitimate. In other words, it is at this point of disjuncture, where hospitality appears, however fleetingly, as a trace of the ethical in the specific relationships between students. To reiterate, this is not to say that teachers can instruct students directly to be responsible (as an openness to the other), but to claim that they can attend to those moments where students respond to another's passionate position with generosity and welcome—even when, and perhaps especially when, they disagree with this very position.

Thus educating for a democratic project, one that seeks to live meaningfully with pluralism, is to embrace the imperfection of democracy itself. That is, a democracy that is not a fully ordered, or rule-bound practice, but one that comes from the contestations that arise in divided communities, where the provocation of disagreement can only come from our encounter with difference. Perhaps education can then move beyond an easy appeal to cosmopolitan harmony and dialogic consensus and become a space for facing those conflicts so necessary to the infinite promise of democracy.

NOTES

1. She also advocates for a notion of democratic iteration, which is largely inspired by Derrida and which I have discussed in chapter 2. For my purposes here, however, it is the way normative discourse ethics is used by Benhabib to trump all forms of communicative, democratic dialogue that sets up a particular relation to conflict.

2. This is not to suggest that cosmopolitanism is a unified philosophy, theory, or outlook. Yet, insofar as certain strands of cosmopolitanism put cross-cultural issues and democratic practices at the centre of their thought, they place much faith in dialogic and/or deliberative procedures. This is to be distinguished from current discussions within political theory that advocate for "cosmopolitan democracy," which generally focuses on the nature and prospects of global governance through trans-national institutions (see, for example, Archibugi 2003; Archibugi, Held, and Köhler 1998). I will not be addressing this here. Instead, my focus is on the idea of dialogue and deliberation in those democratic models seen to be commensurate with promoting cross-cultural understanding as part of the cosmopolitan project. For the remainder of the chapter, I am not making any sharp distinction between dialogic and deliberative forms of democracy and will be treating these terms interchangeably in order to signal a particular relation to conflict.

3. Although Laclau and Mouffe's work influenced the direction of critical pedagogy for a time in the 1980s–1990s, there has been little sustained attention directed to the connection between conflict and democracy, and how best education can promote

democracy in ways that acknowledge this connection. For some recent work on radical democratic theory in education, see Biesta (2006); Ruitenberg (2007); and Todd and Säfström (2008).

4. It seems to me that we must also be wary of importing a parliamentary form of debate into schools as if this were an adequate model for democracy, when democracy is itself so much more than this. See my discussion below on the very understanding of democracy as introducing instability into any given social order.

5. The difference between seeing pluralism along these lines and seeing it as part and parcel of an ontological condition will be highlighted further below in my discussion of Mouffe and Rancière.

6. This is a far more complicated notion in Rancière's work than I can go into here. What Rancière proposes is that with the name of the "the people" it is not simply that there exists an exclusion of certain groups and individuals, but that they are "included" in political discourse as excluded. See his discussion on this point in Rancière (1998, 11 passim).

7

Educating the Sexed Citizen: Irigaray and the Promise of a Humanity That Is Yet to Come

> Humanity seems past. Philosophies and religions are in a period of taking stock. The dominant discipline in the human sciences is now history. Sociology, which shares the spotlight with it, is dedicated to the description of what already exists. We should be what apparently we are, what we have already shown of ourselves. As for the rest, our becoming would be prescribed by our genes, or by what has already been deciphered of them. Our growth is to have stopped one day. We are to have become at best objects of study. Like the whole living world, destroyed little by little by the exploration-exploitation of what it is instead of cultivating what it could be become.
>
> Luce Irigaray, *Between East and West*

"Humanity seems past." Irigaray's provocative words strike quickly at the heart of what many of us tend to hold dear: that human life and the conditions under which it is lived matter deeply to the very purpose and idea of education itself. What sense are we to make of such a brash claim? Ought we to read this statement as declaring the death of humanity as such, as a testament to the loss of our capacities to be humane? Or, ought we to read Irigaray's words as depicting the passing of humanity as an *idea*, one that has simply gone out of fashion in the turn to technocratic ways of thinking? Or, is it that humanity only *seems* past, which would simultaneously signal the impossibility of humanity to exist fully in the present and the possibility that the time for humanity is not wholly lost?

It is, in fact, with the latter question that Irigaray's recent work is most in conversation (2001a; 2001b; 2002a; 2002b). Yet, rather than returning to a familiar humanism, her hopeful resurrection of humanity lies in reinventing it. To this end, Irigaray has devoted a substantial portion of her work to articulating the conditions of civil life in a way that reflects the division of humanity along the lines of sexual difference. Thus not only is she concerned to animate a whole new idea of humanity, but she also seeks to "put" sexual difference into the practical sphere of citizenship, democracy, and human rights.

Given the recent emphasis in education on the changing nature of citizenship in the global era, Irigaray's work would seem to be a timely intervention—but in fact has been little explored in this context. Her emphasis on educating for

117

civil coexistence between men and women as being first and foremost about a politics of sexuate rights (that is, rights which help to create and sustain new forms of civil identity for both men and women, and thus cannot be universal) speaks quite directly to the growing complexity surrounding citizenship in a cosmopolitan frame. Yet, despite an increasing emphasis on an expanded citizenry (world, European, and postnational citizenship come to mind) which is often invested with the cosmopolitan ideals of human rights and liberal democratic forms of life, little mention is made about how *the* citizen is also a sexuate subject and operates within the terms of masculinity and femininity in a given social sphere. Indeed the liberal citizen remains abstracted from the embodied lives of individuals and puts into question the extent to which any notion of the citizen can actually work toward establishing equality and freedom for those individuals if their specificity is not taken into account. We see this in relation to the great stir caused by Muslim girls wearing different forms of dress to school. For although the official discourse is concern for women's equality (and a fear of Muslim militancy—which is not always so readily admitted in public), can this not be seen as yet another instantiation of how the image of the liberal public citizen ought not to exhibit such particular signs of femininity? It is, of course, not that all signs of femininity are proscribed in public, but why is it that this aspect of dress seems to matter so much and why are their rights as women to wear religious clothing (to say nothing of the religious or cultural reasons for wearing *niqab, burqa, jilbab*, or *hijab* that are supposed to be protected) being put under such continued scrutiny?

For Irigaray, the omission of the sexuate subject from discussions of civil rights is consonant with a distorted picture of humanity that cannot fail but to produce inhumane relations, based as it is on a view of oneness and sameness. In other words, the idea of humanity which is supposed to be cultivated through citizenship, democracy, and human rights education means very little, in her view, if it elides the very recognition that humanity is—at least—two. Her work, therefore, bears some significance for my overall project of (a) rethinking cosmopolitanism through its double commitment to the universality of rights and to human pluralism, and (b) facing humanity through confronting its current limitations.

This chapter takes a different form of exposition than previous ones do in turning primarily to the thought of a single philosopher. It is not that the term "sexual difference" appears solely in Irigaray's work—indeed, Julia Kristeva, Monique Wittig, and other French feminists have used this term in their different challenges to the position of the feminine as other in "masculine" theories of subjectivity and humanity. Yet, it is in Irigaray's thought alone where sexual difference becomes *the* driving force for a reconception of democratic politics, based on the civil relation *between* the sexes. Hence I turn to Irigaray's work here not simply because it presents a critique of universality and the modernist idea of humanity, but because it also proposes political possibilities for moving our thinking beyond depictions of humanity in terms of what *is* and what *has been*. By this I mean that Irigaray sees that the focus on humanity both in terms of tradition and of what currently exists actually serves to justify certain inequities and injustices. Instead, she seeks to open up the question of humanity to a revolution of thought in suggesting that we turn our attention to the "cultivation" of what humanity "could become." This shift, I argue, stages an opening to the future that is not based on preconceptions of humanity, but which allows for the possibility for renegotiating humanity as a future-oriented democratic project.

Yet, readers will perhaps note the dissonant ring of "cultivation" here in relation to what I've discussed elsewhere in this book. In previous chapters I have made much critical noise about cosmopolitan appeals to a "shared" humanity and the "cultivation," "flourishing," or "caring for" that often accompany such appeals. However, I do see a fundamental difference between these and Irigaray's call for the "cultivation of what could become:" for the former, cultivation is about the fulfillment of human potential that is already latent within the subject, while for Irigaray, the "could become" suggests that we cannot know beforehand what that call precisely entails. I read her use of the term cultivation here as one that necessarily implies the *facing of humanity as a project of possibility*, and not the cultivation of humanity as a project of fulfillment. That is, as I discuss in this chapter with respect to her claims about civil life in particular, it is through the possibility of facing the *inhumanity* embedded in the universal claim that humanity is *one* that we are given hope for promoting humanity—and hence citizenship and democracy—on new terms. Within this appeal to "what could become" lies the urgent plea to find ways to express a humanity that *is not yet*.

It is with this in mind that this chapter addresses two primary questions: how does a notion of sexual difference as central to the idea of humanity that *is not yet* contribute to rethinking the promise of democratic citizenship? Moreover, how does the idea of facing sexual difference reframe education's relation to this promise?[1] In what follows, I explore Irigaray's rather complex ideas about sexual difference and relate these to her promotion of sexuate rights, democracy, and equality. Throughout, I discuss criticism regarding her position, raised primarily by her feminist readers, in order to clarify my own stance. The concluding section focuses on what Irigaray's rendering of humanity as always already being two can offer an educational discussion on the cosmopolitan direction in democratic citizenship.

SEXUAL DIFFERENCE IS *YET TO COME*

Luce Irigaray has spent—and continues to spend—her philosophical (and activist) career writing about, in, and through a notion of sexual difference. Part of the *écriture féminine* movement of the 1970s and 1980s, Irigaray's early work is known for its lyrical and evocative style, circling around key texts of the philosophical and psychoanalytic canon, and mobilizing new metaphors in the creation of a writing style that can craft, in her terms, new possibilities for feminine subjectivity. For this, and for her later insistence on her sometimes formulaic renderings of female civil identity, her work has been severely critiqued by some feminists for its essentialist nature, and has been perceived by some—even those more sympathetic to her project—as bordering on hyperbole and excess.[2] My own turn to Irigaray here falls into what has been seen to be a "return" to her thought in recent years by critical feminist readers who point out ways of engaging with Irigaray in the political sphere.[3] These critics view her insight into how sexual difference operates within and through embodiment and language actually gives us a strategy for opening up the terms of humanity itself to a more pluralistic reading of human experience.

Jean-Joseph Goux (1994) claims that Irigaray "clarifies two confusions in current discourses: 1. To overthrow patriarchal and phallocentric power does *not* mean denying the difference between the sexes but living the relation between them differently; 2. To assert the difference between the sexes is *not* at all the same thing as positing an essential femininity (or masculinity)" (181). But what does Irigaray mean by sexual difference in the first place, particularly if it seeks to resist essentialism? It is perhaps instructive to begin with what, in my view, it is not. Irigaray is not defining sexual difference in absolute terms. It is not as though there is a singular female identity as opposed to, or as distinct from, an essential male identity. Neither does sexual difference pertain to the differences between men and women on anatomical or biological terms. Nor is sexual difference another name for the ways in which men and women are sexualized differently in society through gender roles. Thus, to be clear, difference neither refers to a pregiven nature, nor to purely socio-cultural determinants.[4] With this said, how are we to understand difference here?

Irigaray (1985a; 1985b) herself begins her theorization of sexual difference through an exploration of what she refers to as the male and female imaginaries—that is through the field of fantasy and body image (or morphology) which serves to support particular conceptions of subjectivity. Through her close (indeed deconstructive) reading of psychoanalytical and philosophical texts and her careful attention to social and cultural organization, she reveals how the category of woman has been positioned as other within an imaginary picture of the human subject as universal, as one, as self-same.

The Male Imaginary as "Universal"

Through her early reading of key psychoanalytic concepts (including Jacques Lacan's mirror stage and Freud's Oedipus complex), Irigaray strives to articulate the ways in which "the body and its morphology are imprinted upon imaginary and symbolic creations" (Irigaray 1993a, 68).[5] She seeks to understand how the "phallus"—as the image of, as opposed to the actual, penis—operates to sustain a certain position for women within what she refers to as the "patriarchal symbolic." That is, the entry into language for the subject rests on the access one has to the phallus, and it therefore represents the way in which subjectivity becomes possible within the culture of patriarchy. This is an important point, given that she interprets the philosophical and political ideas of humanity and the citizen as partially exhibiting these same tendencies, as we shall see. She establishes a connection between, on the one hand, *phallocentrism*—as a way of thinking that privileges the phallus—and, on the other hand, *phallomorphism*—as a way of imag(in)ing the world in terms that privilege the male body as a standard.

Irigaray claims that the projection of the male imaginary acts like a mirror, reflecting back onto itself a phallic image in which only one sex is expressed. In patriarchy, the male imaginary is a *social* imaginary which seeks to construct fictions that sustain its self-illusion. Accordingly, the male imaginary operates through a language that claims to "designate him [the male] perfectly" (1985a, 233). For instance, the Oedipal myth as a phallic *image* is only a representation of a truncated reality—a reality which cannot recognize its own imaginary projections. It tells the story of a supposedly universal sexual difference, through the singular gaze of the male, reflecting back an image with which men are able to identify, with which men may recognize themselves as self-same.[6] In this respect, the male imaginary also necessarily privileges male identification and identity because it supports cultural articulations of maleness and masculinity, *not* because it lies in some immediate relation to male anatomy. Irigaray claims that the patriarchal symbolic does not, however, recognize itself as illusion or as being isomorphic. Instead, it sees itself as expressing the universal, rendering everything in its own (illusory) image.[7] In this way, the Oedipus complex—like other theories of human being—functions for Irigaray on two, interconnected levels. First, these are *symbolic* constructions; they offer a *theory* of subjecthood, a *discursive* construction that involves a *narrative* of how the subject *is*. Secondly, they are also *imaginary* projections, (re)presenting an *image* of the subject through a male *morphology* (body-image), offering images of what the subject looks like, of what identity is, using only the male body as the *ideal*, as the *standard register* against which human agency and subjectivity are measured. The point that Irigaray brings to light here is how these symbolic "stories" of human being, are already saturated with imaginary formulations of the supposed truth of sexual difference.[8]

In sum, the male imaginary functions in two ways. First, it operates as an agency of patriarchal discursive practices, subtending these practices, acting as a support without which symbolizations and narratives such as Oedipus would be, literally, unthinkable. However, secondly, within patriarchy, the male imaginary operates as a *hidden* fantasy. It remains unacknowledged within patriarchy. Patriarchy takes the symbolic as its own truth and denies the social fantasy which supports that truth. Irigaray sees it as her project to articulate this unacknowledged fantasy that organizes patriarchy to unveil what is hidden. As Whitford (1991) notes of Irigaray's project, "the coherence of a conceptual system does not imply its *truth*, but may be the coherence of its *phantasy*" (69). Irigaray underlines the point that patriarchy creates its own hermeticism by failing to recognize its own unconscious otherness. And, it cannot admit the unconscious, or *irrational* basis of its own construction without dismantling itself. Quite simply, if patriarchy allowed itself to recognize the fantasy of its own truth, it would cease to be patriarchy. By implication, then, any new reconfiguration of society needs to acknowledge the imaginary core of its symbolic practices. Hence by *saying* what has been unsaid, Irigaray challenges the patriarchal symbolic, attempting to intervene in conventional modes of universality. In this sense, the hermeticism between the patriarchal symbolic and the male imaginary is not complete or total, which leaves room for Irigaray to propose an alternative social imaginary: a female imaginary that recognizes its own specificity and does not claim a universal identity but reasserts difference into ways of rethinking identity itself.[9]

The Female Imaginary as "Difference"

In these same early works in which she critiques patriarchal theories of subjectivity, Irigaray also boldly analyzes the *condition* of a female subjectivity that is *yet to come* through the space in between nature and culture. Yet, this otherness is not simply to be understood as that which is excluded or marginalized from some proverbial masculine center. Judith Butler (1993) has depicted Irigaray's views of the feminine along two trajectories: the specular feminine and the excessive feminine. The first corresponds to how women have been objectified within the representational system subtended by the male imaginary, and depicts how they have been rendered as a "specular image" of that projected imaginary. The second corresponds to how the feminine exceeds the limits of the symbolic and is capable of imagining anew the relations between the sexes. The feminine is, one might say, both specular and spectacular.

The specularization of women finds its fullest treatment in *Speculum* (1985a) and in Irigaray's critiques of Freud and Lacan in *This Sex which is Not One* (1985b). She charges that the reflection in the mirror Lacan speaks of in his mirror stage only reflects male modes of identification and of relating to the world. The mirror of psychoanalysis forms an image of femininity and female sexuality that is based on a fantasized projection of what woman *is*. "Woman, in this sexual imaginary, is only a more or less obliging prop for the enactment [*mise-en-acte*] of man's fantasies" (Irigaray 1985b, 25). In other words, women have no power over the representational systems which tell each of us who she is, why she is, and how she is. The male imaginary, the fantasy of the male body as One, is *contingent upon* an other who is not One, or "not all," as Lacan professes.[10] In other words, it is the conception of femininity as *other* that keeps intact male identity as *self-same*. As Whitford (1991) notes, women have become the "tain of the mirror" (34), the layer without which the male imaginary mirror would simply be another piece of glass. In effect, women exist "behind the screen of representation" (Irigaray 1985b, 9). Irigaray writes:

> Thus I have become your image in this nothingness that I am, and you gaze upon [*mires-tu*] mine in your absence of being. This silvering at the back of the mirror might, at least, retain *the being*—which we have been perhaps and

which perhaps we will be again—though our mirage has failed at present or has been covered over by alien speculations. (1985a, 197)

But what is this imaginary outside of male fantasy? What does Irigaray mean by "perhaps we will be again" the being re-tained in the silvering of the mirror? How is the female imaginary both within and outside male imaginary-symbolic constructions?

In fact, Irigaray recognizes that her description of the condition of woman as merely a prop of male fantasy does little to challenge patriarchal inscription of female identity. That is, it is not enough to *critique* the patriarchal symbolic, but one must *resymbolize* it in order to open up possibilities for the expression and creation of "female identity" based on difference. Thus, she is not arguing, like Simone de Beauvoir, that women are only "other" (or second) to the masculine subject; Irigaray instead posits woman as other *in and for herself*, one who exists as something more than a simple reflected image. She exists on the other side, as it were, of male projection. That is to say, her difference is not "determined" by masculine discourse (as some feminist theorists concerned with the social construction of identity postulate). Instead, difference arises out of a disjuncture: the space opened up by women's existence that cannot be contained within patriarchal discourse. Sexual difference is therefore not something that is measured against the standard of a masculine version of humanity or subjectivity, but is something that also exists as resistant to such enclosure.

Irigaray's most passionate—and most provocative—claim is that woman resists this enclosure because of her bodily relation to her world, to her environment. Irigaray thereby turns to corporeal specificity and female morphology as elements that can be used to mobilize female agency at the symbolic level. And it is this turn, in particular, that has caused some critics to see this as a lingering essentialism in her work. However, she quite carefully, in my view, puts forth the idea that it is not as though bodies have an unmediated relation to the world, but rather, that one's body-image, or morphology, acts to mediate experience of that world; it is the female imaginary which mediates the relation between a woman's body and the world she finds herself in. The rub here, however, is that while man has projected his imaginary onto ideas of humanity and human subjectivity as universal and gender-neutral, the female imaginary has yet to find adequate expression. Irigaray's goal is for women to *appropriate* their own otherness (not mere specular reflection), in order to compel society to articulate this otherness as a civil identity. As already "other," the female imaginary is not concerned with establishing itself as self-same, but with rewriting identity in and through its difference. This is why, for Irigaray, the female imaginary holds the potential to disrupt the universality of the one by insisting on difference as a condition of being and becoming. In this sense, the female imaginary, relating to another logic of morphology, opens up the possibility for reframing identity, humanity, and universality as something beyond unity and homogeneity. It is this seemingly counterintuitive move (counterintuitive at least for those of us so habituated to the stasis implied in such terms) which Irigaray uses both as leverage for analysis and for advancing concrete political change.

Thus one of the driving forces behind her later work, which I want to focus on more thoroughly below, has to do with finding ways of symbolizing the imaginary in and through culture in a manner that respects the different morphologies operating for men and women. Paradoxically, though, insofar as such representation is *yet to come*, sexual difference as such does not yet fully exist in the social and political spheres. The political and ethical hope for humanity, so Irigaray claims, lies precisely in working toward a representation of a sexual difference that has as yet no positive content. In her eyes, "to confuse the part for the whole taints the negative with an imaginary positivity" (Irigaray 1996, 36). Thus her project is not simply to supplant the male imaginary with a female one, which would just be another claim to yet another pseudo-universality, but to work with the negativity of sexual difference itself. It is in the very anticipatory moment of what sexual difference could become where Irigaray locates democratic politics. Thus her phrase, "democracy begins between two" (2001a), captures the idea that democracy is to begin its work from the "between" space of a sexual difference that has not yet been symbolized. This is a far cry from conceptions of democracy based on the liberal subject who is presumed free, autonomous and rational already. And this is indeed the "impossible politics" (Deutscher 2002) of Irigaray's project—it works as a "labor of the negative." Irigaray is hopeful of the power of such a politics: "With this new elaboration of the negative, it may be possible for another era of human becoming ..." (Irigaray 1996, 14).

SEXUATE RIGHTS OF CITIZENS: AN IMPOSSIBLE POLITICS

To move from the question of sexual difference to *sexuate* rights indeed seems quite impossible, as Penelope Deutscher (2002) suggests, since advocating for sexuate rights presumes that we can put into concrete, positive terms the negativity of a sexual difference that does not yet exist. Indeed, in contrast to the poetic, lyrical invocations of the predicament of female subjectivity so characteristic of her early work, some of Irigaray's latest writing reads more like a series of assertions, which many of her critics have found frustratingly oversimplified. For example, "becoming a woman means acquiring a civil dimension which is appropriate to 'feminine identity', a culture which corresponds to one's own body and specific genealogy ..." (2001a, 36). Although there are problems with some of her rhetorical moves, I nonetheless think that Whitford (1991) is right in stating that Irigaray's proclamations cannot be taken at face value. That is, as I stated above, what she signals with "feminine identity" is not a unified entity, but one that gestures toward the difference inherent in the feminine itself. This is not to say that she avoids paradox or contradiction, or has escaped a certain "monodiscursivity," as Deutscher puts it (2002, 72), but that her reference to seemingly trite overstatement needs to be read in tandem with her earlier deconstructive readings of difference and identity.

Her later writing does appear, though, to be quite distant from the earlier concerns with feminine agency and writing through corporeal metaphors. On the one hand, her critique of patriarchy has lost some of the brittleness it once had. On the other hand, her turn toward more normative political, social, and educational issues (she was for a time involved in the Reggio Emilia schools in Italy), has taken away some of the radically queer edges of her work, which has consequently left her open to charges of heteronormativity (Butler 1993). Indeed, her shift in focus from the scene of the feminine body and women's relations amongst themselves to the space between the feminine and the masculine seems, on the surface, to undermine her earlier desire to mobilize the female imaginary toward the production of new symbolic spaces. However, my own view is that her focus on civil rights is an extension of her earlier views and not a complete break from them. She conceives of the connection thus: "The exploitation and the alienation of women are located in the difference between the sexes and genders, and have to be resolved in that difference, without trying to abolish it, which would amount to yet another reduction to the singular subject" (2001a, 126).

Irigaray's project in these later works is about contending with what she claims is "the real ethical tragedy facing us" today: that there is no dialectical relationship between the genders (1993b, 110). This is the major theme that runs throughout her calls for a renewed model of civil coexistence. Moving therefore from counterposing a critique of patriarchy with an agentic female subjectivity that is yet to come, she insists on two things: that it is both men and women who are disadvantaged (albeit differently) by the dream of symmetry that universal appeals to humanity (and the citizen) invoke; and secondly that part of the solution to this problem is not only that women have to find modes of symbolic representation for themselves (which is still important for Irigaray), but that the very relation *between* the sexes has yet to be represented in all its complexity. "A culture of life does not, in fact, exist. A culture of the body, a culture of the natural sensibility, a culture of ourselves as living beings, is still lacking" (2001a, 57). This is an important shift, and one I think that is derived from her concern to transform civil space along precisely these lines of relationality that lie within the notion of a humanity as two in order to promote what she calls a "peaceful revolution" (1994).

RELATIONSHIP OF COEXISTENCE, OR HUMANITY AS TWO

Irigaray, in commenting on the advent of European citizenship, proposes that the time has come for the development of a *relationship of coexistence*: "the task of connecting natural and civil coexistence is therefore particularly urgent if we are to move towards an enlarged community such as the European community" (2001a, 52). She is adamant that such an accomplishment does not simply involve women's calls for equality with men (based on having the *same* rights), or tinkering with existing social and political models of coexistence, but a fundamental transformation of thought and being—the likes of which we have not seen before. Irigaray's political—and ethical—project lies in the capacity to imagine different conditions for the way culture can be symbolized along the register of difference. "For it is not a matter of changing this or that within a horizon already defined as human culture. It is a question of changing the horizon itself—of understanding that our interpretation of human identity is both theoretically and practically wrong" (1996, 20).

As we have seen above, Irigaray has critiqued universality from the point of view both of the masculine subject it projects through its self-mirroring and of the neutrality it paradoxically claims in its own image. And this, while affecting women in most distressful and violent ways, also plays a part in man's estrangement from himself. "As a citizen he is expected to renounce his sexed singularity in order to realize a universal task in the service of the community. In the name of this alleged universality, he apparently has the right and duty to represent the entire human species in public life" (1996, 22). An instance of this, Irigaray charges, has to do with the ways in which humanity, and consequently our conceptions of being together with others, have been thoroughly based on "needs and instincts" which appear as seemingly sexual-neutral terms (1996; 2001a; 2002a; 2002b). The need to eat, sleep, have community and shelter—these have been used to underscore an idea of humanity that is indivisible. For Irigaray, such reductionist thinking has "enabled the question of sexual difference to be shelved" (1996, 43). In other words, while not denying these needs, the cultural articulation of securing civil rights cannot be based on supposedly sexual-neutral appeals to "biology" or even "sociality."[11] The question of civility, of coexistence between men and women, would then become masked behind naturalistic accounts of human be*ing* as a singular existence.

> No one nature can claim to correspond to the whole of the natural.... There is no 'Nature' as a singular entity. In this sense, a kind of negative does exist in the natural. The negative is not a process of consciousness of which only man is capable. More to the point, if man does not take account of the limit inscribed in nature, his opposition to the natural does not accomplish the labor of the negative. (1996, 35–36)

Instead, Irigaray sees that the task of human *becoming* is to move from an account of the natural as one, to a divided humanity rooted in the ways men and women form their subjectivities along sexuate lines. Thus when she writes of the passage from "natural" to "civil" identity, she is emphasizing the sexed aspect of subject formation via our embodied relation to the world—an embodiment, as we have seen, that is inextricably interwoven with the imaginary aspects of morphology. As such, it is not as though sex (as given in nature—as if even this weren't questionable) determines the outcome of what that becoming will be for women and men, but that our whole idea of humanity needs to reflect the ways in which subjectivity is structured differentially for them. For Irigaray, the problem of sexual difference is to move out of our "natural immediacy," which reflects a way of thinking about the body simply on biological or anatomical terms, toward a civil identity that can begin to recognize the difference between the sexes on cultural terms. And this, she sees, is not only an issue for women, but for humanity itself. "Strictly speaking, there is still no civil law in our era that makes human persons of men and women. As sexed persons, they remain in natural immediacy. And this means that real persons still have no rights, since there are only men and women; there are no neuter individuals" (1996, 21).

On this view, Irigaray is obviously highly critical of an idea of humanity that is posited on a model of aggregation: "society is not made up of one + one + one neutral and separate individuals, but of individuals who are linked together, particularly through sexed relationships" (2001a, 118). Thus rights—civil rights based on a becoming of humanity, a sexual difference that is yet to come—need to reflect, according to her, both halves of humanity, which refuse to occupy a singular position as a universal. But it is not as though Irigaray rejects universalism altogether. Irigaray's revisioning of what is "universal" is located, rather, in a humanity that is two and the relation that this entails: "Managing to respect the other of sexual difference, without reducing the two to the one, to the same, to the similar … represents a *universal way* for attaining the respect of other differences" (2002a, 137, emphasis added). Thus the universal aspect of humanity lies in the irreducibility of the sexes and the relation between them, which that very irreducibility makes possible.

As in the work of Levinas, with which Irigaray continues to be in conversation, Irigaray sees that alterity or otherness is necessary for relationship itself: without difference, there is no possibility of exchange, only an immersion into unity. The other is "transcendent" in the sense that s/he remains out of my grasp, remains outside any totality I seek to impose on him or her. There is always an invisibility to this alterity that I cannot possess. "Certainly, I will never be able to understand you, I will never grasp who you are: you will always remain outside of me. But this not being *I*, not being *me*, or *mine*, makes speech possible and necessary between us" (2001b, 19). However, unlike Levinas, Irigaray sees that transcendence also appears in the "sensible" dimensions of desire as well— a desire that is recast beyond possession. The intersubjective relation, Irigaray claims, is therefore not an abstract conjecture, but one marked by corporeal experience. Transcendence makes its appearance, then, through this realm of the sensible, where alterity allows for "sensibility and thought to come together" (2001a, 115). That is, the question of coexistence needs to reflect this "sensible transcendental," this relation to the other *as* other, the one we touch, smell, caress, and hear. Yet, she cautions, "this is not, then, an affection which seduces the other into denouncing the intellect and the spirit, falling back into unmediated sensibility, but instead a determination to lead the lived experience of the sensibility towards coexisting with the other, thanks to a measure of respect, rationality and thought" (2001a, 117). Thus Irigaray here is not talking about some "private" intimacy that can then inform the "public" sphere, but a rethinking of the public (through respect, rationality, and thought) as a relation of difference that is at once both transcendent and sensible. What this means is that the relationship of coexistence is about representing what lies *between* the two in a way that disregards neither their radical separateness nor their singularity as individual subjects. In this, Irigaray seeks out new language for defining civil rights, democracy, and equality, one that takes seriously the development of rights for individual men and women, on the one hand, and the relations between them, on the other hand.

SEXUATE RIGHTS, DEMOCRACY, AND EQUALITY

When it comes to discussing sexuate rights for individuals, Irigaray is particularly concerned with the way women have traditionally been "specularized" through the masculine assumptions underlying them. Thus she turns more of her attention to the articulation of a culture of rights for women than for men. "In order to attain the status of a civil person, woman must pass from natural identity, especially an imposed natural identity, to civil identity. Her most radical and indispensable (r)evolution is situated there" (2002a, 112). Yet, it must be said that she begins with women's sexuate rights for two reasons: first, because she thinks that women have suffered particularly through laws and rights which reflect a patriarchal genealogy (regulating inheritance, marriage, and reproduction "on behalf of women"); and secondly, that amending the rights of women will go a long way in pursuing an "*oeuvre* of justice" (1996, 14). Indeed, she writes: "The properties of feminine identity remain yet to be thought, not beginning from the violent actions of the masculine, but through a cultivation of the to-be woman which may even be capable of redirecting man to his own to be" (2001b, 72). Irigaray's entire point with recasting rights as a labor of the negative is the cultivation of human becoming, which for women as for men means not simply being entitled to rights, but incurring duties and responsibilities as a result of them. Thus her feminism is not simply about a politics of affirmation, but a politics of responsibility through the recognition of the other.

As coauthor, along with Renzo Imbeni, of a draft code of citizenship for the European Union, Irigaray sees the need to translate the ethical imperative of developing relations between the sexes into political formulations that can begin to create new forms of coexistence (2001a, 69–72). (The code itself was submitted to the European Parliamentary Commission for Women's Rights and received only a curt reply.) Here, as elsewhere, she is concerned with rewriting existing codes and rewording legislation in order to shift the emphasis away from what she perceives to be a masculine economy of the self-same. It is worth quoting her and Imbeni at length:

> The lack of legislation appropriate to women can be seen today in various ways: in particular, in the scandals and trials concerning the violence of which they are victims. National civil codes as well as constitutions, and the *Universal Declaration of Human Rights* all lack the terms relating to specific rights which would enable such crimes to be judged. Thus rape is defined as a crime and not as rape, which fails to protect the woman as such and leaves the ordinary citizen unaware of the felony he commits when he rapes someone. The same is true as regards the free choice of maternity which is defined, at its best, as permission to have an abortion without penal consequences: such a formulation of

the law reveals its complicity with patriarchal power which retains the right to legislate over a woman's body, even if she is of age.... As long as such rights are lacking, crimes involving women are considered almost exclusively in the penal context which does not promote civil peace. What is more, no preventative legislation exists: one which would entrust a woman with responsibility for herself as a citizen and which, by considering her as a civil individual, would give the community the responsibility of preventing the crimes involving her, involving both of them. (2001a, 71–72)

Irigaray's emphasis here is on women's right to choose a way of be*ing*, as opposed to simply being "given permission" to undergo certain actions upon her body. This right of be*ing* is crucial for Irigaray insofar as it signals the possibility that women can *become* subjects that have not as yet been defined for them. Irigaray's appeal to specific rights in order to further the "becoming" of identity, means shifting the symbolic structures and legal frameworks that continue to define women in a specular fashion. Ironically, the supposed autonomy granted to individuals as citizens is lacking, for Irigaray, when we examine closely the ways in which women's rights are formulated either according to need (the right to food, clothing, and shelter—second generation rights) or according to political freedom (the right to freedom from state interference—first generation rights).[12] Thus she takes issue with the fact that not only do civil rights have little affirmative value in processes of human freedom and becoming, but that they actually constrain subjectivity for women in continuing the tradition that positions them beyond human freedom itself. "Certainly these philosophers [of the Enlightenment] did not believe that it was enough to shout 'I want to be free' in order to be so.... Rather, they considered the problem of how to be free in themselves, placing it in terms of their own subjectivity, in terms of their own consciousness. They asked themselves: what can freedom be for me, a human subject?" But they did the asking, Irigaray charges, "as if it were the universal model of every human consciousness" (2001b, 85–86).

What is so striking about the reformulation she and Imbeni attempt here, is that they reveal the ways in which rights are usually minimally concerned with the prevention of discrimination and optimally with the security of basic needs. What this leaves out of the picture, of course, is a sense of positive freedom connected with the emergence of subjectivity itself. This sense of freedom (even as a necessary fiction) would have to facilitate and enhance the prospects for individuals not simply to be citizens but to become equal subjects in their own right. And such equality in turn depends on keeping open the negativity of sexual difference itself. Although the paradox, as I have noted, cannot be fully overcome, the political project that Irigaray suggests attempts to live within this aporia by promoting rights that act (minimally) as a redress to the violence imposed by rights and civil laws themselves. Although she offers no definitive resolution, her attempt to fathom for women another starting point for their becoming subjectivity in the social and political sphere means an assertion of equality that does not yet exist symbolically. So, the problem is that if civil rights form the bedrock of a just, democratic society—indeed such rights often act as the signifier for the democratic state—and if those rights are sorely lacking in attending to a divided humanity, then wherein lies equality for women?

Equality cannot lie in liberal appeals to the citizen, according to Irigaray, for this would be tantamount to demanding that women submit to the very universality which has curtailed their freedom in the first place. "Today, our desperation and impotence often express themselves in the form of slogans. We proclaim that we want to be free, equal, brothers. But we do so without considering the meaning that these words have in the context of our era and without thinking about the conditions in which liberty, equality, and fraternity are practicable" (2001b, 85). Thus she charges that some of our most cherished notions in liberal democracies actually remain mere surface phenomena—fictions which are neither necessary nor related to the specificities of individual lives. "As I am only half of the world, I am not free in the way this is generally conceived. I am free, on the other hand, and as I should be, to be what or who I am: one half of human kind. In that sense, and in that sense only, right—my right—is a function of respect for life" (1996, 41).

In this way, it would be foolhardy for women to seek equality with men on the same terms, as this leads to a reinscription of their submission to the specular image of the feminine which is precisely what women should be resisting in the name of their own equality. Equality, therefore, is not premised on sameness, but on the extent to which the becoming of women's subjectivity can be reflected in the political sphere so that they can "enjoy equivalent opportunities" (2001a, 1). Irigaray is adamant that "with regard to this task, claiming to be equal to a man is a serious ethical mistake because by so doing woman contributes to the erasure of natural and spiritual reality in an abstract universal that serves only one master: death" (1996, 27).

Indeed, this idea of death is what Irigaray sees permeating democracy itself. That is, insofar as sexual difference is denied as part of the temporal structure of life, as part of a project of human becoming, democracy aligns itself on the side of what is already dead: "a society in neutral mode loses sight of the line separating life from death. Although life, obviously, is always sexed, death on the contrary no longer makes this distinction" (2001a, 37). More to the point, Irigaray claims that without a respect for difference, such a society is "capable of all forms of holocaust" (2001a, 37). That is, a society founded on the extinguishment of life (based on difference and otherness) can only reproduce itself through this continual killing of otherness in the name of the universal. This establishes what Zakin (2007) refers to as "totalitarian democracy," a democracy that seeks to reduce everyone— all difference—into its universal fold. As Zakin notes, "only a necropolis denies the temporality that inheres in sexual difference ..." (184).

It is thus in seeking to remove democracy from the arms of its own drive to death, that Irigaray puts into question the very term "democracy" itself: "I am not sure that we should retain the word 'democracy', power of the people. It would be better, I believe, to discover a new term which would guarantee to all wo/men rights which would not alienate the rights of each wo/man. I am searching for this new word ..." (2001a, 100). In suggesting that democracy begins with difference and not universality, it cannot be based on an aggregate notion of the people, which would amount to pure abstraction and artifice: "A democratic politics does not begin with an adding of 'yeses', with a crowd electing whoever is going to govern them; it can only be based on a two which is not reducible to one plus one abstract individuals ..." (2001a, 26).

Thus in putting democracy on the side of life instead of death, it is humanity as—at least—two which emerges as the condition for politics. Yet this democratic politics is not simply a plea for harmony between the sexes, but implies a struggle to articulate the equality of male and female subjects as sexuate. Irigaray writes: "Democracy cannot have its basis in any form of power, even if shared, other than one in which men and women coexist as sovereign beings: a women *or* a man, capable of sharing a right of this sort to exist in a community made up of women *and* men" (2001a, 39). I interpret Irigaray's entire project of articulation, symbolization, and representation as, in effect, a form of "doing" democracy. That is, in asserting an equality based on sexual difference that is yet to come, she is trying to destabilize the social order of inequality. In Jacques Rancière's sense, she asserts equality as conflict into the given system of inequality that currently defines women's right to be and to become. This search for a new language of becoming, then, reveals, I think, the power of Irigaray's thought to continually construct a democratic politics within a "horizon of sexual difference" (2001a, 3). Like all horizons, it is never within our reach and "as long as there are no laws or rules which all women—and all men—may refer to and invoke when making their decisions, there can be no democracy, however attractive the immediate allegiance of a collectivity to a proposition may be" (2001a, 2). I interpret this statement as meaning not that democracy will be achieved once we secure for all men and all women civil rights appropriate for their subjective becoming, but that within the horizon of the negative of sexual difference, that struggle for democracy remains, in the words of Derrida (1997), always "to come." Irigaray's project of promoting sexuate rights seeks, therefore, to do away with the hubris of democracy for all, particularly when we know that "all" is a signifier for abstractions which simply do not exist; as Irigaray claims, only women and men exist, asexuate subjects do not. Democracy therefore becomes a project of finding ways for the relations between existing women and men to reflect their becoming equally, through their difference

But if democracy is also about the appearance of equality along sexuate lines, is it enough to focus on sexual, as opposed to cultural, religious, or ethnic, difference? Are these not equally important to the pursuit of citizenship and human becoming and in defining how sexual difference itself can be expressed?

WHITHER CULTURAL DIFFERENCE?

One of the most important, and intriguing, aspects of Irigaray's project involves her move toward a more cosmopolitan direction; one which she understands has the possibility of civil rights beyond the borders of the nation-state. She embraces the idea that the rights of "individuals" need to find expression in "the organization of supranational community identities" (2001a, 70). This, to her mind, will ward off the all-too-close identification that civil rights currently have with the nation-state and consequently will avoid "the risk of falling back on nationalisms, fundamentalisms, racisms, etc." (2001a, 70). It is in making calls like these that Irigaray shows some awareness of the complexity of citizenship in "post-national" contexts. Irigaray, like Julia Kristeva (1993) in this regard, is, for instance, acutely aware of how differences across cultures have conjured up fear within individual European nations—and this at a time when the building of a collective European citizenry has become so prominent on the political agenda. "The opening-up of frontiers" has led to the unconscious fear that "entry into enlarged community will increase the split between our belonging to a natural state and the new citizenship or that this citizenship will dissolve natural identity into an abstract identity managed by others—not us, not me ..." (2001a, 51). It is a mistake, Irigaray claims, to deny such fears for the task at hand is to dispel them.

Indeed, Irigaray notes that the apparent responses that have arisen out of these fears reveal a paradoxical commitment:

> It is not possible, for example, to advocate abandoning national sovereignty for the needs of the construction of the European Union and to claim, elsewhere, to integrate immigrants into a nation. Such inconsistencies come to confront one another sooner or later; which does not contribute to the development, nor even to the maintenance of a civil community.... Rather than turning to norms incapable of finding a solution for new conditions, it is preferable to question the resources of the situation and to discover a possible positive structuring of them. (2002a, 135)

Such a paradox, Irigaray claims, is constructed on a denial of the already existing ways in which communities are culturally mixed and have, in practice, so to speak, found means of coexistence that are not yet reflected in law and rights. As she exclaims, "Institutions evolve less quickly than reality!" (2002a, 133). Thus in seeking a possible positive restructuring of the norms of belonging which have traditionally guided our ways of thinking (and institutionalizing) the citizen, the task is to be open to a reformulation of belonging itself. She comments that "instead of asking how to treat this fundamental socio-cultural innovation, we often worry about diverse forms of integration that sterilize its potentials rather than promoting its fertility" (2002a, 133–134). Indeed, she sees the lived practices of coexisting in culturally mixed families, friendships, and collegial relations as actually offering preliminary solutions to knee-jerk institutional responses to fear of the cultural other. "Looking closely at this, do we not find ourselves faced with laboratories where, in miniature, the historical becoming of humanity is worked out? Cultural elements that children would have learned with difficulty all year long at school are offered to them at home, or with friends, as bits of daily life" (2002a, 134).

Irigaray thus sees that it is the task of democracy to reimagine relations anew, and she calls for new "cultural elaborations" of between-sexes, between-races, between-traditions (2002a, 139). Such elaborations, of course, echo the strategy of the "between," which, as we have seen above, Irigaray uses in the pursuit of representing the negativity of sexual difference. And, like this strategy, she is adamant that through our relations to others—our corporeal, embodied experience of alterity—new forms of thought can be found. Indeed, she claims that we need to reform our own thinking of national identity in ways that echo our rethinking of sexual difference itself. We do this

> by refusing to subject the respect of the other to the assertion of the same, the present or future to the past. By accepting that the development of a civilization does not inevitably consist of the accumulation of goods, of products, of knowledge inside an unchanged horizon.... Political agendas, like educational ones, need new formations, perspectives, words, and logics in order not to take the ideals of the past for progressive generosity. (2002a, 145)

Yet, her writing on cultural difference seems also to reveal a mode of thought whereby sexual difference takes priority, since it cuts across all societies, cultures, and religions. Indeed, in calling for the return to the self—and the distance from the self this entails—women and men, she claims, will be in a better position to meet the cultural and sexual other (2001a, 51–52). She seems therefore to map sexual difference onto cultural difference—as if through dealing with one, we automatically deal with the other. Thus it appears that despite her willingness to dispel the fears of paranoia and defensiveness which run rampant in the face of "immigration" the question of cultural coexistence seems nonetheless to find itself subsumed into the framework of sexual difference—both in terms of the strategies she relies on to champion it and the analysis of it as a problem. Is sexual difference, for instance, more "fundamental" than religious, cultural, or social differences of various stripes? And if so, how can one assure that in addressing a sexual difference that is *yet to come* through sexuate rights—through building a culture composed of two genders—that all women and men, whatever their cultural background, will have the right to human becoming? Even generous readings of her work in this regard (Spivak 1993; Deutscher 2002) admit of the difficulties here. One of the ways these critics have articulated the possibilities of Irigaray's project has been to see her thinking not in terms of providing *the* singular answer to questions of human difference; indeed, they emphasize that cultural differences reveal themselves in their aporetic state differently than sexual difference does. This requires, then, a different form of analysis, and a different set of possible strategies. It is not that Irigaray is totally ignorant of the state of civil relations across cultures, races, and religions, but that there is a tendency to assume that these differences can be treated from the position of sexual difference itself.

Her critics are, in this respect, less optimistic than Irigaray herself is that sexuate rights can indeed ameliorate/eliminate other conditions of intolerance, violence, and hatred. Instead, they view her as opening up a space where the traces of sexual difference might at best *inform* new articulatory practices for civil community, but do not serve a redemptive function for all aspects of difference within that community. Moreover, her philosophical argumentation for showing how sexual difference is tied to human subjectivities, to a humanity that is two, is simply absent with respect to the advent of other differences. That is, she often slides—as I have echoed here—the "at least" two into some of her formulations of humanity. This is not to suggest that Irigaray does not think seriously about human pluralism in terms of other registers of difference, but that these take a back seat to the driving force and raison d'être of promoting the becoming of sexuate subjects.

Nonetheless, with this said, I do think that Irigaray is concerned with transforming democracy and the civil relations within it in terms of the question of human becoming, in terms of a project that faces humanity as a possibility and that faces the violence it commits to difference under the name of its universality. And it is this promotion of democracy, equality, and sexuate rights through facing humanity that informs her ideas about education.

EDUCATING THE SEXED CITIZEN

To recapitulate briefly one of the major issues discussed above: attempting to navigate the negative of sexual difference through positive advocacy of sexuate rights demands admitting that one does not quite know the content of what one is advocating for. Deutscher (2002) thus sees that Irigaray

> argues both that sexual difference is excluded from culture and that sexuate rights should recognize sexual difference…. Yet, by definition, she can not know or name what she anticipates. Does she even know it is sexual difference? This is the paradox of an Irigarayan philosophy of sexual difference: the emptiness of its own brackets. (120)

In posing the question of sexual difference, though, as opposed to providing us with a fixed definition, Irigaray's work raises the stakes of how we conventionally go about thinking of other forms of difference (as threat, as exotic, as strange), as if we knew what they were as well. Insofar as sexual difference cannot be taken for granted, but remains only as the possibility of a new horizon, it demands that we, both women and men, develop a new sensibility to the other, which requires distancing ourselves from commonplace assumptions about men's and women's needs. Indeed, she claims that "if some cultures appear to us as more foreign than the other gender, this is because we have not yet experienced the distancing that lies in what is closest to us" (2001a, 5–6). The lesson here, despite the paradoxes that positive formulations of sexuate rights fall into, is that thinking through the negativity of sexual difference allows us to put into question at least our own assumptions about human becoming as always already entailing a teleology.

It is this direction with respect to how we encounter others that guides her thought on how education can contribute to the project of human becoming. Although Irigaray's commentary on education is passionate, it is not her primary concern and so remains largely underdeveloped and somewhat naïve. Yet, on the question of citizenship in particular, she offers some fruitful beginnings of how a reworking of humanity as two builds upon both respect for the irreducibility of the other gender and respect for myself as a singular being. "Education in civil life becomes an education in being, rather than in having: being oneself, being with others, male and female, being in and with nature, being in a moment of History, etc.... Relations with individuals are thus prioritized" (2001a, 9). Shifting the emphasis to relationality, Irigaray sees education in citizenship more in terms of a life-sustaining project as opposed to a set of knowledges to be acquired. Hers is a passionate pedagogy whose focus is on sensibility and attentiveness to those conditions that can open up the possibility for sexual difference. It requires, as she puts it, "an education in love between the genders" (2001a, 16).

Irigaray's insistence on educating for what is not-yet recasts education as an ethical and political project of becoming. Unlike other feminist pedagogies which focus on liberating women and girls from the conditions of discursive, social, and cultural instantiations of patriarchy through a politics of affirmation (of affirming girls' or female identity), Irigaray, rightfully in my view, asks us to consider what it might be like to think and practice civil forms of life based on a revisioning of a future, where those identities no longer hold, but must be re-imagined. Educating the *sexed* citizen challenges any general aim of education as a "learning to become" (Todd 2003) so long as it ignores different ways of becoming which are shaped by imaginary mediations of experience. It is not that currently we are "free" from such imaginary projections about what constitutes the good citizen, and which rights are required to protect such a citizen. It is simply that such an imaginary does not recognize itself as such and thus poses as the universal in a way that thwarts recognizing differences between and amongst us.

Educating for sexual difference, then, means giving up the fetish of nation as the defining feature in determining civil rights. It is not that states are unimportant, but Irigaray's point is that the ethnic and masculine constructs of nation are inadequate models for grounding civil life. Neither are cosmopolitan models entirely feasible alternatives; these merely reassert humanity as a principle of one and consequently lay claim to human rights as though differences between men and women were incidental. Irigaray's project suggests that educating for citizenship requires an education in what has yet to be thought, and it requires not the cultivation of "humanity" as race, or species, but the cultivation of relations of generosity and yes, indeed, love which respects the difference between us.

Let us return for a moment to the example of Muslim girls' dress in schools (discussed in chapter 5). Allowing ourselves to think about the sexed citizen, I propose, would open up the question as to what kind of imaginary is operative in perceiving *hijab, niqab, jilbab,* or *burqa* as being provocative. As a marker of sexed subjectivity (not simply a religious one), it seems to challenge a certain (masculine) projection of what constitutes a citizen. This explains the recourse to national stances on integration, and the accusation that Muslims have failed to adapt to the nations in which they live. Thus these girls become signs of cultural and religious differences and are made invisible as specifically sexed subjects in their own right. They are either turned into mere neutered representations, non-sexualized symbols of Muslim militancy, or into signs of existing gender inequality—poster girls for violations of so-called women's rights. Whichever way, their own right to a sexed way of being is constantly being denounced as the wrong one.

If democracy is about the assertion of equality as conflict, then sexual equality demands a recognition of difference that lies in fundamental opposition to what has not yet been named. Moreover, if education is about "creating citizens" in the name of democracy, then it needs to think about how sexual difference as an assertion of equality cannot merely mean the addition or incorporation of "women's concerns" into the already existing social order. Indeed, sexual equality seems to suggest that there is conflict about something that is *not yet.* Thus when we think about educating for democratic citizenship, what are we saying about citizens themselves? As we see from the conflict Muslim girls pose to national understandings of a democratic citizenry, the question becomes how to offer a reading of that conflict in ways that might suggest democratic possibility. This is not to claim that because there is conflict there automatically is democratic possibility, but that aspects of this conflict might actually be suggesting something about the nature of sexual difference as an assertion of equality in the public sphere. And thus, I think, the real challenge facing us here should not focus on the question of integration, but how to open up educational spaces of relationality in which these girls can exercise practices of human becoming as specifically female subjects in their own right.

NOTES

1. My argument here will focus explicitly on citizenship in relation to the nation, democracy, and rights. In this, I am not making direct claims about the theories of cosmopolitanism but take up nonetheless the core tension of these theories, concerned as they are with the universality of rights and the recognition of human pluralism.

2. Irigaray's work on sexual difference has occupied an important place in the eighties' debate on essentialism in feminist theory. It was often cast as either being expressive of a biological determinism or as enacting a strategic essentialism. While this debate remains important for theorizing women's identity and sexuality, it is not my intent here to rehash these arguments in any detail. For a

particularly relevant discussion on essentialism and Irigaray see, for instance, Schor (1994); Fuss (1989); Butler (1990); and various essays in Schor and Weed (1994). For an early critique of Irigaray that charges her with essentialism see Fauré (1981). For anti-essentialist comments see Holmlund (1991) and Burke (1981).

3. This return is captured in the title of a recent volume: *Returning to Irigaray: Feminist Philosophy, Politics, and the Question of Unity* (Cimitile and Miller 2007). Also see Deutscher (2002); Stone (2006); Ziarek (2001) for recent engagements with Irigaray's thought beyond the earlier concerns with essentialism.

4. A recent book by Alison Stone (2006) situates Irigaray's work within the German naturalist philosophical tradition, claiming that Irigaray promotes her understanding of sexual difference on naturalist grounds. My problem with this approach is that it loses sight of Irigaray's post-structural (and psychoanalytic) affinities.

5. For a discussion of morphology, see Grosz (1989, 113–119).

6. This does not mean that all men, in fact, do identify with it. However, Irigaray is attempting here to underline the male imaginary as supporting a social order (that of patriarchy) that codifies maleness and femaleness in very particular ways and which always already privileges the former. Indeed, as we will see below, her view changes slightly in her later work claiming that the male imaginary actually truncates men's subjectivities as well, not only women's.

7. Irigaray coins the term "hommologous" to underscore the isomorphism of the patriarchal system. Here she plays on the French *homme* meaning man and *homo* meaning same. She also coins the term hom(m)o-sexuality to illustrate repressed homoeroticism as the primary libidinal relation of patriarchy (1985b, 170–191).

8. As I discuss below, sexual difference, for Irigaray, is yet to come, but this does not prevent her from analyzing how certain universal theories of subjectivity make "truth claims" about sexual difference—truth claims which she obviously sees as fantastical projections.

9. It may, at first sight, seem ironic to call forth a female imaginary and claim its non-essential character. However, I interpret Irigaray here as championing a feminist, political alternative that rejects identity as meaning self-same. In this way, the female imaginary involves a social fantasy of difference, rather than a social fantasy of identity.

10. This famous dictum appears in Lacan's *Encore* seminar; the key texts appear in Mitchell and Rose (1985).

11. This is reminiscent of Badiou's (2007) observation that current thinking about humanism often starts out from biological considerations. See my discussion in chapter 1.

12. See my discussion in chapter 5 of these two types of rights and feminist positions on them.

8

Teachers Judging Without Scripts, or Thinking Cosmopolitan

Particular questions must receive particular answers; and if the series of crises in which we have lived since the beginning of the century can teach us anything at all, it is, I think, the simple fact that there are no general standards to determine our judgments unfailingly, no general rules under which to subsume the particular cases with any degree of certainty.

Hannah Arendt, 1966 speech, quoted in *Responsibility and Judgment*

What is inhuman is to be judged without anyone who judges.

Emmanuel Levinas, "The Ego and the Totality"

As we have seen in previous chapters, cosmopolitanism comprises, in both its historical and current invocations, a political and ethical mission to embrace a sense of worldliness outside the confines of national belonging, where our neighbors are no longer those who are "just like us," but who exist in a global, as opposed to a national, neighborhood. It is a shift away from patriotism—"the virtue of the vicious," as Oscar Wilde once quipped—toward a new understanding of our place and loyalties in the world. Thinkers such as Ulrich Beck (2006), Peter Kemp (2005), and Karl-Otto Apel (2000) even posit that the future of Europe depends upon the capacity to embrace a cosmopolitan "ethic" and to begin to think differently about our belonging in the world.[1]

But what constitutes the kind of thinking that a cosmopolitan ethic seeks to encourage? And what difficulties does this raise for teachers who are being called upon to educate youth along the lines of this ethic? It is by way of conclusion to this book that this chapter responds to such questions. In line with my discussion of cosmopolitanism's fault lines in chapter 2, a cosmopolitan ethic reveals a commitment to notions of world, transnational, or global citizenship, and also frames its pursuit of global justice largely along two lines: universal rights, on the one hand, and a respect for diversity, on the other, both of which trace their modern lineage to Kant's (1991) understanding of cosmopolitanism in his 1795 essay, "Perpetual Peace." A cosmopolitan ethic, then, invites both an appreciation of the rich diversity of values, traditions, and ways of life as part of the human condition *and* a commitment to broad, universal principles that can secure the flourishing of that diversity. It encourages an openness toward others—their cultures, their values—in seeking justice which moves beyond the narcissism of the nation-state.

Yet, I wish to raise two concerns here that are central for thinking about what relationship a cosmopolitan ethic might have to education. The first one has not so much to do with the inherent tension found within the ethic itself, but how it has failed to be adequately addressed. That is, there is a simultaneous appeal to embrace human rights (which entails a universalist ethic) and to respect cultural differences (which entails an eminently more particularistic emphasis) within cosmopolitanism. This double demand inevitably creates a contradictory logic that cannot be remedied by emphasizing one commitment over the other without, it seems to me, sacrificing the project of cosmopolitanism itself. Rather than suggesting, as has been the tendency with those who support cosmopolitanism, that human rights simply trump all other cultural values as a condition of transnational belonging (e.g., Nussbaum 1997; Kemp 2005; Apel 2000; Anderson-Gold 2001),[2] I think this contradictory logic is really begging a different ethical question: for is it not more a matter of how we *adjudicate* in concrete circumstances, across our differences and in light of rights, that is really at stake here? As already addressed in previous chapters, it seems to me that privileging rights on principle denies the very cornerstone of human plurality upon which cosmopolitanism is usually grounded. Moreover, as I have argued, it ignores the ways in which claims to universality themselves are products of cultural translation (Butler 2000), which means that judgments are also similarly implicated in precisely such translation processes. This does not mean that all judgments are equally valid, as though privileging the diversity within cultures, traditions, and beliefs over rights were the relativist response to universality we are looking for. My suggestion here is instead to make the difficulties of judgment itself a central part of any cosmopolitan outlook, acknowledging that it is precisely the difficulties to be countenanced in adjudicating between rights and particular contexts where the heart of cosmopolitan thought truly can be found. That is, it is a cosmopolitan outlook that seeks to face humanity and to confront the internal divisiveness of its own conceptual heritage that is at stake here.

My second concern has to do with this cosmopolitan ethic (or any ethic, for that matter) becoming yet another script that teachers or anyone else should supposedly recite, as though it held all the answers to our human predicament in the 21st century. Teachers in particular are frequently bombarded with various kinds of directives that are supposed either to "help" their practice in becoming better teachers or to be "implemented" in the name of a better future. The problem with this application model of theory to practice is that it risks leaving out of the equation the here-and-now realities in which teachers are engaged, and it also risks encouraging an uncritical—dare I say thoughtless—stance toward those ideas that are meant to be implemented. With the case of the inherent divide

within cosmopolitanism, this is particularly evident in terms of how teachers negotiate and reconcile their commitment to respecting the diversity of values and traditions, on the one hand, with their commitment to universal principles, on the other hand. My point is that if we are going to concede that cosmopolitanism has something important to say with regard to how education might be rethought beyond the nation-state, then it behooves us to consider the whole question of how teachers might live justly within the aporetic space created by a dual commitment to transnational, universal principles of human rights *and* an attentiveness to the unsettling play of cultural and social diversity.

I focus here on one of the dilemmas to be faced in taking cosmopolitanism seriously, namely the difficulty of *judging what is just* in the context of an increasingly divergent public—and classroom—discourse about values, rights, and equality. In other words, how might judgment help us think differently about the relation between education and cosmopolitanism beyond the script of a cosmopolitan ethic? I propose in what follows that everyday teaching practices and the difficulties of judgment that teachers face are tied already to what Kant referred to as our "cosmopolitan existence" and what Arendt has taken up in her radical focus on human pluralism. In this sense, teaching can be seen as being *implicated* in a cosmopolitan approach as opposed to being the vehicle through which a cosmopolitan ethic is implemented. To explore what is at stake in making judgments in an educational context, I draw on both Hannah Arendt's and Emmanuel Levinas's notions of judgment and thinking. What both emphasize is the strong connection between our capacity for thought and our capacity to judge as conditions arising from human plurality, from our "cosmopolitan existence." As Kant himself identified, cosmopolitanism as an expression of respecting diversity and of according others rights demands a capacity for "enlarged mentality," or, in other words, a capacity to think beyond oneself in order to judge. Thus, what I explore here is the educational significance of thought and judgment as conditions for reframing the universalism-particularism problem found in a cosmopolitan ethic. My argument is that there is a world of difference between educating for cosmopolitanism, which entails a faith in principles, and "thinking cosmopolitan," which entails an aspiration for justice for my neighbors. Thus I wish to keep alive the criticisms of cosmopolitanism I have made throughout this book while focusing on a renewed understanding of the cosmopolitan project insofar as it can become oriented toward facing humanity and all the imperfections this entails. In short, rethinking cosmopolitanism in ways that face humanity requires thinking cosmopolitan. In this, I move from a fixed notion of what cosmopolitanism as an "ism" is and focus on the active engagement of human pluralism within a context that is not purely shaped by universal principles. Indeed, by placing thinking at the heart of judgment, I wish to mobilize a notion of thought that resists scripts, even those as seductive as cosmopolitanism. For the question remains, how do we promote a particular project of global justice without turning it into a prosthesis for thinking?

TEACHING, JUDGING, THINKING

There are two aspects of teaching and judging I wish to draw out here in order to situate them in relation to rethinking cosmopolitanism: first, that teaching is inherently involved in making judgments; and secondly, that judgment is central to justice. With respect to the former, the judgment of teachers is perhaps most obvious in matters of assessment and evaluation; but it is in facing the range of human diversity in their classrooms, that teachers' judgments are an everyday matter, constantly deciding, evaluating, comparing, and prioritizing students' competing individual demands and needs. More often than not, such judgments happen without much reflection: the immediacy of their required response often does not allow teachers much time for thinking. Instead, relying on well-worn strategies and rules of engagement, teachers frequently perform their professional role, like a character in an old, familiar play. Such rules help teachers to respond quickly, efficiently; and I certainly appreciate the need for teachers to do so. However, strictly speaking, a judgment is precisely that which cannot be made by adhering, relatively unthinkingly, to a rule or principle. It requires decision, by a singular subject, by a teacher as an individual who says, in her particular encounters with others, "I decide." Thus it is not a role we are talking about when we talk about judgment in this sense, but a person who, although a professional and part of a profession, makes decisions in all her singularity. Indeed, in my experience, teachers frequently discuss the tensions they face in the classroom between making decisions as teachers and making decisions as "persons." It is as though the role at times speaks through them as opposed to their speaking through the role. But at the end of the day, to echo Levinas, roles do not judge; there is something inhuman about claiming that there is no *one*, no person, who judges.

Regarding the second point, judgment is also that which is a necessary, if difficult, condition of justice, thus making the practice of judging in teaching a practice of justice as well. Judgments are statements of our prioritized responsibilities and of the results of our weighing the elements of a situation in order to reach a verdict. They say something about us to the world, and thus signal our own implication in it. That is, being able to decide who speaks when and to whom; giving priority to one student's story over another's; judging the truth value of what a student is telling you; deciding whether or not to punish a particular act of disobedience; assessing when a student's behavior warrants a call home; protecting one student from harm at the hands of others; judging how to respond to disruption; deciding if a particular behavior is racist or sexist, and if so, how to handle it—all these and more illustrate times when our judgments as teachers are actually partaking of something more than general rules or regulations can account for. They are decisions made about particular cases, which at the very least require interpretation of rules, and at most sometimes demand abandoning them altogether. As Arendt has warned us, if we have learned anything from the horrors of the 20th century, it is not to put so much faith and trust in rules as the safeguards to our actions. Instead, what we need to reflect on is how judgment demands thinking beyond the standard scripts. That is, to think about our roles as opposed to letting those roles determine our thinking. This is particularly acute when it comes to a seemingly benevolent script such as cosmopolitanism, for it simply cannot provide the answers it sometimes professes to be able to offer. This means we need to reconsider what is at stake in our judgments as teachers with respect to others, and it means assessing the place of thinking in judgment more generally.

LESSONS FROM EVIL

No philosopher has generated as much controversy, perhaps, as Hannah Arendt has done with her phrase "the banality of evil." A discussion on the place of thinking in judgment ironically must begin with this and its appearance in Arendt's report on the notorious 1961 trial of Adolf Eichmann. Arendt claims in a postscript written a year after the initial publication of *Eichmann in Jerusalem* that she was merely offering an account "strictly on the factual level" of phenomena she witnessed daily at the trial in coining the phrase. Here, Arendt for the first time develops the idea that it is the sheer inability to think that enables someone to perpetrate evil acts. No demonical possession, no diabolical depth: Arendt attributes simply (!) a thoughtlessness, a superficiality, and a "remoteness from reality" (Arendt 1994, 288) to Eichmann's comportment throughout the trial, and in particular to the detached way in which he used language, unthinkingly parroting stock phrases without any sense of what they seemed to be signifying. Arendt observes that even at the gallows, moments before his execution by hanging, Eichmann's last words to the world are a series of contradictory clichés strung together. As Shoshana Felman (2002) remarks on the same event, "Eichmann does not *speak* the borrowed (Nazi) language: he is rather *spoken by it, spoken for* by its clichés, whose criminality he does not come to realize" (213, n. 4).

It is precisely this chilling inability to recognize human consequences, to weigh and to judge authentically beyond a mere parroting of rules, that is, for Arendt, one of the hallmarks of Nazi Germany. Although Arendt identified evil in all its banality, she did not assume that evil was ordinary; neither did she think that it did not have a unique human face. The danger with asserting that "there is an Eichmann in us all," or that one was merely following orders (what Arendt refers to as the "cog-theory of evil"), or that one shouldn't judge "lest ye be judged," or that one cannot judge because one wasn't there, is the assumption that there is no unique agent—and therefore, nothing human—about the deeds being committed. Indeed, ironically, these ideas fall in precisely with Eichmann's defense: that evil deeds are not committed by a person, but that a person's role is merely the vehicle through which such deeds are enacted (if it was not me, then it would be someone else—what Zygmunt Bauman refers to as responsibility "floated" [1993, 18]). Arendt is adamant that it is the individual who is to be judged and that judging requires seeing the one being judged in her or his humanity. Indeed, commenting on the apparent fear people seem to have about judging, Arendt claims that "behind the unwillingness to judge lurks the suspicion that no one is a free agent, and hence the doubt that anyone is responsible or could be expected to answer for what he has done" (Arendt 2003, 19).

The Eichmann case taught Arendt two important lessons: (a) that the absence of independent thought in relation to words, to rules, to standards, leads to a failure of judgment; and (b) that the apparent easiness of this absence should indicate a deep suspicion about how rules and standards themselves function. With respect to the latter point, she writes:

> it was as though morality, at the very moment of its total collapse within an old and highly civilized nation, stood revealed in the original meaning of the word, as a set of *mores*, of customs and manners, which could be exchanged for another set with no more trouble than it would take to change the table manners of a whole people. (Arendt 2003, 43; cf 50)

Thus, for Arendt, it is perilous to be complacent and take any rules or standards at face value; she claims that we need "to start thinking and judging instead of applying categories and formulas which are deeply engrained in our mind ..." (2003, 37). Insofar as general rules of morality are "taught and learned until they grow into habits" (2003, 189), they will always risk leading us awry unless we have the ability to think the particular case from outside the terms of the universal. So, for Arendt, it is not so much that thoughtlessness leads to bad judgment: rather it leads to no judgment at all.

Before moving on, I want to sum up what I see, in turn, as Arendt's lessons for education: first, that we would do well to think better of educating values as "habits of mind" (even those cosmopolitan values that we find compelling) for even when we think our values are best, we must recognize that we are not necessarily educating for thinking; and secondly, that making judgments, in Arendt's sense of the word, requires us to think, which means that judgments must be re-personalized even as they are made within the context of our roles as teachers. Thus, Arendt challenges the idea that education can ever be the fulfillment of an "ism," at least not without risking thoughtlessness—and perhaps, consequently, even evil. But how are judgments made exactly, and what has this to do with thinking and promoting more just relations to others, both within and outside the classroom?

THINKING FOR JUDGMENT

At first blush it is easy to see how thinking and judgment might be linked here. One reflects on the standards or the rules one is called upon to use in order to inform one's decisions about what to do with particular cases. To some degree, this is the relation Arendt proposes; but it is not the whole story. For do not thinking and judgment actually do different things?

In depicting how judgments are made, Arendt wishes to move out from underneath the history of philosophy—and religion—which centers the self as a unified entity isolated from others in making judgments. Taking issue with such prescriptions as "Love thy neighbor as thyself," Arendt sees that there is a type of narcissism at play: the self as center of the world as opposed to the self as being in the world with others. So, although she proposes that "morality concerns the individual in his singularity" (2003, 97), it is a funny sort of singularity in that the self exists in the plural: I am I as I appear to others, and I am also myself to myself. Thus being different is part of the very nature of the self—all things identical with themselves are at the same time different from what they are not.[3]

Thinking, for Arendt, is therefore the conversation the I has with itself. It needs no others to engage with; it is, in fact, a necessary retreat from the world of appearances. Thinking is not an activity like others, like an action upon the world, but an internal conversation which has the job of representing to the self things in the abstract: it deals with invisibles. Moreover, thinking does not lead to any "solid axioms" or moral rules of engagement. As Arendt writes, "we cannot expect any moral propositions or commandments, no final code of conduct from the thinking activity, least of all a new and now allegedly final definition of what is good and what is evil" (2003, 167). Thinking is a meditation, a resultless enterprise not fixated on deliberating, or reaching conclusions. It examines unceasingly all creeds, suppositions, standards, and rules. In this sense, thinking poses a danger to established thought. Yet this is a necessary danger, lest one merely becomes subservient to established rules of order. Thus the alternative cannot lie in discouraging thinking:

> By shielding people against the dangers of examination, it teaches them to hold fast to whatever the prescribed rules of conduct may be at a given time in a given society. What people then get used to is not so much the content of the rules … as the possession of rules under which to subsume particulars. (2003, 178)

The radicality of Arendt's conception of thinking lies in the acknowledgment that thinking "does society little good … it does not create values, it will not find out, once and for all, what 'the good' is, and it does not confirm but rather dissolves accepted rules of conduct" (2003, 188). This is a truly revolutionary counterresponse to the ways in which education is often conceived as the purveyor of values and right-thinking standards and as the cultivator of the moral capacity of youth in teaching them appropriate virtues. For what Arendt emphasizes here is the distinction between thought and judgment, the distinction between knowing a rule of conduct and adjudicating our behavior accordingly. This begs the question of how we reconcile thinking with judgment when the latter seems to be very much about deciding as opposed to restlessly ruminating, and what role education has to play in this reconciliation.

Judgment is indeed very different from the activity of thinking as Arendt depicts it. Judgment is not about invisibles, but is concerned with actual persons and circumstances. It is the arbiter of right and wrong in particular cases. Judgment requires that I take others into account, and although I do not conform to their judgments (indeed blindly doing so would not be judgment at all), Arendt is clear that judgment is not purely subjective. I do not simply take my own thinking into account, but that of those others who are prepared to judge themselves. It is here that Arendt establishes the importance of community between fellow-judges. Thus, it is with them that I am in a community of common sense—what Arendt, following Kant, calls "the mother of judgment." It is this intersubjectivity that keeps judgment alive, and not the solo performance of the thinking ego. Judgment is, quite simply, an engagement in a world rich with diversity; it is a cosmopolitan activity. Commenting on Kant, Arendt writes: "One judges always as a member of a community, guided by one's community sense, one's *sensus communis*. But in the last analysis, one is a member of a world community by the sheer fact of being human; this is one's 'cosmopolitan existence'" (Arendt 1992, 75). Moreover, Arendt links this directly to Kant's political hopes for peace. As in his essay "Perpetual Peace," where he articulates his cosmopolitan vision most directly, Kant's critique of judgment situates peace as "the necessary condition for the greatest possible enlargement of the enlarged mentality" (Arendt 1992, 74). In this sense, Arendt sees that judgment itself involves qualities of the cosmopolitan project insofar as it takes place in a broad community of fellow-judges: "When one judges and when one acts in political matters, one is supposed to take one's bearings from the idea, not the actuality of the being a world citizen and, therefore, also a *Weltbetrachter*, a world spectator" (1992, 75–76).

So, how could thinking be related to judgment if the former is always about invisibles, the latter about particular, lived circumstances in a manifold human landscape, a specifically *cosmopolitan* landscape? Arendt (2003) claims that judgment is the "by-product of the liberating effect of thinking" (189); thinking kicks off, as it were, this engagement with the world. It is thus that judgment becomes a *realization* of thinking (188) and it thus is in this sense both determinant and reflexive. Nevertheless, it is not clear to me why thinking has such power to jumpstart the faculty of judgment. Indeed, it is not clear how the solitariness of thinking lends itself to the social, intersubjective sphere of judging. What moves me out of my solitude to come back to the world and offer my judgment in a community of fellow-judges?[4] Given that Arendt's claim is that judgment requires thought to mobilize it—for without thought, we are back to nonjudgment and evil—there is a piece missing from her picture which distorts, I think, the place judgment has in our relations to others. It is a particularly important relation that, in my view, has vital consequences for teaching in general and for "thinking cosmopolitan" in particular.

THE PROVOCATION OF THE OTHER

I believe Arendt is correct in assuming that thinking is a dangerous, critical enterprise, particularly welcomed in times of moral and political conformity. And I agree that thinking is, at least in part, a resultless, restless conversation that I have with myself, and is, by its nature, not of society in the same way that our other activities are. Yet, although I might think in solitude, I want to challenge the idea that thinking *derives* wholly from myself. Arendt was correct in identifying that alterity, or otherness, is fundamental to the internal conversation, but in my view that alterity comes from something exterior to the self—it is precisely what is not-me that enables conversation—whether that conversation happens internally or otherwise. That is, she claims that I am I to myself, but I am also I as I appear to others. Although this leads her to posit a necessary and fundamental social aspect to the nature of the split within the self, there is something about this latter, social aspect that begs the question as to what role the other plays in the formation of my thinking. I want to spend a little time on this here, drawing on the work of Levinas, in order to develop the view that it is precisely because thought comes from the other and not from myself that thinking can be seen to be essential to judgment, and to justice more generally.

It is perhaps helpful to begin this tack with a depiction of what thinking is not for Levinas (1987): "A particular being can take itself to be a totality only if it is thoughtless. Not that it is deceiving itself or thinking badly or foolishly; it is not thinking" (25). This particular being that doesn't think is what Levinas (1987) calls a living being—a being who lives in "ignorance of the exterior world" (25) and who experiences the world only through sensation (26); it is, in short, the biological being whose inner world is undisturbed by the messiness of the outside world around it, its consciousness remaining without problems. "This consciousness is not concerned with situating itself relative to an exteriority, does not grasp itself as part of the whole (for it precedes all grasping); it is a consciousness to which the term the unconscious ... or instinct corresponds" (1987, 26). The portrait of being that Levinas paints here does not represent an actual person who lives entirely in thoughtlessness, but rather depicts an aspect of the ego whose tendency is to totalize its reality, to see its reality as an extension of itself.

In contrast to this, Levinas situates the thinking being as one who is not only in and of the world, but who also recognizes that world as exterior to it. Thus a thinking being is one whose inwardness is dependent upon the presence of an other: the inner world is inner because there is an exterior world from which it is distinct, and to which it is opposed. Thought "establishes a relationship with an exteriority which is not assumed. Qua thinker man is the one for whom the exterior world exists. From that moment on, his so-called biological life, his strictly inward life, is illuminated with thought" (Levinas 1987, 27). One might say that "man" is a totality no longer. The ability to think, then, is set in motion by something outside oneself, not, as in Arendt, by an interior split. As Levinas (1987) writes, "thought begins with the possibility of conceiving a freedom external to my own ... [Indeed] conceiving of a freedom external to my own is the first thought" (28). What it means to think, for Levinas, is a consciousness of my outer world, a consciousness that others exist independently of me, a taking in of something unfamiliar and new. Moreover, consciousness itself is not possible without this exteriority.

Thought thus enables a relation between two, the self and the other, whereas thoughtlessness remains contained within the one, the same. With thinking established as that which is fundamentally connected to alterity—to a radical difference, to a not-me—Levinas simultaneously establishes the ethical character of judgment: the I or ego is susceptible to others in the outside world, to what lies exterior to it. It cannot think without the disruption that only an exterior relation can provide. So although the consequence of thinking may indeed be the conversation one has with oneself, that conversation is provoked into existence by otherness and is not self-constituting.

Recognizing that we do not exist simply as I and other in the world, Levinas introduces the term "third party" to formulate the link between thinking and judgment, or justice. This third party is the *referent* for the human plurality which marks our social and political life. The third is the other's other, the other's neighbor, and hence my own neighbor as well. With this admission comes the difficult task of having to prioritize my attention and my responsibility with respect to my neighbors, in the plural. What was once an ethical responsibility, a total openness to the unique other, changes with the entry of the third party who pulls me away from "this proximity ... away from responsibility prior to all judgment" (Levinas 1998c, 195). Thus this necessity to judge founds thinking; it compels us to evaluate, compare, and thematize. We are already strangely in the realm of justice as we think.

Thus what do we think about as we judge? What kinds of considerations do we need to take into account and what is it that we give up when we judge? It is worth quoting Levinas (1996) at length here:

> Doubtless, responsibility for the other human being is, in its immediacy, anterior to every question. But how does responsibility obligate if a third party troubles this exteriority of two where my subjection of the subject is subjection to the neighbor? The third party is other than the neighbor but also another neighbor, and also a neighbor of the other, and not simply their fellow. What am I to do? What have they already done to one another? Who passes before the other in my responsibility? What, then, are the other and the third party with respect to one another? Birth of the question.
>
> Comparison is superimposed onto my relation with the *unique* and incomparable, and, in view of equity and equality, a weighing, a thinking, a calculation, the comparison of incomparables ... the necessity of thinking together under a synthetic theme ... and through this, finally, the extreme importance in human multiplicity of the political structure of society, subject to laws and institutions ... (168)

In Levinas's view, judgment does not have to be kick-started by thinking, for thinking is already caught up in the bonds of responsible justice by virtue of the self's encounter with exteriority. We can see here, then, that the thinking subject is one who of necessity betrays the ethical covenant of infinite responsibility even as that covenant informs how justice ought to guide our judgments. Justice, for Levinas, is thus an ideal for thought (I have discussed this ideal in terms of Lyotard's interpretation of Kant in chapter 4) which nonetheless grows out of the initial obligation the I has for the other. And it is I, the thinker, who has unique responsibility in the plurality of human faces, in the multitude of neighbors. It is the suffering, now, of my neighbors and not just the singular other, which moves me to judgment. As Richard Cohen has remarked, "Love thy neighbor as thyself" is transformed by Levinas into "Love thy neighbor *is* thyself."

So, as with Arendt, adherence to rules or standards is not part of the substantive nature of justice for Levinas. Justice, although an ideal, has no content. It cannot tell us *what* to decide, it can merely inform us that, through a reminder of the initial obligation that we have for the other, we merely must decide. Thus it is not that universal principles, such as respect or human rights, have no meaning, rather it is that they cannot provide the content of our decisions. As Catherine Chalier (2002) has noted with respect to Levinas, contra Kant, "universal philosophical concepts are put to the test of singularity" (83). Concepts like respect, for instance, are not abstract principles emanating from a prior conception of justice waiting to be applied to my relation to others. As Levinas claims, "respect is not the result of justice.... The one respected is not the one to whom, but the one with whom one renders justice" (1987, 43). Again with Arendt, Levinas posits the intersubjective element of justice as a coendeavor amongst equal subjects who always must be reminded that I am singularly responsible to unique others and their suffering. Like Rancière's (1995) emphasis on the originary equality that exists between humans (albeit in a context of a social order of inequality), Levinas insists on this equality as the very condition of justice. Yet, it is the memory of the other's "useless suffering" that informs this equality (Levinas 1998b).

At this point, I want to interject this Levinasian story of thinking (and Arendt's for that matter) with an Irigarayan question concerning sexed subjectivity.[5] The "man" of whom Levinas speaks above is, of course, deeply problematic from the perspective I have taken in various chapters here. For if humanity itself is at least two, then the thinking being itself can no longer simply reflect one side of subjectivity—man—however much we insist on the concreteness of that subject's relation to the other. Is there a way to speak of a thinking being, in Levinasian terms, that recognizes the sexuate nature of subjectivity so that the different ways the two sexes inhabit the world through their morphologies matters? That is, if my being in the world conditions the way I encounter exteriority, then it would seem to be crucial that the ways in which that world is mediated by a sexed body actually makes a difference to a thinking being. This is in no way to suggest that one can relegate some essential aspects of thinking to each of the sexes, but to recognize that in the relation between self and world, different kinds of encounters with the other open up different opportunities for thought. This latter point is one that I think is entirely commensurate with the spirit of Levinas's idea that it is concrete encounters between self and other which give rise to thought. Although Levinas's philosophy is incapable of providing the necessary groundwork for thinking this aspect of human pluralism, my point is that there is nonetheless room in it for complicating how thinking comes into being differently for each subject, dependent as it is on the concrete relation to the other that the subject has.

I read thinking as central in judgment not only because of what thinking can do (critique, challenge, reflect), but that it does so fundamentally in relation to human plurality. Thinking has a fundamentally cosmopolitan quality, one that, I think, can incorporate an understanding of the sexed difference of humanity on Irigarayan terms. Thought is not simply a flight into solitude, but a relation across radical difference where my thinking is enabled by the provocation of others. This means that although thinking is a distinct form of conversation, it nonetheless is occasioned by the conscious recognition of exteriority and the freedom of others. Thus both Arendt and Levinas are right in asserting that rules or standards (morality, quite simply) are not the stuff of judgment; rather it is the unique thinker who is responsible for the judgments he or she makes.

THINKING COSMOPOLITAN IN EDUCATION

Thinking cosmopolitan, on this view, presents a shift from a focus on the principles of cosmopolitan*ism* to a focus on how the pluralism of existence itself is involved in mediating and translating principles in and through concrete situations with others. It is not that the inherited tradition of cosmopolitanism has nothing important to say to us in terms of rights, hospitality, and broader notions of belonging, but that it fails to address adequately the field of human plurality, with all its so-called inhumanity, conflict, and antagonism by relying too readily on humanity and universality to deliver us from our sins. Moreover, as I have discussed in the immediately preceding pages, it is precisely the way we judge and how we think that matters deeply to creating conditions that can begin the difficult work of facing humanity in education.

In proposing that "thinking cosmopolitan" provides us with some insight into judgment, I am wary, however, of promoting yet another rule or standard against which teachers evaluate their own judgments. Instead, I think we would do well to think, rather, of judgments as *moments that fix thinking in time*, that implicate teachers in the here and now of their work. For judgment is, ultimately, about implication: it is a definite decision that breaks with the duration of thought. And it reveals precisely the point where teachers feel the pull between the professional and the personal most profoundly: judgment commits "me" to something. There is a basic paradox to be faced in teaching when it comes to judgment, for if judgment is that which exceeds rules, and devotes itself to particular cases, then it is clear that teachers must perform as teachers in ways that cannot do justice to others. By this I mean that teachers' decisions often are made in the context of the rules of the profession and the culture of the school, with the result that the particularities of a case are neglected in the exigency of coming to a decision. Thought is not always possible in teaching. But how much thoughtlessness can we tolerate and how much can we hide behind the veil our professional roles afford us?

It seems clear that where we draw that line has precisely to do with personal, not professional, judgment. It is not that all professional judgment is an unthinking reliance on rules and standards. Indeed, I would hope that a notion of the professional, of the teacher's role itself, could allow for the paradoxes and tensions teachers often experience. Moreover, I would hope too that that role could also incorporate personal aspects of the teacher herself. But, in cases of a sensitive nature, such as cultural conflict, for example, where a cosmopolitan ethic cannot provide us with a useful guide, then we also seem to require a much fuller language for how we make judgments in ways that do not forget the nature of justice in the process. For it is precisely here where teachers are most likely to fall back on routine and procedure in an attempt to escape the discomfort and unease that conflicts entail.

Given the kind of work teachers do, there is often not a lot of time for thinking and so we need to reflect on how we can propose a thoughtful orientation to our judgments; that is, to think about our roles as opposed to letting those roles determine our thinking. Such a thoughtfulness, whose nature I hope has now become clear, refuses both the simplicity of self-righteous moralizing and the anonymity provided by standards and rules. It is a thoughtfulness which carries within it a cosmopolitan sense: a thought that is born from others who are my neighbors. And so, how do teachers carry out judgments concerning complex matters of values, rights, and equality, for instance, without falling back *unthinkingly* on abstract rules? It seems to me that "thinking cosmopolitan," as opposed to "thinking according to cosmopolitanism" allows us some room for acknowledging the ideal of justice that prevails in making judgments, and puts human diversity at the centre of what too often appears to be a solitary enterprise. For cosmopolitanism, it seems to me, is precisely about an openness to the indefinite, and if we are going to attempt to inaugurate forms of belonging that resist the narrow nationalisms which have thus far shaped so much educational content, then it means having to think "without a banister" as Arendt was fond of saying (cited in Arendt 2003, xxxvii). And this includes even those banisters—like cosmopolitanism—that we believe actually might be of the most help.

NOTES

1. My use of the term "ethic" here is not meant to suggest that all writers who advocate for cosmopolitanism do so under the name of an "ethic," but they do commonly agree on a shared set of values that are central to their cosmopolitan outlook, and it is this to which I am referring: world citizenship, empathy with global "neighbors," commitment to human rights, respect for human diversity in all its manifestations.

2. For differences within the literature on cosmopolitanism, see for example Derek Heater's (2002) discussion which takes a more equivocal position and

focuses on the pros and cons of cosmopolitan and communitarian arguments with respect to world citizenship. Appiah (2006) in his discussion of cosmopolitanism and its ethical dimensions focuses on commonalities across differences (particularly with respect to certain "universal" values) and makes appeals to "humanity" without sufficiently addressing the specific tensions between rights and human pluralism that inevitably arise when discussions are forged on how one decides—and who is to decide—on what is common between us.

3. See Arendt's (1978) discussion on these points in more detail in the first book of *The Life of the Mind: Thinking*.

4. Although Arendt (1978) discusses in *Willing*, the second book in *The Life of the Mind*, that the I returns to the world in action where "a We is always engaged in changing our common world, stands in the sharpest possible opposition to the solitary business of thought, which operates in a dialogue between me and myself" (200), she nonetheless does not attribute to the Will the capacity to aid in making judgments. Will, though central to Arendt's conception of political action and freedom, is little discussed in direct relation to the connection between thinking and judgment.

5. I confine myself here to a brief "Irigarayan" intervention for the very reason that Irigaray herself has spent little time on the nature of judgment. Although we have seen in chapter 7 her views on the way established thought has been subtended by a male imaginary, her work largely has focused on the mobilization of language for critique and transformation and has not paid so much attention to thinking directly. I suspect that a reason for this is that she would read the philosophical discussion on thinking as itself representing a truncated view of humanity. Nonetheless, my own view is that both Arendt and Levinas, by focusing on the concrete, the particular and the singular open a space through which Irigaray's concerns for the sexuate nature of being can be taken into consideration. Although there is far more to be said on the complications of importing Irigaray's thought into this space, this is beyond the scope of this chapter—and indeed warrants a book-length study in itself.

Epilogue:

Toward an Imperfect Education

The various chapters in this book have sought to reframe attention to certain features of cosmopolitanism—namely, human rights, democracy, and citizenship—by exploring the problematic idea of humanity they are often based upon. I have mapped this assumption of humanity onto the fault lines of cosmopolitanism and identified these as part of its inheritance of a divided modernity. In particular, I have focused on the paradoxical commitment to universal rights and respect for cultural diversity and have shown how this cannot be resolved through an emphasis on rights as moral "trump cards" that will somehow temper the relativistic tendencies of human pluralism. Indeed, by focusing on processes of negotiation and cultural translation, I have argued that universal claims themselves are always subject to refinement, redefinition, and reformulation. Without this possibility, it seems to me, we risk an abstraction that seems to live a life of its own and thus becomes petrified into lifeless precepts that have little to do with the ongoing human communicative practices through which values, commitments, and "universals" are in fact posited.

Overall, two major claims have occupied center stage in my argument. The first has been that the idea of humanity underpinning cosmopolitan efforts in education currently diminishes the potential to deal with human pluralism meaningfully. The task of challenging the sameness upon which an idea of humanity is based is not to assume that there are no common bonds, no bridges to be built, no sharing of values, principles and perspectives. It is, rather, that such commonalities grow out of the very differences that structure the plurality of human life. If there is any commonality to be found, it lies in the different ways in which we are radically uncommon to each other, diverse in existence and therefore unique in one's being. Hence my contention that the idea of humanity needs to be rethought in terms that privilege otherness and difference as a condition for justice. It is in relation to others who are not like myself that thought and the capacity to judge across the divide that separates me from my neighbor are provoked. It is, I have claimed, this radical disjunction of pluralism that is needed in order to have just and thoughtful relations in the first place. Moreover, this means that if humanity is fundamentally plural, then it cannot be posited as a singular, unified portrait of what we think constitutes the perfect subject. Pluralism by its very nature resists an idea of humanity that seeks to contain everyone within a totalizing image.

Secondly, connected to my emphasis on pluralism has been the stress placed on conflict, antagonism, disagreement, and the potential for violence. A major assertion has been that if we are to take justice seriously, then it is the conflictual dimensions of the human condition that warrant our attention. That is, working toward the amelioration of the plight of others cannot be achieved through ignoring the very human aspects of conflict or relegating to them to some realm of the "inhuman" that no longer has any connection to an idea of humanity itself. What this does, as I have suggested, is to erase "imperfection" in the name of the perfectibility of the human subject. It is not that those cosmopolitanists who call for the development of our capacities for reason, empathy, and understanding are ignorant of the existence of human conflict around the globe. It is, rather, that terms such as "cultivating" humanity reveal the extent to which the capacity for violence falls outside the purview of what is meant by humanity here. This disavowal of the humanness of violence lends itself to an idealized account of humanity that is inadequate for tackling the seriousness of conflict and antagonism. A critical point of departure for me has been to resist the assumption that education ought to overcome these imperfections by refocusing its attention on this idealized image. Instead, collectively, the chapters have centered on the idea that the real, and perhaps formidable, task of education is to *face* humanity, in all its imperfection.

Education, on this view, cannot be aligned with cultivating humanity, promoting virtues, or implementing principles per se, but is intimately tied to the practices through which engaging our human limitations is seen to provide the best possibilities of keeping open the "language game of justice" (Lyotard), of transforming "antagonism into agonism" (Mouffe), of focusing on "human becoming as—at least—two" (Irigaray), of "affirming human rights through critique" (Derrida), of "attending to the suffering of others" (Levinas), and of recognizing the singularity of judgment within the horizon of our "cosmopolitan existence" (Arendt). How I am viewing the potential for working toward an imperfect education is very much rooted in a shift from a cosmopolitanism that, on the one hand, seeks to encapsulate pluralism within universal commitments or, on the other hand, seeks to ignore the very heart of cosmopolitan right as a right of humanity by focusing solely on cultural diversity and hybridity. Indeed, the former leads to a profound denial of human plurality in its principled approach, while the latter treats the whole question of universality as some antique relic that no longer holds in the postcolonial and postmodern world of globalization. For education, the shift that I am advocating gives up on the idea of "ism" altogether, and focuses on the adjectival possibilities of the term cosmopolitan. In speaking, for instance, of a cosmopolitan existence as framing the horizon for judgment and thought, emphasis is placed on the ways individual subjects negotiate, both morally and politically, the particular contexts, traditions, and circumstances through which they live their lives.

Turning to cosmopolitan thinking and judgment requires a recognition of the imperfection of both the principles we hold and the human condition we are part of. It lives within the paradox of the inherited legacy of cosmopolitanism by recognizing as its task the very movement between posited universals and diversity of specific cases. Moreover, it recognizes that situated contexts are the only ones through which we continually negotiate and translate what is given us in the world in order to create something new. Education, as Arendt points out, is concerned with a "world that is out of joint." It is an imperfect world that no solutions concerned with perfectibility can possibly respond to adequately. My simple take is that educating in such a world demands an education of humility not hubris. No universal principles can secure justice, since its promise lies in keeping open the question of justice itself. No fixed idea of humanity can substitute for the humanity that is always yet to come and never unified. No consensus can bring about equality or democracy, which require dissensus and disagreement. No right can secure the well-being of a human life without acknowledging its never-ending place in processes of negotiation and translation. No principles or virtues can guarantee the moral betterment of society if individuals apply them unthinkingly *as* principles. And, finally, no human being can be expected to become an abstract idea of itself, even one infused with the capacity for rationality, empathy, and understanding.

This means that education is eminently banal even as it aims to rise above the dissonant, daily rumbles of social life. Educational projects that define their aims in terms of peaceful coexistence, the elimination of discrimination, abuse and violence, and the promotion of justice across cultural differences are crucial for creating possibilities for social transformation. My point has been to question neither the existence of these aims in educational thought and practice nor their necessity for moving us toward alternative visions of social life other than the received ones. Rather, I have questioned the underlying assumptions, their omissions, and their formulas for getting us there. The quest and challenge is to resignify what they mean in specific contexts and the everydayness of human relationality. Thus the claim that education is banal means having to give up not on our aims, but on the ways in which we think about them.

Such thought, I suggest, is cosmopolitan insofar as it participates within a horizon of human diversity and difference, and has relevance for two dimensions of education. First, it asks us as educationalists to consider the ways in which our concepts and principles, however dearly we hold them, continually undergo change in relation to the specific contexts in which we find ourselves and in relation to the language we use to talk about them. The cosmopolitan aspect comes in at the moment we recognize that meeting an other who is not like me is not only an *encounter* with another's point of view, but is an *exchange*: it is itself a provocation and potential source of new thought. It means that we cannot prepare in advance what this exchange will offer us, and we cannot assume that even our most well-defined principles are impervious to alteration. Particularly when it comes to relatively firm ideas about human rights, democracy, and citizenship, educational encounters are about exchanges that have the potential to transform the ways in which we think and speak about them. In other words, in giving up the idea of the perfectibility of principles and in accepting their incomplete and imperfect character, we gain the possibility of insight that only an openness to exchange can grant us.

Secondly, if we accept that education is banal in this sense I've suggested above, it is well-nigh impossible to insist that cherished principles can ever be transferred onto "impressionable" youth. Rather, the educational focus is on the processes of negotiation and translation that youth employ in their engagement with rights, democracy, and citizenship. This requires, it seems to me, an entirely different emphasis on engaging students around these issues, one that highlights the fractured nature of the ideas themselves and the dilemmas they pose to social life. As I discussed previously in relation to human rights, education is often perceived to be instrumental, a vehicle through which students learn about rights and how to apply them to particular cases of abuse, but are rarely engaged in the very dilemmas of judgment as an everyday exercise in negotiation. Similarly, teaching youth how to conduct rational argument misses the extraordinary manner in which democracy is an ongoing, antagonistic struggle that no amount of rationality can smooth over. Moreover, exploring issues of citizenship as a mere series of already inscribed entitlements and obligations obfuscates the ways in which particular subjects are constrained within them, and leaves to the side, therefore, the hope that it can be otherwise.

Developing a perspective of specificity in education is not some sly maneuver that ushers relativism in the backdoor. It is rather a complex moral and political engagement with pluralism that allows us to focus on the ways in which individuals, and their becoming, matter to the furthering of justice—and education itself. Far from being a top-down approach, it enables us to put particularity and universality in conversation with one another and to confront the limitations and possibilities that inhere within inherited ways of thought as they come into contact with the students we teach. Most of all, it compels us to confront the difficulties and imperfections that all interhuman exchange entails as an indelible feature of our cosmopolitan existence. Humanity, in this light, is no mere abstraction, but is a responsibility that grows from my proximity to actual others. So, although we do not share humanity, we do share a world with others and this demands nothing more and nothing less of us than to face the individuals we share it with. Can this not be where a renewed cosmopolitan project in education begins?

References

Ahmed, Leila. 1992. *Women and Gender in Islam*. New Haven, CT: Yale University Press.

Aloni, Nimrod. 2002. *Enhancing Humanity: The Philosophical Foundations of Humanistic Education*. Dordrecht: Springer Publishers.

Anderson, Amanda. 1998. "Cosmopolitanism, Universalism, and the Divided Legacies of Modernity." In *Cosmopolitics: Thinking and Feeling Beyond the Nation*, edited by P. Cheah and B. Robbins, 265–289. Minneapolis: University of Minnesota Press.

Anderson-Gold, Sharon. 2001. *Cosmopolitanism and Human Rights*. Cardiff: University of Wales Press.

Andreopoulos, George J. 1997. "Human Rights Education in the Post–Cold War Context." In *Human Rights Education for the Twenty-First Century*, edited by G. J. Andreopoulos and R. P. Claude, 9–20. Philadelphia: Pennsylvania University Press.

Andreopoulos, George J., and Richard Pierre Claude, eds. 1997. *Human Rights Education for the Twenty-First Century*. Philadelphia: Pennsylvania University Press.

Apel, Karl-Otto. 2000. "Globalization and the Need for Universal Ethics." *European Journal of Social Theory* 3 (3): 137–155.

Appiah, Kwame Anthony. 2006. *Cosmopolitanism: Ethics in a World of Strangers*. New York: Norton.

Archibugi, Daniele. 1998. Principles of Cosmopolitan Democracy. In *Re-imagining Political Community: Studies in Cosmopolitan Democracy*, edited by D. Archibugi, D. Held and M. Köhler, 198–228. Stanford: Stanford University Press.

Archibugi, Daniele. 2003. Cosmopolitical Democracy. In *Debating Cosmopolitics*, edited by D. Archibugi, 1–15. London: Verso.

Archibugi, Daniele, David Held, and Martin Köhler, eds. 1998. *Re-imagining Political Community: Studies in Cosmopolitan Democracy*. Stanford: Stanford University Press.

Arendt, Hannah. 1959. *The Human Condition*. New York: Anchor Books.

Arendt, Hannah. 1965. *Between Past and Future: Six Exercises in Political Thought*. New York: Meridian.

Arendt, Hannah. 1978. *The Life of the Mind*. New York: Harcourt.

Arendt, Hannah. 1992. *Lectures on Kant's Political Philosophy*. Chicago: University of Chicago Press.

Arendt, Hannah. 1994. *Eichmann in Jerusalem: A Report on the Banality of Evil*. New York: Harcourt.

Arendt, Hannah. 2003. *Responsibility and Judgment*. Edited by J. Kohn. New York: Schocken Books.

Arendt, Hannah. 2004. *The Origins of Totalitarianism*. New York: Schocken Books.

Assemblée Nationale du France. 2004. Le loi encadrant, en application du principe de laïcité, le port de signes ou de tenues manifestant une appartenance religieuse dans les école, collèges et lycées publics.

Badiou, Alain. 2007. *The Century*. Translated by A. Toscano. Cambridge: Polity Press.

Bauman, Zygmunt. 1993. *Postmodern Ethics*. Oxford: Blackwell.

Bauman, Zygmunt. 1999. *In Search of Politics*. Stanford: Stanford University Press.

Baxi, Upendra. 1997. "Human Rights Education: The Promise of a Third Millennium?" In *Human Rights Education for the Twenty-First Century*, edited by G. J. Andreopoulos and R. P. Claude, 142–154. Philadelphia: University of Pennsylvania Press.

Beck, Ulrich. 2006. *The Cosmopolitan Vision*. Translated by C. Cronin. Cambridge: Polity.

Benhabib, Seyla. 2002. *The Claims of Culture: Equality and Diversity in the Global Era*. Princeton: Princeton University Press.

Benhabib, Seyla. 2004. *The Rights of Others: Aliens, Residents and Citizens*. Cambridge: Cambridge University Press.

Benhabib, Seyla. 2006. *Another Cosmopolitanism*. Oxford: Oxford University Press.

Berlin, Isaiah. 2002. *Liberty*. Edited by H. Hardy. Oxford: Oxford University Press.

Biesta, Gert J.J. 2006. *Beyond Learning: Democratic Education for a Human Future*. Boulder, CO: Paradigm Publishers.

Binion, Gayle. 1995. "Human Rights: A Feminist Perspective." *Human Rights Quarterly* 17 (3): 509–526.

Bohman, James, and Matthias Lutz-Bachman, eds. 1997. *Perpetual Peace: Essays on Kant's Cosmopolitan Ideal*. Cambridge: MIT Press.

Breckenridge, Carol A., Sheldon Pollock, Homi K. Bhabha, and Dipesh Chakrabarty, eds. 2002. *Cosmopolitanism*. Durham NC: Duke University Press.

Brems, Eva. 1997. "Enemies or Allies? Feminism and Cultural Relativism as Dissident Voices in Human Rights Discourse." *Human Rights Quarterly* 19 (1): 136–164.

Burggraeve, Roger. 2002. *The Wisdom of Love in the Service of Love: Emmanuel Levinas on Justice, Peace and Human Rights*. Translated by J. Bloechl. Milwaukee: Marquette University Press.

Burke, Carolyn. 1981. "Irigaray Through the Looking Glass." *Feminist Studies* 7 (2): 288–306.

Burke, Carolyn, Naomi Schor, and Margaret Whitford, eds. 1994. *Engaging with Irigaray*. New York: Columbia University Press.

Butler, Judith. 1990. *Gender Trouble: Feminism and the Subversion of Identity*. New York: Routledge.

Butler, Judith. 1993. *Bodies That Matter: On the Discursive Limits of "Sex"*. New York: Routledge.

Butler, Judith. 2000. "Restaging the Universal: Hegemony and the Limits of Formalism." In *Contingency, Hegemony, Universality*, edited by J. Butler, E. Laclau and S. Žižek, 11–43. London: Verso.

Calhoun, Craig. 2003. "The Class Consciousness of Frequent Travellers: Towards a Critique of Actually Existing Cosmopolitanism." In *Debating Cosmopolitics*, edited by D. Archibugi, 86–116. London: Verso.

Chalier, Catherine. 2002. *What Ought I to Do?* Translated by J. M. Todd. Ithaca: Cornell University Press.

Cheah, Pheng. 1998. "Given Culture: Rethinking Cosmopolitical Freedom in Transnationalism." In *Cosmopolitics: Thinking and Feeling Beyond the Nation*, edited by P. Cheah and B. Robbins, 290–328. Minneapolis: University of Minnesota Press.

Cimitile, Maria C., and Elaine P. Miller, eds. 2007. *Returning to Irigaray: Feminist Philosophy, Politics, and the Question of Unity*. Albany, NY: State University of New York Press.

Coomaraswamy, Radhika. 1994. "To Bellow Like a Cow: Women, Ethnicity, and the Discourse of Rights." In *Human Rights of Women: National and International Perspectives*, edited by R. J. Cook, 39–57. University Park, PA: Pennsylvania State University Press.

Cornell, Drucilla. 2003. "Facing Our Humanity." *Hypatia* 18 (1): 170–174.

Critchley, Simon. 1999. *Ethics, Politics, Subjectivity*. London: Verso.

Critchley, Simon. 2004. "Five Problems in Levinas's View of Politics and the Sketch of a Solution to Them." *Political Theory* 32 (2): 172–185.

Critchley, Simon. 2007. *Infinitely Demanding: Ethics of Commitment, Politics of Resistance*. London: Verso.

Derrida, Jacques. 1978. "Violence and Metaphysics: An Essay on the Thought of Emmanuel Levinas." In *Writing and Difference*, 79–153. Chicago: University of Chicago Press.

Derrida, Jacques. 1997. *Politics of Friendship*. Translated by G. Collins. London: Verso.

Derrida, Jacques. 1999. *Adieu to Emmanuel Levinas*. Translated by P.-A. Brault and M. Naas. Stanford: Stanford University Press.

Derrida, Jacques. 2000. *Of Hospitality*. Translated by R. Bowlby. Stanford: Stanford University Press.

Derrida, Jacques. 2001. Talking Liberties. In *Derrida and Education*, edited by G. J. J. Biesta and D. Egéa-Kuehne, 176–185. London: Routledge.

Derrida, Jacques. 2002. *On Cosmopolitanism and Forgiveness*. Translated by M. Dooley and M. Hughes. London: Routledge.

Derrida, Jacques. 2003. "Autoimmunity: Real and Symbolic Suicides." In *Philosophy in the Time of Terror: Dialogues with Jürgen Habermas and Jacques Derrida*, edited by G. Borradi, 85–136. Chicago: University of Chicago Press.

Derrida, Jacques. 2005. *Rogues: Two Essays on Reason*. Translated by P.-A. Brault and M. Naas. Stanford: Stanford University Press.

Deutscher, Penelope. 2002. *A Politics of Impossible Difference: The Later Work of Luce Irigaray*. Ithaca: Cornell University Press.

Enslin, Penny, and Mary Tjiattas. 2004. "Cosmopolitan Justice: Education and Global Citizenship." *Theoria: A Journal of Social and Political Theory* 104: 150–169.

Fauré, Christine. 1981. "The Twilight of the Goddesses, or the Intellectual Crisis of French Feminism." *SIGNS* 7 (1): 81–86.

Felman, Shoshana. 2002. *The Juridical Unconscious: Trials and Traumas in the Twentieth Century*. Cambridge: Harvard University Press.

Fine, Robert. 2003. "Taking the 'ism' out of Cosmopolitanism: An Essay in Reconstruction." *European Journal of Social Theory* 6 (4): 451–470.

Fine, Robert, and Robin Cohen. 2002. "Four Cosmopolitan Moments." In *Conceiving Cosmopolitanism: Theory, Context and Practice*, edited by S. Vertovec and R. Cohen, 137–162. Oxford: Oxford University Press.

Føyn, Sissel H. 1994. "1993- A Breakthrough for Increased Focus." *European Journal of Education* 29 (4): 355–362.

Fuss, Diana. 1989. *Essentially Speaking*. New York: Routledge.

Gallagher, Anne. 1997. "Ending the Marginalization: Strategies for Incorporating Women into the United Nations Human Rights System." *Human Rights Quarterly* 19 (2): 283–333.

Gallop, Jane. 1983. "Quand nos lèvres s'écrivent: Irigaray's Body Politic." *Romanic Review* 74: 77–83.

Gereluk, Dianne. 2008. *Symbolic Clothing in Schools*. London: Continuum.

Gibbs, Robert. 2000. *Why Ethics? Signs of Responsibility*. Princeton: Princeton University Press.

Goux, Jean-Joseph. 1994. "Luce Irigaray Versus the Utopia of the Neutral Sex." In *Engaging with Irigaray*, edited by C. Burke, N. Schor and M. Whitford, 175–190. New York: Columbia University Press.

Grosz, Elizabeth. 1989. *Sexual Subversions*. Sydney: Allen and Unwin.

Habermas, Jürgen. 1996. *Between Facts and Norms: Contributions to a Discourse Theory of Law and Democracy*. Translated by W. Rehg. Cambridge: Polity Press.

Hansen, David. 2008. "Education through a Cosmopolitan Prism." Conference presentation. *Philosophy of Education Society*. Cambridge, Massachusetts.

Heater, Derek. 1991. "The Curriculum Jigsaw and Human Rights Education." In *The Challenge of Human Rights Education*, edited by H. Starkey. London: Cassel, Council of Europe Series.

Heater, Derek. 2002. *World Citizenship: Cosmopolitanism Thinking and Its Opponents*. New York: Continuum.

Held, David. 2005. "The Principles of Cosmopolitan Order." In *The Political Philosophy of Cosmopolitanism*, edited by G. Brock and H. Brighouse, 10–27. Cambridge: Cambridge University Press.

Heller, Agnes. 1992. "Rights, Modernity and Democracy." In *Deconstruction and the Possibility of Justice*, edited by D. Cornell, M. Rosenfeld and D. G. Carlson, 346–360. New York: Routledge.

Holmlund, Christine. 1991. "The Lesbian, the Mother, the Heterosexual Lover: Irigaray's Recodings of Difference." *Feminist Studies* 17 (2): 283–308.

Honig, Bonnie. 1999. "'My Culture Made Me Do It'." In *Is Multiculturalism Bad for Women?*, edited by S. M. Okin, J. Cohen, M. Howard and M. Nussbaum, 35–40. Princeton: Princeton University Press.

Honig, Bonnie. 2006. "Another Cosmopolitanism? Law and Politics in the New Europe." In *Another Cosmopolitanism*, 102–127. Oxford: Oxford University Press.

Ignatieff, Michael. 2000. *The Rights Revolution*. Toronto: House of Anansi Press.

Ignatieff, Michael. 2001. *Human Rights as Politics and Idolatry*. Princeton: Princeton University Press.

Irigaray, Luce. 1985a. *Speculum of the Other Woman*. Translated by G. C. Gill. Ithaca: Cornell University Press.

Irigaray, Luce. 1985b. *This Sex Which Is Not One*. Translated by C. P. with and C. Burke. Ithaca: Cornell University Press.

Irigaray, Luce. 1993a. *An Ethics of Sexual Difference*. Translated by C. Burke and G. C. Gill. Ithaca: Cornell University Press.

Irigaray, Luce. 1993b. *Sexes and Genealogies*. Translated by G. C. Gill. New York: Columbia University Press.

Irigaray, Luce. 1994. *Thinking the Difference: For a Peaceful Revolution*. Translated by K. Montin. New York: Routledge.

Irigaray, Luce. 1996. *I Love to You*. Translated by A. Martin. New York: Routledge.

Irigaray, Luce. 2001a. *Democracy Begins between Two*. Translated by K. Anderson. New York: Routledge.

Irigaray, Luce. 2001b. *To Be Two*. Translated by M. M. Rhodes and M. F. Cocito-Monoc. New York: Routledge.

Irigaray, Luce. 2002a. *Between East and West: From Singularity to Community*. Translated by S. Pluháček. New York: Columbia University Press.

Irigaray, Luce. 2002b. *The Way of Love*. Translated by H. Bostic and S. Pluháček. New York: Continuum.

Kant, Immanuel. 1906. *On Education*. Translated by A. Churton. Boston: D.C. Heath & Co.

Kant, Immanuel. 1991. "Perpetual Peace: A Philosophical Sketch." In *Political Writings*, edited by H. S. Reiss, 93–130. Cambridge: Cambridge University Press.

Kant, Immanuel. 1997. *Critique of Practical Reason*. Translated by M. Gregor. Cambridge: Cambridge University Press.

Kant, Immanuel. 2003. *To Perpetual Peace: A Philosophical Sketch*. Translated by T. Humphrey. Indianapolis: Hackett Publishing.

Kemp, Peter. 2005. *Världmedborgen: Politisk och Pedagogisk Filosofi för det 21 Århundradet. [World Citizens: Political and Educational Philosophy for the 21st Century]*. Translated by J. Retzlaff. Göteborg: Daidalos.

Kristeva, Julia. 1991. *Strangers to Ourselves*. Translated by L. S. Roudiez. New York: Columbia University Press.

Kristeva, Julia. 1993. *Nations without Nationalism*. Translated by L. S. Roudiez. New York: Columbia University Press.

Kristeva, Julia. 2000. *Crisis of the European Subject*. Translated by S. Fairfield. New York: Other Press.

Laclau, Ernesto, and Chantal Mouffe. 2001. *Hegemony and Socialist Strategy: Towards a Radical Democratic Politics*. 2nd ed. London: Verso.

Levinas, Emmanuel. 1969. *Totality and Infinity: An Essay on Exteriority*. Translated by A. Lingus. Pittsburgh: Duquesne University Press.

Levinas, Emmanuel. 1985. *Ethics and Infinity*. Translated by R. A. Cohen. Pittsburgh: Duquesne University Press.

Levinas, Emmanuel. 1987. "The Ego and the Totality." In *Collected Philosophical Papers*, 25–45. The Hague: Martinus Nijhoff.

Levinas, Emmanuel. 1994. "The Rights of Man and the Rights of the Other." In *Outside the Subject*, 116–125. New York: Columbia University Press.

Levinas, Emmanuel. 1996. Peace and Proximity. In *Basic Philosophical Writings*, edited by A. T. Peperzak, S. Critchley and R. Bernasconi, 161–169. Bloomington: Indiana University Press.

Levinas, Emmanuel. 1998a. *Otherwise Than Being or Beyond Essence*. Translated by A. Lingis. Pittsburgh: Duquesne University Press.

Levinas, Emmanuel. 1998b. "Useless Suffering." In *Entre Nous: On Thinking-of-the-Other*, 91–102. Translated by M. B. Smith and B. Harshav. New York: Columbia University Press.

Levinas, Emmanuel. 1998c. Uniqueness. In *Entre Nous: On Thinking-of-the-Other*, 189–196. Translated by M. B. Smith and B. Harshav. New York: Columbia University Press.

Levinas, Emmanuel. 1999a. "The Rights of the Other Man." In *Alterity and Transcendence*, 145–149. New York: Columbia University Press.

Levinas, Emmanuel. 1999b. "The Violence of the Face." In *Alterity and Transcendence*, 169–182. New York: Columbia University Press.

Levinas, Emmanuel. 2001. "Philosophy, Justice, and Love." In *Is It Righteous to Be? Interviews with Emmanuel Levinas*, edited by J. Robbins, 165–181. Stanford: Stanford University Press.

Levinas, Emmanuel. 2003. "Humanism and An-Archy." In *Humanism of the Other*, 45–57. Urbana, Ill.: University of Illinois Press.

Linklater, Andrew. 1998. *The Transformation of Political Community*. Cambridge: Polity Press.

Lister, Ian. 1991. "The Challenge of Human Rights for Education." In *The Challenge of Human Rights Education*, edited by H. Starkey. London: Cassell, Council of Europe Series.

Løvlie, Lars, Klaus Peter Mortensen, and Sven-Erik Nordenbo, eds. 2003. *Educating Humanity: Bildung in Postmodernity*. Oxford: Blackwell.

Lyotard, Jean-François. 1988. *The Differend: Phrases in Dispute*. Translated by G. Van den Abbeele. Minneapolis: University of Minnesota Press.

Lyotard, Jean-François. 1991. *The Inhuman: Reflections on Time*. Translated by G. Bennington and R. Bowlby. Cambridge: Polity Press.

Lyotard, Jean-François, and Jean-Loup Thébaud. 1985. *Just Gaming*. Translated by W. Godzich. Minneapolis: University of Minnesota Press.

Malcomson, Scott L. 1998. "The Varieties of Cosmopolitan Experience." In *Cosmopolitics: Thinking and Feeling Beyond the Nation*, edited by P. Cheah and B. Robbins, 233–245. Minneapolis: University of Minnesota Press.

Mitchell, Juliet, and Jacqueline Rose, eds. 1985. *Feminine Sexuality: Jacques Lacan and the École Freudienne*. New York: W.W. Norton.

Mignolo, Walter D. 2002. "The Many Faces of Cosmo-polis: Border Thinking and Critical Cosmopolitanism." In *Cosmopolitanism*, edited by C. A. Breckenridge, S. Pollock, H. K. Bhabha and D. Chakrabarty, 157–188. Durham, NC: Duke University Press.

Moellendorf, Darrel. 2005. "Persons' Interests, States' Duties, and Global Governance." In *The Political Philosophy of Cosmopolitanism*, edited by G. Brock and H. Brighouse, 148–163. Cambridge: Cambridge University Press.

Mouffe, Chantal. 1993. *The Return of the Political*. London: Verso.

Mouffe, Chantal. 2000. *The Democratic Paradox*. London: Verso.

Mouffe, Chantal. 2005. *On the Political*. London: Routledge.

Noddings, Nel, ed. 2005. *Educating Citizens for Global Awareness*. New York: Teachers College Press.

Nussbaum, Martha. 1994. "Patriotism and Cosmopolitanism." *Boston Review* 19 (5) http://www.soci.niu.edu/-phildept/Kapitan/nussbaum1.html).

Nussbaum, Martha. 1997a. *Cultivating Humanity: A Classical Defense of Reform in Liberal Education*. Cambridge, MA: Harvard University Press.

Nussbaum, Martha. 1997b. "Kant and Cosmopolitanism." In *Perpetual Peace: Essays on Kant's Cosmopolitan Ideal*, edited by J. Bohman and M. Lutz-Bachman, 25–58. Cambridge, MA: MIT Press.

O'Hare, Ursula A. 1999. "Realizing Human Rights for Women." *Human Rights Quarterly* 21 (2): 364–402.

Okin, Susan Moller. 1999. "Is Multiculturalism Bad for Women?" In *Is Multiculturalism Bad for Women?*, edited by S. M. Okin, J. Cohen, M. Howard and M. Nussbaum, 7–24. Princeton: Princeton University Press.

Osler, Audrey, and Hugh Starkey. 2003. "Learning for Cosmopolitan Citizenship: Theoretical Debates and Young People's Experiences." *Educational Review* 55 (3): 243–254.

Papastephanou, Marianna. 2002. "Arrows Not Yet Fired: Cultivating Cosmopolitanism Through Education." *Journal of Philosophy of Education* 36 (1): 69–86.

Parekh, Bhikhu. 2000. *Rethinking Multiculturalism: Cultural Diversity and Political Theory*. Basingstoke: Palgrave.

Perry, Michael J. 1997. "Are Human Rights Universal? The Relativist Challenge and Related Matters." *Human Rights Quarterly* 19 (3): 461–509.

Pessoa, Fernando. 1998. "They spoke to me of people and of humanity." In *Fernando Pessoa & Co. Selected Poems*. New York: Grove Press.

Pollis, Andrea, and P. Schwab. 1979. "Introduction." In *Human Rights: Cultural and Ideological Responsibilities*. New York: Praeger.

Pollock, Sheldon, Homi K. Bhabha, Carol A. Breckenridge, and Dipesh Chakrabarty. 2002. "Cosmopolitanisms." In *Cosmopolitanism*, edited by C. A. Breckenridge, S.

Pollock, H. K. Bhabha and D. Chakrabarty, 1–14. Durham, NC: Duke University Press.

Preis, Ann-Belinda S. 1996. "Human Rights as Cultural Practice: An Anthropological Critique." *Human Rights Quarterly* 18 (2): 286–315.

Rancière, Jacques. 1995. *On the Shores of Politics*. Translated by L. Heron. London: Verso.

Rancière, Jacques. 1998. *Disagreement*. Minneapolis: University of Minnesota Press.

Rancière, Jacques. 2004. "Who is the Subject of the Rights of Man?" *South Atlantic Quarterly* 103 (2/3): 298–310.

Reardon, Betty A. 1995. *Educating for Human Dignity: Learning about Rights and Responsibilities*. Philadelphia: University of Pennsylvania Press.

Reardon, Betty A. 1997. Human Rights as Education for Peace. In *Human Rights Education for the Twenty-First Century*, edited by G. J. Andreopoulos and R. P. Claude, 21–34. Philadelphia: University of Pennsylvania Press.

Rhodes, Aaron. 1994. "Editorial." *European Journal of Education* 29 (4): 347–353.

Robbins, Bruce. 1998. "Introduction Part I: Actually Existing Cosmopolitanism." In *Cosmopolitics: Thinking and Feeling Beyond the Nation*, edited by P. Cheah and B. Robbins, 1–19. Minneapolis: University of Minnesota Press.

Rosemann, Nils. 2003. "Human Rights Education: Towards the End of the UN Decade." *Mennesker & Rettigheter: Nordic Journal of Human Rights* 4 (Autumn): http://www.hrea.org/erc/Library/rosemann03.pdf.

Rousseau, Jean-Jacques. 1974. *The Social Contract*. Translated by C. Sherover. New York: New American Library.

Ruitenberg, Claudia. 2007a. "Educating Political Adversaries: Chantal Mouffe and Radical Democratic Citizenship Education." Conference Presentation *Philosophy of Education Society of Great Britain*. Oxford, UK.

Ruitenberg, Claudia. 2007b. "How to Do Things with Headscarves: A Discursive and Meta-Discursive Analysis." In *Philosophy of Education 2006*, edited by D. Vokey. Urbana, Ill: University of Illinois Press.

Säfström, Carl Anders. 2005. *Skillnadens Pedagogik: Nya Vägar inom den Pedagogiska Teorin [A Pedagogy of Difference: New Trends in Educational Theory]*. Lund: Studentlitteratur.

Säfström, Carl Anders, and Gert J. J. Biesta. 2001. "Learning Democracy in a World of Difference." *The School Field* 12 (5/6): 5–20.

Schor, Naomi. 1994. "This Essentialism which is Not One." In *Engaging with Irigaray*, edited by C. Burke, N. Schor and M. Whitford, 57–78. New York: Columbia.

Schor, Naomi, and Elizabeth Weed, eds. 1994. *The Essential Difference*. Bloomington: Indiana University Press.

Seymour, Mike, and Henry M. Levin, eds. 2005. *Educating for Humanity: Rethinking the Purposes of Education*. Boulder, Co.: Paradigm.

Smart, Barry. 1998. "The Politics of Difference and the Problem of Justice." In *The Politics of Jean-Francois Lyotard: Justice and Political Theory*, edited by C. Rojek and B. S. Turner, 43–62. London: Routledge.

Spivak, Gayatri Chakravorty. 1993. *Outside in the Teaching Machine*. New York: Routledge.

Spivak, Gayatri Chakravorty. 2004. "Righting Wrongs." *South Atlantic Quarterly* 103 (2/3): 523–581.

Starkey, Hugh. 1991. "The Council of Europe Recommendation on the Teaching and Learning of Human Rights in Schools." In *The Challenge of Human Rights Education*, edited by H. Starkey, 20–38. London: Cassell, Council of Europe Series.

Stasi, Bernard. 2003. "Commission de reflexion sur l'application du principe de laïcité dans la republique." Rapport au Président.

Stone, Alison. 2006. *Luce Irigaray and the Philosophy of Sexual Difference*. Cambridge: Cambridge University Press.

Tan, Kok-Chor. 2004. *Justice Without Borders: Cosmopolitanism, Nationalism and Patriotism*. Cambridge: Cambridge University Press.

Tibbits, Felisa. 1994. "Human Rights Education in Schools in the Post-Communist Context." *European Journal of Education* 29 (4): 363–376.

Todd, Sharon. 1998. "Veiling the Other, Unveiling Our 'Selves': Reading Media Images of the Hijab Psychoanalytically to Move Beyond Tolerance." *Canadian Journal of Education* 23 (4): 438–451.

Todd, Sharon. 2003. *Learning from the Other: Levinas, Psychoanalysis and Ethical Possibilities in Education*. Albany, NY: State University of New York Press.

Todd, Sharon. 2008. "Welcoming and Difficult Learning: Reading Levinas with Education." In *Levinas and Education*, edited by D. Egéa-Kuehne, 170–185. London: Routledge.

Todd, Sharon. forthcoming. "'She's Not One of Us': Muslim Girls, Schooling the Redefinition of Nation." In *Teaching Religion in a Multi-religious Society*, edited by J. Berglund and L. Roos. Stockholm: Södertörn University Press.

Todd, Sharon, and Carl Anders Säfström. 2008. "Democracy, Education and Conflict: Rethinking Respect and the Place of the Ethical." *Journal of Educational Controversy* 3 (1): http://www.wce.wwu.edu/Resources/CEP/eJournal/.

Tomaševski, Katarina. 2001. *Human Rights in Education as a Prerequisite for Human Rights Education*. Stockholm: Swedish International Development Agency.

Turner, Brian S. 2002. "Cosmopolitan Virtue, Globalization and Patriotism." *Theory, Culture, and Society* 19 (1–2): 45–63.

Van der Veer, Peter. 2002. "Colonial Cosmopolitanism." In *Conceiving Cosmopolitanism: Theory, Context and Practice*, edited by S. Vertovec and R. Cohen, 165–179. Oxford: Oxford University Press.

Vertovec, Steven, and Robin Cohen. 2002. "Introduction." In *Conceiving Cosmopolitanism: Theory, Context and Practice*, edited by S. Vertovec and R. Cohen, 1–22. Oxford: Oxford University Press.

Vertovec, Steven, and Robin Cohen, eds. 2002. *Conceiving Cosmopolitanism: Theory, Context and Practice*. Oxford: Oxford University Press.

Wang, Zhihe. 2002. "Toward a Postmodern Notion of Human Rights." *Educational Philosophy and Theory* 34 (2): 171–183.

Whitford, Margaret. 1991. *Luce Irigaray: Philosophy in the Feminine*. London: Routledge.

Yuval-Davis, Nira. 1997. *Gender and Nation*. London: Sage.

Zakin, Emily. 2007. "Between Two: Civil Identity and the Sexed Subject of Democracy." In *Returning to Irigaray: Feminist Philosophy, Politics and the Question of Unity*, edited by M. C. Cimitile and E. P. Miller, 173–204. Albany, NY: State University of New York Press.

Ziarek, Ewa Płonowska. 2001. *An Ethics of Dissensus: Postmodernity, Feminism, and the Politics of Radical Democracy*. Stanford: Stanford University Press.

Zubaida, Sami. 2002. Middle Eastern Experiences of Cosmopolitanism. In *Conceiving Cosmopolitanism: Theory, Context and Practice*, edited by S. Vertovec and R. Cohen, 32–41. Oxford: Oxford University Press.

Index

About the Author

Sharon Todd is Professor of Education at Stockholm University and Mälardalen University. She is author most recently of *Learning from the Other: Levinas, Psychoanalysis, and Ethical Possibilities in Education* (SUNY Press, 2003).

Lightning Source UK Ltd.
Milton Keynes UK
UKHW021826220120
357435UK00016B/227